Praise for the first edition of *Democracy in Small Groups*

"John Gastil brings good judgment, common sense, acute observation skills and a wealth of concrete experience to this study of democracy in small groups. Citizens, business people, churchgoers, workers—all those concerned with how to make a small group democracy work in practice—will find much to help them in this book."

-- Jane Mansbridge, author of *Beyond Adversary Democracy* and Adams Professor of Political Leadership and Democratic Values at the John F. Kennedy School of Government, Harvard University

CONTENTS

DEMOCRACY IN SMALL GROUPS

Communication, Participation, and Decision Making

2nd Edition

© 2014 by John Gastil

Library of Congress Cataloging-in-Publication Data

Gastil, John

Democracy in Small Groups / John Gastil – 2nd ed.

This is a work of nonfiction. Names, characters, places, and incidents are hopefully not merely the product of the author's imagination, nor that of the sources the author has cited, hypothetical examples notwithstanding. Any resemblance to actual persons, living or dead, events, or locales is entirely intentional.

Manufactured in the United States

A Note on References

Complete references for the second edition of *Democracy in Small Groups* appear in the chapter endnotes, which hyperlink back to the original sources on the Internet, whenever possible. A full bibliography of sources is available online at the Zotero online reference site.

The full url is
https://www.zotero.org/groups/democracy_in_small_groups_2nd_edition_2014.

PREFACE TO THE SECOND EDITION

Democracy in Small Groups should help those who want to make the small groups in their lives more effective, deliberative, and democratic. Clear concepts and sound theories can help us understand and change the world, and I hope to provide both. This book also stands on a foundation of social scientific research and political theory, and I hope scholars continue to use it as they study small-scale democracy, group decision making, and public deliberation. With that purpose in mind, I have updated many of the book's references and connected each chapter with contemporary scholarship.

One of the members of the co-operative workplace at the heart of this book recently spoke with me about these two purposes. In his words, the book's value comes from its blend of scholarly and practical content. "The model that Mifflin Co-op represented," Norm Stockwell explained, "is not often taught in academic circles." Norm has seen people enter the nonprofit sector with an "AT&T/IBM mentality" of hierarchical decision making that devalues consensus processes and employee empowerment. He recommends *Democracy in Small Groups* to people "because it gives an academic validation to a collective decision-making process that's different from the bigger-is-better model taught in business schools."[1]

Perhaps this is so, but *Democracy in Small Groups* came into existence more serendipitously than Norm might have guessed. The book's thesis grew out of the peculiar mix of influences in my life. I witnessed intensive group process growing up as a Quaker in San Diego and while attending Swarthmore College, which maintains a consensus tradition that dates back to its roots in the Religious Society of Friends. As an avid debater in college, high school, and at my family's dinner table, I also appreciated the need to temper strong argument with a deeper current of mutual respect.

I saw no sign of such respect while working on my mother's 1992 Congressional campaign. In that contest, and the many others I managed and assisted through the 1990s, I saw clearly the divergence between American political traditions and the aspirations of democratic theory. Running for office is an exercise in public relations, over-simplification of complex policy problems, and sometimes even the demonization of one's opponent.[2]

I knew a different kind of public talk was possible because I had spent a summer at the Kettering Foundation, which preaches the gospel of public deliberation. Their National Issues Forums showed that even partisans could have substantive conversations when given the necessary information and structure to deliberate.[3] My Kettering internship in 1991 inspired me to write the first edition of this book on the hope that it could promote honest group discussion and mitigate the trend toward cynical political talk.

Far from a naïve modern ideal, the deliberative imperative flourished during our nation's first and only Constitutional Convention.[4] It surged again early in the twentieth century, when public meetings became wildly popular affairs and American educators trained their students to become effective discussion leaders.[5] Deliberation also had a role in the radical activism that celebrated consensus processes during the feminist, anti-war, and civil rights movements of the 1960s and 1970s.[6]

During the twenty years since I published *Democracy in Small Groups*, both the physical and intellectual landscape the book describes changed dramatically. The Mifflin Street Community Co-op, which served as the book's central case study, reached the end of its run as an historic grocery cooperative when it closed its doors in 2006.[7] The ascendance of Whole Foods and other competitors have posed challenges for such stores, but consumer co-ops still thrive in Madison, Wisconsin and across the United States.[8]

I wrote *Democracy in Small Groups* to aid the wider set of associations that seek to govern themselves democratically— particularly those working for democratic social change. Those groups have become ever more sophisticated in their decision-making methods. In the early 1990s, counter-cultural group processes pioneered in the 1960s remained obscure, but they reached new audiences through organizationally complex anti-globalization protests and their offspring. Organizers of the Occupy Wall Street encampments, for instance, re-engineered the human megaphone and mass-consensus procedures for a younger generation.[9]

More subtly, democratic decision making has become normative in mainstream organizations. *Democracy in Small Groups* became a recommended resource for all sorts of organizations, from the Unitarian Universalist Association (not surprising) to the American College of Nurse-Midwives and NASA. Countless others who never saw my book still chose—or felt compelled—to adopt democratic norms, even if operating under a formal hierarchy.

This fact struck me most clearly during an arbitration process I witnessed at the University of Washington. The ombudsperson brought out a worksheet that she and others used to help both businesses and not-for-profits understand the most common grievances. When viewed through a wide-angle lens, every single one of these complaints underscored an appetite for more democratic governance and social relations in the workplace. Employees wanted "fairness," a "seat at the table," more "equal treatment," to be "treated with respect," or just "to be heard." The bulleted list was a disorganized string of more than twenty woes, but I think a manager or supervisor would better understand its gist if one simply recognized that the average American—even those who don't vote with any regularity— want employers who embrace democratic values.

The most fundamental shift since 1993 occurred among scholars and civic reformers. When I began researching this book, I sent letters to two political scientists, Benjamin Barber and Jane Mansbridge. Both took the time to reply, and both advised reading (judiciously) the writing of German social theorist Jürgen Habermas. By their lights (and mine), there wasn't much else out there that spoke to democratic group process.

Two decades later, Mansbridge, Barber, and Habermas stand at the center of a crowd of writers on "deliberative democracy." This modern strain of democratic theory holds that the most effective form of self-government privileges reason, argument, respect, and dialogue in its formal institutions and in the wider public sphere. Deliberative democratic theorists rejected representative democracy's limited ambition for public engagement, but they also cringed at participatory democracy's pursuit of mass mobilization without regard to the quality of the public's judgment.

This philosophical shift inspired hundreds of researchers to study the actual practices of small and medium-sized groups, particularly those convened specifically to engage in "democratic deliberation." Dozens of articles on the subject now appear in scholarly journals each year, and research teams devoted to studying the subject have emerged, such as the Center for Democratic Deliberation and the McCourtney Institute for Democracy at Pennsylvania State University, where I now work.

It was my good fortune to have the opportunity to follow the counsel of political scientist Samuel Popkin, who advised me to choose a research subject where ground had already been broken but excavation had only just begun. *Democracy in Small Groups* was my first substantial contribution to this literature, and though my own thinking on the book's subject has evolved over the years, I continue to believe in the soundness of the book's core argument and theoretical framework. That said, I made substantial revisions to most chapters, and I updated and expanded this edition's endnotes, with the assistance of Robert Richards, Robert Marriott, and Alexander Cook. These now have URLs linking directly to versions of the articles and books cited, even to the exact pages quoted whenever possible, and the entire set of references for this book also appears in Zotero as a public group library, which can be accessed through this endnote.[10]

Thanks to the research assistance of Meera Faw, and especially Robert Richards, who offered many substantive suggestions for the updated references, I now have the privilege of sharing with readers this twentieth anniversary edition of *Democracy in Small Groups*.

I dedicate this new edition to the memory of my late uncle, Raymond Gastil, who generously critiqued my work as I stepped into his shadow. Uncle Ray counseled temperance in one's partisan appetites but gluttony in the pursuit of knowledge. May this new edition provide ample cognitive calories for those working toward a more democratic world.

Uncle Ray, visiting his childhood home
in Alpine, California

CHAPTER 1

Introduction

Rhonda has taught fifth grade at Eucalyptus Elementary School for ten years. She almost quit over discipline problems, but when she allowed the kids to create their own class activities, they became more attentive. Now Rhonda holds weekly planning meetings in her classes. Assembled as small groups, her students make small decisions together on projects, playground activities, and the books Rhonda reads to them.

Tony wanted to get more involved in his community, so he worked as a volunteer with the Jefferson Neighborhood Council. After a year, he joined the council's planning board. It strictly followed the procedures in *Robert's Rules of Order* for both minor and major decisions. Like other volunteers, he began to see the board members and their meetings as rigid and unwelcoming. He quit after three months and stopped working with the council.

Lisa and Alejandro were determined to raise their children differently from how they had been raised. They tried to create an open, egalitarian family atmosphere for their three adopted daughters. The family used consensus to assign chores and plan outings, and their daughters became adept at arguing and, to a lesser extent, listening. When the children launched a chore-strike over allowances, Lisa and Alejandro refused to negotiate. The eldest daughter charged them with hypocrisy.

These scenarios offer a glimpse of the promise and problems of small group decision making. Democratic procedures often provide the best path to sound judgment and effective implementation, but even the most conscientious classroom, community group, or family faces hazards when it commits to a democratic process.[1]

Problems begin with our foggy understanding of the key word, "democratic." People normally use that term to critique large-scale political systems, with scholars and activists debating its meaning at length. Only in the past two decades have both researchers and civic reformers taken seriously the idea of democracy *in small groups*.[2]

Abstract principles for democratic political systems provide only a crude blueprint for smaller social scales, so in chapter 2 I provide a working definition of small group democracy. In the third chapter, I focus on the different rules groups can use to finalize their decisions, particularly the trade-offs between majority rule and consensus. Chapter 4 shows what small group democracy looks like in practice through a detailed case study of a legendary food co-op in Madison, Wisconsin. For decades, this group hoped to make every important decision through a democratic process.

In the second half of the book, I examine the challenges of democratic group deliberation. Almost everyone has encountered some of the most common group problems that even the Madison co-op faced, such as exhausting meetings and bitter personal conflicts, and Chapter 5 recounts these struggles and what the co-op did to address them. Chapter 6 reviews the wider literature on small groups to consider additional challenges, from time pressure to geographic dispersion, and the remedies researchers have suggested.

I devote the last two chapters of the book to considering how a renewed appreciation of small group democracy might influence our lives and our wider world. In Chapter 7, I examine the character of democratic conversations, relationships, schools, and families. Finally, in Chapter 8, I consider how the principles of small group democracy could make large-scale political systems more deliberative.

The Meaning of Democracy

Given the ubiquity of the word "democracy," one might doubt the necessity of reexamining it. Hanna Pitkin and Sara Shumer offered a contrary view in the essay, "On Participation":

> At first glance, democracy may seem a battle long won, but that is only because we pay lip service to the term without thinking about its meaning, let alone trying to live by its implications. The idea of democracy is the cutting edge of radical criticism, the best inspiration for change toward a more humane world, the revolutionary idea of our time.[3]

As people demand more power over their lives, their definition of democracy radicalizes.[4] In this way, democracy's meaning has evolved over the centuries, and the term has become applicable to what were once considered apolitical spheres. People now speak of democratic civic associations, democratic business meetings, democratic schools, and even democratic families.

Every time democracy's scope widens, the questions posed by Pitkin and Shumer return. What does democracy mean? How can we live by its implications? These questions are crucial. As Gregory Calvert, former National Secretary of Students for a Democratic Society, argues, even movements committed to democratic social change will fail if they, too, lack a clear definition of democracy.[5]

Democracy embodies powerful philosophical principles that have never been fully realized on large social scales. As Charles Lummis writes, democracy "describes an ideal, not a method of achieving it. It is not an...historically existing institution, but a historical project."[6]

Democracy connotes wide-ranging liberty, including the freedom to decide the course of one's life and the right to play an active role in

3

forging a common destiny. Democracy means social and civil equality that detests discrimination and prejudice. It welcomes a wide range of worldviews and lifestyles into a dialogue to seek mutual understanding, or at least a peaceful coexistence.[7] Even when it entails robust debate, democracy holds out the promise of a cohesive community working together to finding fair and nonviolent ways to reconcile disputes.[8] In sum, democracy embodies all three elements of the famous French Revolutionary slogan, "*liberté, egalité, fraternité.*"[9]

Working from these principles, it is possible to envision the contours of large-scale, democratic utopias, or realistic approximations thereof.[10] But what would a small democratic group look like? How do concepts such as pluralism or freedom of speech embody themselves on smaller social scales? Should all groups strive to be democratic? These are the questions with which I begin.

Democracy at the Small Group Level

All of us have taken part in countless group discussions. These range from informal gatherings to formal meetings held in businesses, civic organizations, and recreational groups. We may not be experts, but we all know something about both the power and pitfalls of group decision making.

We also have our own ideas about the democratic process. Through formal and informal education, we have learned something about both democratic ideals and the behavior of governments that call themselves democratic. For many of us, democracy has come to mean elections, parliamentary debates, voting, lobbying, and the occasional social movement. For others, democracy may mean open discussion, the search for common ground, or egalitarian decision making.

Despite such experience and knowledge, many people have never participated in highly democratic groups. Finding information about such groups is difficult because until recently, studies rarely discussed small-scale democracy. Even twenty years after this book's first publication, the phrase "small group democracy" remains uncommon.[11] Thus, it is necessary to begin with a brief definition of this central term.

A "small group" consists of more than two people who have a perception of common goals, a network of communication, some interdependence, some shared norms, and a perception of wholeness.[12] The "smallness" of a group depends on both absolute numbers and the intimacy of the membership. Imagine a group as a cluster of people in two-dimensional space: the more people the group has, the larger it becomes; however, the closer the members are to one another, the smaller the group becomes. There is no simple delineation between small and large groups, but small groups must have a minimal amount of cohesiveness and fewer than thirty members.[13]

A small group is "democratic" if it has equally distributed decision-making power, an inclusive membership committed to the democratic process, and healthy relationships among its members, and reaches decisions through democratic deliberation. Group deliberation is democratic if its members have equal and adequate opportunities to speak, neither withhold information nor verbally manipulate one another, and are able and willing to listen.

The Time and Place for Democracy

Given this basic definition, should all groups strive to be democratic? If not, when and where can groups use a democratic process? In answering these questions, previous authors have identified a number of key considerations.[14] In Figure 1, these are organized as the branches of a "decision tree." This tree shows the questions that one asks when deciding whether to solve a problem democratically.

Figure 1. A Decision Tree for Small Group Democracy

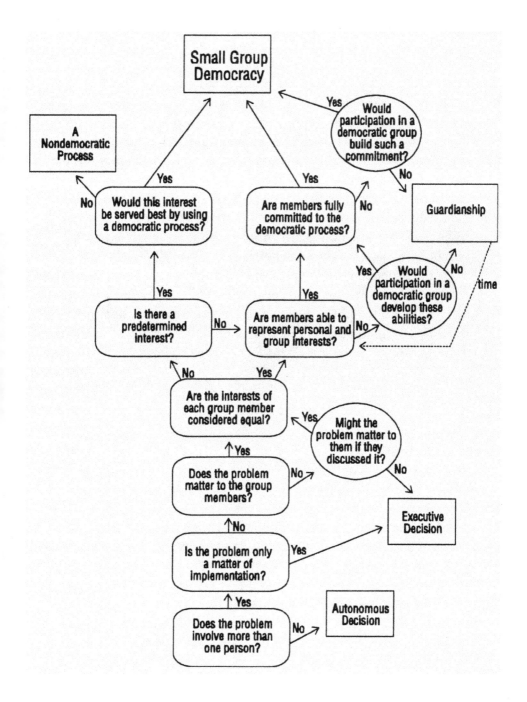

Starting at the trunk of the decision tree, one first assesses the nature of the problem. If the problem involves only one person, an autonomous decision can be reached. Though one might wish to consult others, a group decision is unnecessary.

If the problem involves merely implementing or working out the details of a previous decision, an executive (or judicial) decision-making process is in order. When a group decides to buy a shared computer, for instance, the membership does *not* ordinarily reach a fully detailed agreement and then march out the door together to buy it. Instead, the group authorizes the finance committee to decide on the model and accessories (a matter of detail) and gives the treasurer responsibility for handling any problems that arise in making the purchase (a matter of implementation).

If the problem is of no concern to group members, an executive or delegated decision might be appropriate. Thus, a member of a worker-owned saw mill might make an executive decision to order lumber from a visiting supplier, because the membership has made plain that it only cares about the price paid for the wood it buys.

But note the question in the first oval: Might the problem matter to group members *if they discussed it*? This raises the possibility that members would care if they had the requisite information or insight. This question (like the other two questions in ovals) views the decision-making process as a means for changing the character of the membership. In the case of the lumber co-op, workers might wish to boycott a supplier if they learned through discussion that it was non-union or a rapacious clear-cutter.[15]

If the problem is a serious matter to the group as a whole, the decision tree then poses the most difficult question: Are the interests of each group member considered equal? This isn't a factual matter, but a moral or ethical one. A "no" answer implies that for some reason, the interests of an individual or a subgroup have priority over the interests of other group members. A "yes" means that each member's interests weigh equally in making a decision. Who decides the answer is the crux of many a conflict.

Following the imagery of classical philosopher John Locke, if I were to pick my share of acorns and apples, a group of passers-by could claim that they and I should form a collective that jointly decides what to do with the food I had gathered. I could reply that I have the right to do what I please with my food, since I gathered it using my own labor.[16]

In the case of apples and acorns, one might sympathize with the humble gatherer, but in the modern marketplace, matters are more complicated. Does a factory worker have the right to play a role in management or earn a share of company profits? Do community members have a right to regulate local businesses or tax property owners?[17]

Aside from economic matters, are the interests of a spouse or partner given equal weight when the other is contemplating a career change? Are the disapproving views of my neighbors to be weighed equally with my own preferences when I wish to play my Electric Light Orchestra record on a Saturday afternoon? Criteria for answering these questions of "inclusiveness" appear in Chapter 2, but for now, it is enough to recognize the difficulty of determining when the interests of different people should receive equal weight.[18]

If the interests of group members are considered unequal, an individual (or subgroup) with exclusive authority might still cede decision-making power to the group, simply because there is no pre-determined interest or objective. When the individual does have an objective, one simply employs the decision-making process that best realizes it. Thus, an author with a pre-existing goal (i.e., making a manuscript as good as possible) might forego a fully democratic review process on the belief that such a process wouldn't produce the best possible book. By contrast, an orchard manager might decide that her self-interested goal (profits and high-quality produce) is best served by empowering the orchard workers to make collective decisions about their working hours and conditions.[19]

When the interests of all group members are considered equal, different questions arise. If members are not the best representatives of their own interests (or incapable of effectively participating in democratic deliberations), guardianship may be the best form of decision making.[20] The term "guardian" commonly refers to the adult who holds legal responsibility for the well-being of minors or mentally incapacitated individuals.[21] But groups of competent adults can also select provisional guardianship. Thus, the members of a political action committee might consider each other's interests equal, yet choose to let an experienced member make the decisions about an upcoming press conference. This member becomes the group's guardian with respect to the conference.

More generally, if a group holds a different goal above that of democracy, it might choose to appoint a member (or hire a non-member) to make some decisions on its behalf. In effect, the group decides that a provisional guardian will better serve their interests than would their own democratic process.[22] Thus, a homeowners' association might send a dispute into binding arbitration on the assumption that a neutral third-party will yield a sound decision and avoid the frustration and division that could accompany any further deliberation among residents on the matter.

Even when guardianship is considered optimal, it is important to note the dashed arrow on the decision tree that moves away from it. This line suggests that with the passage of time, the characteristics of the membership may change. Ideally, a system of guardianship develops the skills and character of its members. This idea underlies the authority of teachers and mentors, many of whom strive to make their students or apprentices fully capable and independent.[23]

In addition, it is necessary to consider whether group members assumed incapable of democratic deliberation might become sufficiently skilled through participation in the democratic process.[24] A child unfamiliar with group deliberation might be restless and confused at first, but become adept over time.

If group members are already capable of democratic decision making, but don't all value democracy, they might subvert the democratic process, willfully or carelessly. As with deliberative skills, democratic values might emerge through participation, but it is necessary to gauge whether they would develop in time. If the danger of subversion is high, guardianship might be appropriate. With this concern in mind, a community improvement board might ask that new members serve as observers for their first two meetings, then as full members after developing an appreciation for the board's process.

If these questions lead to the conclusion that small group democracy is appropriate, the last consideration is whether time permits deliberation. If an approaching deadline requires a decision immediately, the group can vote without discussion, but this is far from optimal. (See Chapter 6.) If time allows it, the group can go through a fully democratic process, eventually arriving at a decision.

In sum, though many situations don't call for a democratic process, many others do. Looking at the three hypothetical groups presented at the opening of this chapter, each has decisions that could be made through a democratic process.

Rhonda's sixth grade class learned a great deal by making some of its decisions democratically. No matter how sophisticated her students became at using this process, however, they would never have authority over issues such as hiring teachers or student expulsions.

In the second example, the neighborhood council is ignoring or shielding itself from volunteer and community input. Presuming the volunteers are capable of democratic participation, there is no reason for the council to prevent them from speaking. Unless the council became more receptive, the volunteers might prefer moving to a direct system of decision making and eliminate the representative council altogether.

Finally, the parents of the three adopted daughters found that many family decisions were best made democratically. The parents forgo democracy only when the interests of each family member don't merit equal consideration, as when the mother decides what career to pursue, or in those cases where the parents believe their children lack the wisdom necessary to represent themselves in high-stakes decisions.

If small group democracy were better understood and appreciated, more groups would attempt to make decisions democratically. The original publication of this book was an attempt to test that presumption, and the growing interest in the power of the small group suggests its validity. [25]

CHAPTER 2

Defining Democracy

"In the small group...is where we shall find the inner meaning of democracy, its heart and core." —Mary Parker Follett[1]

A century ago, Mary Parker Follett called for studying democracy in small groups, which she called the "heart and core" of democratic society. Since that time, only a few activists, philosophers, and social scientists have heard her call and produced writings that address the subject of small democratic groups in detail.[2] When combined with the vast literature on large-scale democracy, this body of literature provided enough insight to discern the essential features of a small democratic group.[3] Better still, in the two decades since the first edition of *Democracy in Small Groups*, there has been an explosion of research linking democracy, dialogue, and deliberation in small groups and public forums, and this new edition takes advantage of these sources.[4]

I begin by introducing the concept of a *demos*, a useful shorthand term for a body of people who govern themselves democratically. The demos is usually a large political unit, such as a nation or state, but it can also refer to smaller democratic groups. I define small group democracy by specifying the features of an ideal demos. The ideal is unattainable, but it is something that a group can strive toward.[5] A group will never become fully democratic, but one can estimate its distance from the ideal.

Table 1 outlines my comprehensive definition of small group democracy. Democratic groups exhibit certain forms of power, inclusiveness, commitment, relationships, and deliberation. A group is democratic to the degree it shows these characteristics.[6]

Table 1. A Definition of Small Group Democracy

I. Group Power
    A. Group sovereignty
    B. Equal distribution of ultimate authority
II. Inclusiveness
III. Commitment to the Democratic Process
IV. Relationships
    A. Acknowledgement of individuality
    B. Affirmation of competence
    C. Recognition of mutuality
    D. Congeniality
V. Deliberation
    A. Speaking rights and responsibilities
        1. agenda setting
        2. reformulation
        3. informing
        4. articulation
        5. persuasion
        6. voting
        7. dissent
    B. Listening rights and responsibilities
        1. comprehension
        2. consideration

Group Power

As political theorist Robert Dahl puts it, in any democracy "the people must have the final say." The fundamental meaning of democracy is self-government, and meaningful governance requires power.[7] Thus, democratic groups must have jurisdiction over the items that appear on their agendas.

If a group has no authority, its meetings may be advisory, influential, or many other things, but they can't be *democratic*. If a factory work team can make suggestions but not policy, it would be misleading to call its deliberations "democratic." If the team had control over work schedules but not product design, it could deliberate democratically about times but not products.[8]

Given the primary importance of power in defining small group democracy, I will specify a meaning for this elusive word. Power is the capacity to influence the future behavior of objects or the behavior, beliefs, and emotions of living beings, including oneself. One can use power to do something, and power can be used to prevent or delay something from being done. When I direct power inward, I exercise the power to do something by and for myself (e.g., the willpower to resist cheesecake). When I direct power outward, I exert it against, over, or with someone or something else.[9]

Power resides in both individuals and groups. Individuals have the power to accomplish things by themselves, but sometimes an individual's power is inconsequential unless combined with that of others. Imagine yourself trying to carry a grand piano up a staircase single-handedly. It's impossible for one person, but a dozen people—none of whom possess the muscle to move a piano—can do it by combining their strength.[10]

Group power includes influence over its members' personal behavior. Consciousness raising groups, for instance, seek social change, but the immediate goal is raising individual awareness of behavioral choices—the previously unacknowledged power to transform one's own life. Philosopher Catharine A. MacKinnon explains that women's participation in such groups reveals to them patriarchy's dependence on traditional behavioral routines that we enact daily. Women have the power to change the structure of male supremacy, because it has always depended on their compliance. "Although it is one thing to act to preserve power relations and quite another to act to challenge them," MacKinnon explains, "once it is seen that these relations require daily acquiescence, acting on different principles, even in small ways, seems not quite so impossible."[11]

When power is thought of in this way, it loses many normal connotations. Power doesn't have to imply domination and subordination, nor does the use of power necessarily entail coercion, violence, or corruption. Power can signify an individual or collective capacity that doesn't rob others of their abilities. Any egalitarian, peaceful social movement will have a great deal of power, derived neither from a superior status in an institutionalized hierarchy nor threat and intimidation. Power lies in the collective will of the movement, and the decisions and actions made with this force can be nonviolent and non-coercive.[12]

In any case, a democratic group must do more than possess power. A true demos distributes its power evenly among the group members. Everyone in a small democratic group must have some form of influence or control, and all members must ultimately have equal power with regard to group policies. Some members might be more influential than others, and they might make more decisions by themselves or in committees. But final group authority must be divided evenly among group members, through procedures like consensus or majority rule, discussed in Chapter 3.[13]

Following this principle, a teachers' union could give day-to-day authority over dues collection to a treasurer or finance committee, while still retaining final authority over their money and every other union policy. The union always has the power to overrule a decision made by the single member or committee.

Inclusiveness

Assume, for the moment, that all the teachers' union members have equal final authority, but if the union excludes untenured teachers, is it democratic? If the union makes no decisions that affect untenured faculty, it might be democratic. On the other hand, if untenured teachers must pay whatever dues the union decrees, one could doubt whether the dues were set democratically.

Robert Dahl calls this a question of *inclusion*: People who are significantly affected by the decisions of a demos ought to have full and equal decision-making power within it. This seemingly straightforward requirement presents a paradox. Which comes first, the scope of the demos' power or the composition of its membership? If a group agrees to make decisions that affect only its members, it avoids this problem. Most groups, however, like this hypothetical teachers' union, make decisions that directly and indirectly affect many nonmembers.[14]

For the vast majority of groups, the inclusion problem has no easy solution, and groups can only meet the criterion by degrees. In light of this difficulty, I suggest a clarification: Democratic groups must strive to *include* those people who are profoundly affected by its decisions, *invite* those significantly affected, and at least *consider* the views of those marginally affected.[15]

A co-operatively run book store, for example, might decide that all of its managerial decisions have a profound effect on all employees, so each has equal decision-making authority at the store's monthly planning meetings. Since employee decisions also significantly affect both volunteers and customers, the staff informs those groups of upcoming meetings and welcomes their attendance. Since the store's policies marginally affect the larger community and local authors, the staff holds an annual community meeting (disguised as a festival to encourage attendance), and its website invites readers and authors to email staff with concerns or suggestions throughout the year.

This example shows an attempt to bring people into direct contact with the group, but inclusion can also mean considering the views and concerns of people not present for consequential deliberations. With this in mind, the book store could establish a general rule never to make its most crucial decisions when a staff member was unable to attend a meeting. Recurrent or profound customer concerns should likewise come up for discussion during planning meetings, rather than being addressed solely outside of deliberation.[16]

This broad definition of inclusiveness must be qualified in two respects. As philosopher John Burnheim argues, "Nobody should have any input into decision making where they have no legitimate material interest." Burnheim aims to exclude "intrusive desires about how others should fare." Thus, the book co-op pays no heed to the religious zealots who are offended by the store's books on bisexuality. When Burnheim further requires that material interests be "legitimate," he rejects those interests not "based on entitlements that are morally sound." Thus, the co-op's donations committee refuses to consider requests for financial assistance from a self-publishing firm that preys on authors' vanity. In both cases, the zealots and the publisher are "affected" by the bookstore's decisions, yet the co-op excludes them on the grounds that their affected interests are either intrusive or illegitimate.[17]

In addition, Dahl argues that a demos "must include all adult members of the association except transients and persons proved to be mentally defective." Under exceptional circumstances, a demos can exclude people even if their legitimate material interests are profoundly and directly affected by group decisions. These exceptions include infants and (in some cases) young children, non-residents who are "just passing through" the group's jurisdiction, and people, such as those with severe mental disabilities, who are utterly incapable of making sound decisions on their own behalf or as a member of a group.[18]

Commitment

Small democratic groups have goals besides being democratic, but all of these should remain secondary to their principled adherence to democratic processes.[19] As political scientist Joshua Cohen argues, the members of a demos must share "a commitment to coordinating their activities within institutions that make deliberation possible and according to norms that they arrive at through their deliberation."[20] Group members must internalize democratic values and respect those group decisions that are reached democratically, so long as the decisions themselves are consistent with democratic principles.

Every democratic group needs a set of bylaws or unwritten group norms that protect it against undemocratic maneuvers, and members need to understand both the letter and spirit of those codes. When the group welcomes new members, they must develop a strong commitment to the democratic features of the group's decision-making process.[21]

If a member doesn't like a democratic group's decision, the member can voluntarily withdraw from the group, accept some form of sanction for refusing to follow the decision, or assent to the decision. This requirement guards against those group members who adhere to democratic principles only when they like the group's judgments.[22]

Democratic commitment isn't blind. Fully democratic decisions must be arrived at democratically and have no effects inconsistent with democracy. The decision-making process cannot involve undemocratic actions, such as a group facilitator or chair making autocratic decisions or scheduling a meeting at a time meant to exclude a member who holds a dissenting opinion. Also, the group decision itself must not contradict the principles of small group democracy. For instance, a group decision is undemocratic if it institutes an exclusionary membership policy or places all ultimate authority in the hands of one group member. More generally, political philosopher James Fishkin requires democratic groups to follow the principle of non-tyranny by never permitting the majority to rob the minority of its democratic rights.[23]

Groups can establish their own set of democratic principles in an oral tradition or in written bylaws, but no matter how precise, these principles always have to be interpreted. Their full meaning cannot be articulated outside of the changing contexts of individual group members and settings. If members don't make the effort to consider, practice, and internalize their group norms, interpretations may themselves become undemocratic.

For example, a parliamentary group's membership might decline to challenge or override the ruling of an autocratic chair. A community development organization might interpret inclusiveness in increasingly narrow terms that gradually exclude all but an inner circle. In both cases, the groups might deem their processes consistent with democratic principles, but they are not. A firm commitment to the democratic process can prevent such misinterpretations.[24]

Relationships

Besides sharing a commitment to democracy, the members of a small democratic group enjoy a special kind of relationship with one another—a way of relating consistent with and conducive to the democratic process.[25] Relationships form through shared experiences and the exchange of words carrying relational meanings for group members. Formalized salutations and polite forms of address are some of the most obvious ways our words convey relational significance. Even when a group reviews a treasurer's report, members are often subtly discussing how they think and feel about the treasurer, other group members, and the group as a whole. The utterance, "That was an excellent report," does more than reassure the treasurer of her fiscal acumen.[26]

According to philosopher John Dewey, a fully democratic group respects both the individuality and competence of every member of the demos. The words and deeds of group members create a friendly atmosphere that recognizes the bonds that hold the group together.[27] Political theorist Jane Mansbridge adds that when there is a substantive conflict in material interests among the members of the demos, mutuality and congeniality ought to play a more minor role owing to the risk that appeals for unity might disguise the conflict and manipulate the membership.[28]

Consider two examples. A neighborhood improvement group consisting of like-minded neighbors might place greater emphasis on member relationships. All members of this voluntary association share the common goal of improving neighborhood parks and assisting members of the community. Cementing friendships and emphasizing common identities only strengthens the group. Within a city council, by contrast, there might exist sharp conflicts of interest between developers and those favoring an end to urban development and between suburbanites and inner-city residents. Although the council needs a minimum of comradeship to proceed democratically, seeking consensus might subvert deliberation. The council might discover common interests over time, but an honest adversarial relationship is better than false unity.

Looked at more closely, democratic group relationships have four aspects. Each manifests itself through how members speak to one another, so the following discussion focuses on four varieties of relational talk.[29]

Acknowledgement of Individuality

Recognizing a person's individuality begins with differentiating her from the group as a whole. When one acknowledges the individuality of a group member, one addresses that person as an individual and affirms her identity and interests as potentially distinct from those of the group. I can even acknowledge my own individuality, as when I say, "That's all I can give to the group right now."

The opposite impulse is denial of another's individuality. This asserts that a member's identity and interests are (or should be) subordinate to the group. For instance, at one group meeting I observed, a member insisted that her personal needs were paramount at the moment and compelled her to act accordingly. To this another member responded, "A collective is not where everybody can do what they want and get their needs met.... A collective...is a unit that works for the collective."[30]

In *Rethinking Democracy*, philosopher Carol Gould explains why it's important that democratic group members acknowledge one another's individuality. Democracy, she writes, can be "fully effective only if...people generally relate to each other as equals and with respect for each other's individual differences and interests....The very process of participatory democratic decision making entails such reciprocal recognition."[31]

Affirmation of Competence

As a member of a demos, one assumes that no one else is a more competent judge of one's own interests. More importantly, one generalizes this assumption to others, such that individual group members are seen as their own best judges. "You know yourself better than I do" is a clear affirmation, whereas "Maybe I should decide for you" questions this form of competence.[32]

This idea derives from Dahl's "strong principle of equality." Following this principle, the members of a demos assume that the entire membership is qualified to participate in making collective decisions. At the very least, members assume that none "are so definitely better qualified than the others that they should be entrusted with making the...decisions."[33]

It seems reasonable to go a step farther. Democratic groups assume that all members are capable of judging what is best for the group. Members may misjudge what is in the group's best interest, but no member is thought so superior that other members are deemed incompetent. As Chai Ling, a student leader of the Chinese Pro-Democracy movement, explains, "...Each must have simple faith in other people's intelligence and ability to choose."[34] A group member could affirm the competence of others by simply saying, "I think we should hear from everyone on this, because we all have different visions of the future of this organization."

Recognition of Mutuality

Mutuality is "the willingness to be connected—to take on another's well being and recognize oneself in the other," so affirming mutuality consists of highlighting the interconnection and common identity of group members.[35] Referring to others as "the group" and "the team," or even simply "us" or "we," can constitute a recognition of mutuality. More explicitly, the speaker can ask members to think and act as a group: "We need as a group, as a collective, to figure out a way to get beyond the resentment that taints future negotiations about those same things."[36]

Just as Carol Gould identifies the importance of individuality, she also stresses the need for recognizing how our individual identities connect through social relations. A member of the demos is an individual, yet her identity comes partly from her membership in a social group. Through "reciprocal recognition" we acknowledge one another's membership and conjure the demos itself into being. Any one member's identity as a part of the whole is contingent on the identities of the others.[37] Identification with others has additional importance for democratic groups because it forms much of the basis for the altruism that can help groups seek a common purpose and take into account even the needs of those who exist outside the demos.[38] Only in an extreme form does this pose the kind of conformity hazard associated with "groupthink."[39]

Congeniality

As defined herein, congeniality is the development and preservation of positive emotional relationships and a neighborly or friendly group atmosphere. It includes expressions of kindness, empathy, sympathy, and praise. "Congeniality" may be the best word, because it covers relations ranging from formal cordiality and acquaintance to more informal companionship.

Congeniality can be expressed as humor, such as when a member of a group I observed once joked about the cleanliness of the cellar: "I still think we should just give everybody a shovel and start digging out the basement." It can also take a more direct form, such as when another group member remarked, "I'm just ever so grateful that Steve and Amy and Ray put in the time that they did to get us to this point."[40]

The opposite of congenial talk is rude, hostile, or belittling communication. It can appear in subtle forms, such as a condescending or threatening tone of voice, or in a more blatant manner: "I have to ask you all and beg and plead if I want to even take off a [expletive] weekend." Negative speech can come as a combination of word choice and tone, as in the following quip, which I heard a speaker shout in a rapid burst: "Sometimes I get kinda frustrated with us, because we just want to do everything for the political pureness of it."

Congeniality aids small group democracy the same way a lubricant greases gears, by soothing irreconcilable conflicts of interest or moving individual group members toward a common vision. Mansbridge points out that Aristotle conceived of democracy as nothing less than the political extension of friendship.[41] In less unified groups, political theorist Benjamin Barber suggests that congeniality can serve as a substitute for friendship: "A neighbor is a stranger transformed by empathy and shared interests into a friend—an artificial friend, however, whose kinship is a contrivance of politics rather than natural or personal and private."[42]

If a discussion of congeniality seems too far afield from more traditional conceptions of the democratic process, one can turn to the stodgy classic, *Robert's Rules of Order*, a codebook for public meetings designed, in part, to maintaining decorum. This emphasis on civility, if not friendship, parallels the baseline expectation that citizens should show tolerance toward one another in a large-scale political system.[43] The heightened concern with political civility in modern American politics comes out of this same impulse, and the imperative of maintaining congenial social relations holds as true for small groups as it does for large systems.[44]

Deliberation

Healthy relationships have a mutually reinforcing relationship with open and constructive deliberation.[45] "Deliberation" is discussion that involves judicious argument, critical listening, and earnest decision making. A deliberative process includes a careful examination of a problem or issue, the identification of possible solutions, the establishment or reaffirmation of evaluative criteria, and the use of these criteria in identifying an optimal solution.[46]

The idea of deliberation appears in political cultures ancient and modern, but until recently, it had been underappreciated as the heart of the democratic process.[47] Even deliberative democratic theorists failed to recognize the centrality of jury deliberation in the American system, so the purpose and process of deliberation merits careful consideration.[48]

In one of the earliest modern works on the subject, James Fishkin argued that democracy must mean more than political equality. Democracy's advocates have focused their energy on building "a system which grants equal consideration to everyone's preferences and which grants everyone appropriately equal opportunities to formulate preferences on the issues under consideration."[49] Such equality is essential, but it doesn't encompass the full meaning of democracy.

In Fishkin's view, equating democracy with political equality "neglects the deliberation needed to make democratic choices meaningful." Our preferences are not always well developed. If they are "unreflective or ignorant," they "lose their claim to political authority over us." Since it is through collective discussion and judgment that our preferences become reflective and informed, deliberation is necessary "if the claims of democracy are not to be de-legitimated."[50]

Joshua Cohen is another political theorist who was among the first to stress the importance of deliberation. Cohen argues that a fully democratic group uses an "ideal deliberative procedure" that has four main features. First, participants view themselves as bound only by decisions arrived at through legitimate deliberation. Second, the members of the demos put forward their reasons for advancing, supporting, or criticizing proposals. Third, the process is designed to treat participants equally, and there are no power or resource differences that "shape their chances to contribute to deliberation" or "play an authoritative role in...deliberation." Finally, "ideal deliberation aims to arrive at a rationally motivated consensus." There is no promise that reasoned argument will lead to a consensus, and a democratic process may end in a majority vote. But regardless of the demos' decision-making method, a full consensus can be viewed as the ideal.[51]

When one imagines democratic groups, one might think that the members of such groups should speak for roughly equal periods of time. In fact, it is less important that all members of a collective speak the same amount than each has equal *opportunities* to speak. If one person speaks far more than any other, there may be a problem. The problem, though, is that this speaker is taking away others' opportunities—not that the speaker is simply talking the most. Likewise, if a group member hardly ever speaks, this member may lack speaking opportunities, but it is the presence or absence of opportunities—not the silence—that is at issue.[52] It is inevitable that some members will speak more than others, and the members of small democratic groups have a right to remain silent.[53]

As Dahl argues, members of the demos "ought to have an adequate opportunity, and an equal opportunity, for expressing their preferences as to the final outcome," as well as "for placing questions on the agenda and for expressing reasons for endorsing one outcome rather than another."[54]

These opportunities need to be readily apparent to each member of the demos. They should be "manifest" or "displayed," such that every member recognizes their existence.[55] For instance, a group might formally give opportunities to all, yet never remind shy members they are welcome to speak. A group might have a system for taking turns, yet never explain the system to its newest members. Equality of speaking opportunity must be an explicit goal given the ubiquity of subtle power dynamics, such as gender norms, that can generate subtle inequalities.[56]

For opportunities to be meaningful, members must also have at least minimal communication skills.[57] If some members cannot speak the group's language, dialect, or jargon, their opportunities to speak are meaningless. If the group encourages conversational spontaneity (e.g., interruptions and digressions), members who struggle to "hold the floor" under such conditions may be unable to use their opportunities. If a group member can speak the language and take the floor but is inarticulate, the chance to speak may amount to nothing more than an invitation to mutual frustration.[58]

Like anything, this notion of equal opportunities can be taken too far. It isn't necessary for every group member to be able to speak at every moment. Timely interjections can sustain a discussion's momentum, and groups sometimes need to interrupt long-winded speakers. Similarly, time pressure often makes it necessary for democratic groups to limit each member's speaking turns. The point is that over time and across different topics, speaking opportunities should be equal.

But what if no member has the opportunity to say even a few sentences? In this scenario, opportunities are equal, but inadequate. If there are insufficient opportunities to communicate with one another, deliberation—careful and thorough discussion—is impossible. Under such conditions, a small group might choose to vote in a democratic manner, but the constraints on deliberation move it far from the democratic ideal.[59]

With the rights to equal and adequate opportunities come certain responsibilities. Members of the demos always have the chance to speak, but there are times when they also have a responsibility to speak. A fully democratic decision is impossible if a member of the demos has withheld information that would cause the group to take a different course of action. A group is equally impaired if a member irresponsibly manipulates other group members into accepting a decision they would otherwise oppose.

Having outlined these general principles, it is now useful to distinguish the different forms of speaking that characterize democratic deliberation, including agenda setting, reformulating, informing, articulating, persuading, voting, and dissenting. In turn, each of these forms of talk is defined and related to other aspects of the democratic process.[60]

Agenda Setting

Broadly defined, a group's agenda consists of the issues a group discusses during a meeting. Members can set the agenda by placing, removing, or altering the priority of items on it, and one can also influence the pace at which the group moves through one or more agenda items. Suggesting that the group devote an hour to a given item might lead the group to consider carefully that issue and, as a consequence, give little or no attention to others.

In a democracy, Dahl explains, "The demos must have the exclusive opportunity to decide how matters are to be placed on the agenda."[61] Agenda setting is a vital form of talk, for there can be no debate until an issue is placed on the agenda.[62] Agenda setting is the means by which the demos decides what issues are of immediate concern. If the full membership of the group isn't involved in setting the agenda, the concerns of some members will be ignored in any subsequent discussion.[63]

Reformulation

Reformulation is the redefinition or reframing of an issue already on the agenda and under discussion. Reformulation includes both semantic alterations (e.g., rephrasing a problem) and changes in the content of a proposal (e.g., combining two solutions into one). As an example, two workers at an employee-owned technology startup might have two different ideas for spending a windfall profit. One might want to invest in smart technology that reduces the company's electric bill, and the other might prefer expanding their office space. A third worker might reformulate the issue by joining the two seemingly competing ideas into a proposal for moving the company to a new solar-ready office building.[64]

Reformulation, as Benjamin Barber defines the term, amounts to "language"—the metaphors and terms that define the experiences of the past, the realities of the present, and the possibilities of the future. Barber goes so far as to insist, "We may redistribute goods and make power accountable, but if we reserve talk and its evolution to specialists [or any elite few]...then no amount of equality will yield democracy."[65]

One study of deliberation found that "free flow" of ideas was an essential part of the process, and reformulation might be one of the things such a flow achieves.[66] Groups that lack a creative dynamic likely tend to get stuck in binary debates and miss the opportunity to reassemble or integrate the items on their agenda.

Informing

One of the most common forms of speech during deliberation is the exchange of information to better understand the problem at hand and how to address it. Herein, informing means providing information relevant to an agenda item under discussion without attempting to express one's views or persuade the group to reach a particular decision.[67]

If group members fail to present the pertinent information they possess, they may jeopardize democratic deliberation. Their silence could distort other members' perspectives and result in the expression of uninformed deliberation and judgment. Withholding information could also cause the group to make decisions with unforeseen results that are either undemocratic or unproductive.[68] The natural tendency to discuss most often the information already widely shared among group members only underscores the importance of this issue.[69]

Thus, informing is sometimes more of a responsibility than a right. In a fully democratic group, members always volunteer whatever information they believe the group needs to make an informed decision. Small democratic groups have a tacit "Freedom of Information Act" that grants members access to pertinent information, though members of such groups should share knowledge spontaneously, before anyone has to demand it.[70]

This requirement must not be exaggerated or misunderstood. There always exists useful information that is unknown to *all* of the group's members, and it isn't incumbent on the group to seek out every last bit of knowledge. Group members are only responsible for providing relevant information they know (or can access easily). A conscientious group may do even more to ensure the strength of its information base, but democracy, per se, doesn't require infinite diligence.[71]

Articulation

Articulation involves the expression of one's perspective with regard to an issue on the agenda, without clear persuasive purpose and before a decision has been reached. When articulating a view, speakers are presenting their opinions, interests, and ideas. For example, in a community group's strategy session, a speaker might tell the other group members that she dislikes censorship. The speaker's aim, in this case, might be for other group members to understand her point of view—not to embrace it.[72]

The ability to articulate can't be taken for granted, because people don't always have a clear perspective and the ability to express their point of view. Learning how to recognize and distinguish between self-interest and the interests of the group is an important skill, as is learning how to transform unreflective and disparate opinions into sound group judgments. In general, articulation serves democracy by bringing forward the minority and majority views of the group and filling the well of ideas from which the demos draws.

This form of speech is particularly important when "the perspectives of some citizens are systematically suppressed" during deliberation. Whether such suppression is due to social or psychological pressures, the demos should aim to "insure the expression of...excluded perspectives." Although groups might ideally seek common ground, the more fundamental goal is insuring that "those who are usually left out of...discussions learn to speak whether their perspectives are common or not."[73]

Articulation, however, can amount to more than the expression of one's opinion. Mansbridge explains that democratic deliberation includes a form of articulation analogous to "thinking out loud" on an issue:

> Preferences themselves, let alone interests, are not given. They must be tentatively voiced, tested, examined against the causes that produced them, explored, and finally made one's own. Good deliberation must rest on institutions that foster dissent and on images of appropriate behavior that allow for fumbling and changing one's mind, that respect the tentativeness of this process. Only such safeguards can help participants find where they want themselves to go.[74]

Thus, articulation presents a speaker's point of view, but it can also play a vital role in the formation of one's judgment.

Persuasion

Agenda setting, reformulation and the other forms of speech set the table for debate, where the centerpiece is persuasion. As defined herein, persuasive speech aims to influence the views of other members of the demos with regard to an agenda item. Persuasion can create, reinforce, or change other members' feelings, attitudes, and beliefs about an issue.[75]

Michael Walzer, a lifelong advocate of democracy, explains why persuasion plays such an important role in democratic deliberation:

> Democracy puts a premium on speech, persuasion, rhetorical skill. Ideally, the citizen who makes the most persuasive argument—that is, the argument that actually persuades the largest number of citizens—gets his [*sic*] way. But he can't use force, or pull rank, or distribute money...And all the other citizens must talk, too, or at least have a chance to talk...Citizens come into the forum with nothing but their arguments. All non-political goods have to be deposited outside: weapons and wallets, titles and degrees.[76]

But democracy needs more than mere persuasion. Were there no ethical restraint on rhetoric, the door would open to deceptive or manipulative discourse. Thus, Cohen insists that in a deliberative democracy, members of the demos "are required to state their reasons" when presenting their views on proposals.[77] Political philosopher Bruce Ackerman adds a "consistency requirement," whereby the reasons a person gives at one time must remain consistent with the reasons given to justify other claims.[78]

More fundamentally, Dahl argues that arguments should be backed by systematic research and self-reflection.[79] This requirement of reflection is particularly relevant to arguments that include emotional appeals. Groups reach decisions through both thought and feeling, and just as reasoning can be superficial and uninformed, so can emotions arise from mood and circumstance more than heartfelt convictions.[80]

There are many linguistic devices and strategies that members of a democratic group are wary of using. Euphemisms, loaded words, and jargon often conflict with the need for clarity and precision. Using grammar to disguise arguments or dodge questions also undermines the need for explicit debate. Simplistic, ritualistic, metaphoric, and mythic discourse can forge genuine consensus and unity, but these rhetorical strategies are often used to intoxicate or mystify. They can oversimplify situations and obscure real and important differences in members' perspectives and interests. Concealed and distorted messages make it more difficult for participants to deliberate in an informed, reflective manner. When oratory slips into sophistry, the respectful exchange of perspectives and ideas becomes nothing more than a winner-take-all competition among manipulators.[81]

One might object to these restrictions, arguing that they need to be balanced with a recognition of the speaker's present situation and goals. In this view, democratic ends can justify undemocratic methods of persuasion. However, as rhetoric scholar and political organizer Robert A. Kraig argues, it is dangerous to permit speakers to weigh seemingly just ends against unjust means:

> If we take a longer-term perspective…, then the ends and means of rhetoric are not as distinct…The character of a community, a movement, an institution, or a nation, is in many respects the product of the rhetorical transactions by which it is constituted and maintained. In this sense, dehumanizing rhetoric leads to dehumanized institutions…. Rhetorical means are not merely the neutral instruments of the rhetor's immediate political ends but are the building blocks of the future.[82]

In sum, since every attempt at persuasion affects both listener and speaker, members of the demos restrain themselves from using manipulative discourse, both because of its unethical character and its long-term damage to the character of the demos.

Voting

Although rarely described as a form of communication, voting is the formal expression of preferences with regard to a set of alternative positions. This includes both preliminary tallies, such as "straw polls," and decisive balloting or voice votes, anonymous (secret ballot) and public (raised hand or voice vote) forms of expression, and consensual and majoritarian methods of decision making. Voting is only required at the decisive stage of deliberations, and a demos can choose among a wide variety of democratic voting methods, as I discuss further in Chapter 3.[83]

Voting is the only form of talk that democratic theorists universally recognize as essential. Without the vote, all other forms of deliberation become virtually meaningless. As Dahl writes,

> At the decisive stage of collective decisions, each citizen must be ensured an equal opportunity to express a choice that will be counted as equal in weight to the choice expressed by any other citizen. In determining outcomes at the decisive stage, these choices, and only these choices, must be taken into account....[84]

Dissent

Even after a proposal has passed, some members might present a dissenting opinion to remind the group of the minority viewpoint. This amounts to articulating a preference for a position that lost in a decisive vote. Like voting, dissent is an essential feature of any theory of democracy. After a group reaches a decision, there must be an opportunity for the expression of dissent, whether it consists of lingering doubts or steadfast opposition.

This form of democratic speech allows those who opposed a group decision to put their objections on record for future reference. Barber cherishes this form of democratic talk because "it is in the aftermath of a vote that dissenters may feel the greatest need to speak their pain." The dissenter says, "'I am part of the community, I participated in the talk and deliberation leading to the decision, and so I regard myself as bound; but let it be known that I do not think we have made the right decision.'" This doesn't change the decision, but it does "bear witness to another point of view" and thereby keeps the issue, at least informally, on the agenda.[85]

Listening

Speaking counts as one half of the deliberative process, for democracy's first art is listening.[86] If group members won't listen to one another, there is little point in talking. Imagine a planning group where the treasurer talks over everyone's head. The other members are missing out on information that they may need to make a fully informed decision. Alternately, if one group member refused to listen to the treasurer's arguments, the group may have difficulty arriving at anything close to a consensus. These examples show the importance of comprehension and consideration in small group democracy.

Comprehension

Comprehension means understanding another person's speech. In a demos, the listener must be able to grasp the ideas a speaker presents and the gist of the speaker's message. A group's members can come to understand one another's (and one's own) views only through comprehending each other's statements.

This form of listening is essentially a right. The members of a demos have equal and adequate opportunities to comprehend what others say. If unable to comprehend the words or ideas of other speakers, group members are doubly deprived. They will have difficulty seeing an issue from the perspective of the group as a whole, and they lack access to information and insight that could help develop their own perspectives. Therefore, there needs to be a right to understand the language of the demos—a right to be spoken to in intelligible terms.[87]

Fishkin gives a glimpse of what full comprehension might look like by drawing on David Braybrooke's conception of "logically complete debate." In such a debate, "the participants, turn by turn, raise proposals and invoke arguments for them," and they take the time necessary to address these proposals and arguments. "As the issue moves toward resolution," writes Braybrooke,

> every participant is aware at every stage of every ingredient still current in the debate—every proposal outstanding; the arguments still pressed on its behalf; the distribution among the participants of favor for the various proposals and of opposition to them, and as well the distribution of conviction respecting the various arguments and of doubt.[88]

There is a practical limit to how far a group can go to ensure mutual comprehension, as I shall demonstrate in Chapters 4–5, but the basic right to comprehension remains essential.

Consideration

It is more common, and equally important, to think of listening as a responsibility. If group members refuse to listen, they undermine the very ideas of dialogue and deliberation. Consideration can amount to passive listening, such as sitting and attending to what another member says. When groups carefully weigh each other's words, brief silences often fall "to give time for what has been said to make its own appeal."[89] To a degree, one can always deliberate in one's mind, as jurors do during a trial.[90]

Consideration can also take a more active form, such as a verbal request for more information or probing questions to clarify a speaker's statements. These active forms of consideration are particularly valuable when the listener is unsure of the speaker's intent.

Sociologist Robert Bellah and the coauthors of *The Good Society* stressed the social value of paying attention to one another: "When we are giving our full attention to something, when we are really attending, we are calling on all our resources of intelligence, feeling, and moral sensitivity."[91] Barber also places great value on this form of listening. "Without it," he writes, "there is only the babble of raucous interests and insistent rights vying for the deaf ears of impatient adversaries."[92]

To distinguish active consideration from passive capitulation, consideration must be reciprocal. Moreover, consideration needn't result in agreement. Group members need to be willing to consider arguments, listening with an openness to consider the reasons given, but whether or not they reach full agreement is uncertain.[93]

In fact, sometimes respectful consideration can change the mind of the speaker, rather than that of the listener. This has been one of the results of the Learning Project, a national program for community organizing and outreach. Organizers working in the program have found that careful listening and probing questions can cause a speaker to reconsider his or her views—even on issues as polarized as the sources of crime and poverty.[94]

Conclusion

To summarize, small group democracy involves a sufficiently powerful and inclusive group, with a membership committed to the democratic process. A demos maintains healthy member relationships and practices a form of deliberation that entails speaking and listening rights and responsibilities.

This amounts to an unattainable ideal for any existing group, and one might question the usefulness of such a utopian vision. Dahl answers this question after presenting his own criteria for an ideal democratic procedure:

One might...wonder whether any system can hope to meet the criteria fully. And, if not, of what relevance are the criteria?...In the real world, no system will fully meet the criteria for a democratic process...However, the criteria serve as standards against which one may compare alternative processes and institutions in order to judge their relative merits. The criteria do not completely define what we mean by a good polity or good society. But to the extent that the democratic process is worthwhile, then the criteria will help us to arrive at judgments that bear directly on the relative worth or goodness of political arrangements.[95]

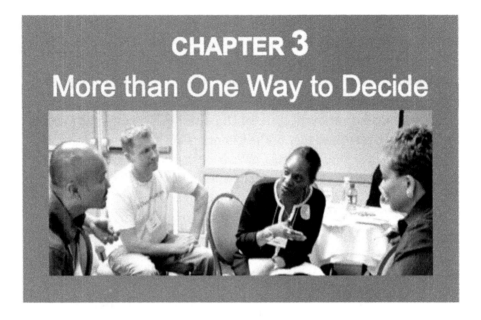

CHAPTER 3
More than One Way to Decide

The Committee for Peace in the Middle East takes pride in its method of decision making. Weekly meetings of volunteers are run by consensus, and the group has never needed a formal voting procedure. Each Tuesday night, a different member facilitates by guiding discussion and discerning when a consensus has emerged. Every meeting also has what members call a "watchdog," who makes certain the facilitator doesn't rush the meeting or intimidate anyone. All members are responsible for noting any signs of discord, but meetings usually proceed harmoniously.

Across town, the Middle East Peace Society holds a different kind of meeting. They pride themselves on their almost ritualistic use of *Robert's Rules of Order*. They elect a chair each year, and this individual oversees monthly meetings-of-the-whole, as well as bi-weekly committee meetings. Meetings are fast-paced, even though members take all critical votes by secret ballot. Rarely does one question the chair's authority, but members say this reflects the group's clear understanding of *Robert's Rules* rather than any sheepishness on the part of the membership.

These two hypothetical groups are similar to many I have joined or observed. If they existed in the same town and had overlapping goals, it is quite possible that each would dislike the other's method of decision making and claim that only their own procedures are fully democratic. Such a claim lacks merit because equally democratic groups can and do use different procedures. There is room for considerable variation within the boundaries of small group democracy.

Four methods of decision making used in small democratic groups are consensus, majority rule, proportional outcomes, and random selection.[1] Consensus tries to reach an agreement acceptable to all members, whereas majority rule allows the passage of proposals supported by a simple majority or supermajority (e.g., two-thirds). In the proportional outcomes method, decisions are segmented and distributed in proportion to the prominence of different views; this is analogous to proportional representation electoral systems, whereby parties receive a share of parliamentary seats in proportion to their percentage of the vote. Random selection presents one more egalitarian option for those situations when a group opts to subject alternative policies to equal chance, rather than equal votes.

Each of these methods fits within a democratic framework, and I will explain their features, advantages, and liabilities. Every democratic group must come to terms with how it makes decisions. Even those groups that operate based on informal norms have implicit decision rules, and without explicit reflection on those, a group's members might discover at an inopportune time that they didn't have the same conception of the rules by which their group reached decisions.[2]

Consensus

Consensus...stresses the cooperative development of a decision with group members working together rather than competing against each other. The goal of consensus is a decision that is consented to by all group members...Full consent does not mean that everyone must be completely satisfied with the final outcome—in fact, total satisfaction is rare. The decision must be acceptable enough, however, that all will agree to support the group in choosing it. —Center for Conflict Resolution[3]

The business meetings of the Religious Society of Friends (Quakers) are commonly cited an example of small group consensus. Consensus logically follows from the Quaker view of spiritual knowledge. Believing that all persons have "that of God" within them, Quakers use consensus to draw out and integrate the insights of each individual, arriving at the best possible approximation of the truth. For centuries, Quakers have found this method effective for addressing issues such as the opposition to war, the abolition of slavery, and the marrying of same-sex couples. They have used it in face-to-face groups ranging in size from 5 to 200 members.[4]

To get a feel for the Quaker way, consider this list of "Friendly Advices on the Conduct of Quaker Meetings for Business:"

1. Suitably prepare thyself for business session by previous group or individual waiting upon the Lord [prayer or meditation].

2. Seek not for information in open business session which thou shouldst have discovered by reading reports and minutes.

3. Let not certain Friends be known for their much speaking. Brevity is desirable in meetings for business as in meetings for worship.

4. If those are tempted to speak much and often, exercise restraint lest thy speaking be not "in the Spirit."

5. Having spoken on a matter of business, it is well for thee to refrain from speaking again till after others have had full opportunity to voice their concerns.

6. Thou shouldst exercise care lest thy presumed convictions be only "points" or even prejudices.

7. Beware lest thou confuse thy own desire with the leading of the Spirit.

8. Should thy concern not meet with the general approval of the meeting, in common courtesy and in true humility withdraw thy concern that the meeting may act in some measure of unity.

9. Temper thy speech with tenderness and forbearance, that Friends may "feel" the promptings of the heart.[5]

Such guidelines reflect a particular theology of decision making inappropriate for many groups. Nonetheless, they convey much of the spirit of consensus, by which even members of secular groups might ask one another to "temper thy speech with tenderness and forbearance."

An example of a semi-formal style of consensus comes from the bi-weekly meetings of Friends Co-op, a housing cooperative I lived in for two years while researching this book. The meeting facilitator would begin by reading a proposal from the agenda and opening the floor for discussion. After members had spoken their minds, the facilitator or another member would try to find a consensus. Members would register their agreement by nodding, verbally assenting, or silently wiggling their fingers (sometimes referred to as "Quaker applause").[6] In the event of continuing disagreement, the group would seek alternative solutions or a temporary resolution.[7]

Consensus relies on information, articulation, and persuasion to clarify and change the minds of group members, and it sometimes, begrudgingly, resorts to compromise.[8] Ideally, each group member provides different perspectives, puts forward knowledge, ideas, feelings, and arguments, and each listens carefully to what the others have to say. When conflicts of interest or desire arise, members aim to reconcile divergent views, often agreeing on a reformulated version of a popular proposal that failed to reach full consensus.

In the event of protracted disagreement, consensus groups continue to look for unanimity, but group members also accept the possibility of a deadlock. If agreement can't be found or time pressure forces an immediate decision, dissenters can register their views without blocking the group. There is a wide spectrum of dissent, ranging from disagreement without "standing in the way" to blocking consensus through a veto.[9] Even in those groups that have a shared terminology for "blocking" a decision, there can exist conflicting interpretations of such a block that range from improving the group's judgment and building community to obstruction and division.[10]

Consensus, however, must be distinguished from a simple "veto power" decision rule. The consensus process seeks to find common ground, whereas the veto power model is necessitated by mutual distrust and unwillingness to compromise. The United Nations Security Council exemplifies the veto system, since its members can't accept any decision that goes against their national interests. The impetus for negotiation is intolerable gridlock, rather than a sense of shared goals and mutual respect.[11]

There are many advantages to using consensus as a means of reaching decisions in small democratic groups.[12] Consensus is the surest safeguard against an unequal distribution of power. In theory, all group members have full power. In practice, those who abuse the blocking privilege often find themselves constrained by more informal social pressures, so a balance emerges between members' autonomy and their shared purpose.

Consensus can also bolster members' commitment to democracy. It radically empowers group members, often making them aware of both their autonomy and their responsibility to the group. Through consensus, members can come to cherish their democratic rights and duties. At the very least, the feeling of satisfaction that comes from consensus decision making can enhance one's appreciation of the democratic aspects of the process.[13] In my own research, I have seen precisely such effects on American criminal juries, one of the most famous bodies that routinely requires unanimity and works with a consensus-like approach to decision making.[14]

Member relations in consensus groups may be nurtured, because the relational aspects of small group democracy are the foundation of consensus. Individuality, competence, mutuality, and congeniality are historically associated with the use of consensus decision making, so it is more likely that consensus groups will direct energy toward maintaining a healthy relational atmosphere.[15] This isn't to say one can't observe relational dysfunction in consensus groups, but such outcomes often reflect the individuals populating such groups more than the dynamics of the process itself.

Consensus also safeguards opportunities to speak. Consensus assumes that the minority viewpoint is crucial, so members may go out of their way to draw out quieter group members. Even in rigorous experimental studies, it has proven a bulwark against gender bias in group participation.[16] Listening may also be enhanced by consensus, since it relies on members understanding and considering what each other says. Without such attention to one another's words, it becomes far more difficult to arrive at a decision acceptable to all.[17]

In addition, consensus increases members' commitment to the group's decisions. One may choose to implement a decision enthusiastically precisely because the group made a favorable compromise to ensure consensus. Or one may willingly implement a decision after recognizing that it was the best decision on which the group could agree. Since no decision emerges until all members can accept it, everyone has responsibility for ensuring its success.[18]

Despite these potential advantages, consensus has its pitfalls. Like any method of decision making, consensus works better in theory than in practice. Its drawbacks are its vulnerabilities—ways the process can fail if members lack sufficient experience, knowledge, or discipline. Over a period of months, groups using consensus can mature substantially and reach increasingly sound decisions by incorporating member information and perspectives.[19] Initially, however, problems are likely.

The more adept members of a consensus group can manipulate the shades of disagreement to alter a group decision. People may have a tendency to approach consensus with a bias against disagreement and conflict, so a member can induce agreement by threatening a conflict if challenged.[20]

Consensus can also take a long time.[21] A group might have a two-thirds majority from the outset, yet many meetings might pass before the majority or minority change their views and reach an agreement. Possible side effects of such a time-consuming process include frustration, missed opportunities, and a weakened commitment to group procedures. The extra effort taken to reach one decision also takes time away from deliberations on other issues.[22] Even if most members are ready for change, the existing policies remain intact if they can't reach a decision. As Jane Mansbridge points out, "Not making a decision...is making a decision to leave the status quo (which may be oppressive, or just inefficient) unchanged."[23]

Majority Rule

Whereas consensus has historic links with groups such as the Quakers, people associate majority rule with representative bodies, such as the U.S. Congress. In the standard model of majority rule, group discussion is framed by a set of written procedures—often based on *Robert's Rules of Order*—and monitored by a chair or parliamentarian. Group members have the power to extend or limit the discussion, with a simple or two-thirds majority required to call for votes, table proposals, etc. Formal voice votes or written ballots render final decisions.

This parliamentary stereotype overlooks the variety of ways democratic groups can use majority rule. Even *Robert's Rules* emphasizes the need for the group to tailor procedures to the skills and styles of its membership. Groups governed by majority rule can choose to proceed more informally by speaking without specified turns and changing proposals without a lengthy amendment process. Also, there are different kinds of majorities. A "simple majority" (i.e., more than 50% of the votes) is most commonly thought of as majority rule, but majoritarian decisions can be based on three-fifths, two-thirds, three-fourths, and any other fraction greater than one half and less than unanimity. Groups can use these different decision thresholds to give minority opinion more power on certain issues or procedural questions.[24]

Just as consensus has its strengths, so does majority rule. This form of decision making ensures equal voting power without giving group members absolute vetoes. When group members disagree even after deliberation, majority rule provides a way to resolve the dispute fairly, without favoring the status quo.[25]

Formal speaking opportunities are also likely to be equal when governed by majority rule. If the group requires a two-thirds majority vote to close debate, discussion continues until the vast majority of group members, if not all, have had their say. Different views are also likely to be aired if speaking turns are alternated between those favoring and opposing the proposal under discussion. Even if one's chances to speak are not adequate or equal in a given instance, they may become so over time.

The same procedures that ensure speaking opportunities also allow quick decisions when a majority emerges. Majority-rule procedures enable a group to close debate and take a decisive vote even when disagreement persists. Majoritarian groups sometimes require a two-thirds vote to revoke an existing policy, but often a simple majority can revise policy. In either case, the group's policies are likely to reflect the views of current majorities.

As with consensus, these strengths are most prominent when members are experienced with the group's method of decision making. Just as the limitations of consensus are exacerbated by inexperience, so are the following hazards of majority rule most prominent when members fail to understand or appreciate the purposes of majoritarian group procedures.[26]

Members of a group using majority rule sometimes find themselves in a "permanent minority," and this situation can become intolerable if exploited or ignored. The membership may divide into two or more blocks, with one being a dominant majority that votes together on a wide range of proposals. Though the majority may be only six of ten members, it will prevail ten out of ten times. If members find themselves stuck in a permanent minority, their commitment to making decisions democratically may wane. Their participation may begin to feel like voluntary servitude more than an opportunity to work within a group of equals.[27]

Even with shifting majorities, this method of decision making can lead to tense relationships among group members. Majority rule often works as a zero-sum game: One subgroup's victory is another's defeat. If the process becomes highly competitive, adversaries may begin to question one another's mutuality and competence, and group discussions can turn into hostile debates.[28]

Just as it can splinter a group, majority rule—when combined with elaborate parliamentary procedures—has a tendency to fragment issues. It can require, as one critic has noted, "a series of often confusing motions, seconds, points of order, and reconsiderations." Such a procedure "has severe limitations in helping a group get a sense of the whole of an issue and in setting some common direction for dealing with it."[29]

Finally, the ability of majorities to close debate can be abused by silencing a minority viewpoint. Once a clear majority is identified, those holding the prevailing view may not listen patiently to the minority. Considering others' arguments presumes the need to work together, but majorities have no short-term need to hear minority opinions.[30]

Proportional Outcomes

The problems associated with majority rule and consensus might lead some groups to a third alternative, the proportional outcomes method. In this system, decisions are designed to reflect the proportions of the group membership that hold different views. Whereas compromise commonly occurs within both consensus and majority rule methods, the proportional outcome method institutionalizes the spirit of compromise.

This approach has intuitive appeal because it embodies basic principles many people learn at an early age. Studies of children in Western countries have found that they gradually develop the ability to distinguish between permanent and shifting group majorities. When a few group members are always in the minority, older children more routinely give the minority a proportional share of influence.[31]

This is easiest when decisions lend themselves to simple division. Imagine a group of five children at a summer camp deciding how to pass five two-hour blocks of time. If each of the proposed activities, such as board games, could be accomplished in two hours, each child could decide how the group would spend two of its ten hours.

In other cases, groups can make compromises and concessions, such that those in the minority are given compensation in proportion to their share of the membership. In the previous example, two children in the minority may agree to do an activity that takes the full ten hours, but only if they get double desserts at lunch or the chance to make the next group decision.

When a minority faction of a group is extremely small relative to the majority, a proportional outcomes approach can go even farther. The group might give the minority limited veto power or a disproportionate amount of representation, just as each state, regardless of its population, receives two seats in the U.S. Senate.[32]

In a way, proportional outcome schemes are a hybrid of majority rule and consensus. Like majority rule, unanimity isn't required. Just as majorities get their power by virtue of their size, the relative strength of voting blocs determines their influence. Like consensus, the proportional outcomes method presumes that all members, including those in the minority, ought to shape the final decision.[33]

These similarities correspond to some of the strengths of proportional outcomes. Depending on how it is practiced, proportional outcomes can have many of the advantages associated with consensus, such as encouraging positive relationships and careful deliberation. It can also reap the benefits of majority rule, since it is egalitarian, allows quick decisions, and reduces the bias toward the status quo.

The unique advantage of this method is its tendency to structure decisions in such a way that members don't always have to choose between compromise or majority rule. Decisions can often be divided proportionally, or compromises can be made across issues, rather than within a single issue. Though other methods can also allow such outcomes, this advantage is built into the basic principles of the proportional system.[34]

Just as the proportional outcome scheme combines the potential strengths of consensus and majority rule, so does it share their weaknesses. To the extent that it emphasizes unanimity, it can invite manipulation and excessive delays. If it leans toward quick decisions, it can result in fewer speaking opportunities and inattentiveness.[35]

Proportional outcomes also have a tendency to factionalize groups, more so than even majority rule. In majority rule, minority blocs have a clear incentive to build coalitions; otherwise, they can become isolated and powerless. In the proportional outcome system, subgroups are never powerless, since they receive a degree of influence commensurate with their size. This makes it easier for a group to split into separate and permanent factions, a condition that limits the group's mutuality, deliberative capacity, and ability to implement truly collective decisions.

Random Selection

If proportional outcomes seems an unusual group decision rule, consider the often-overlooked method of random selection.[36] Like proportional outcomes, groups deploy this rule without conceptualizing it as a group *decision*, but that is precisely what it is. Whether drawing straws to see which castaway has to spear the wild boar or randomly designating a juror as foreperson, groups often use random selection to name an officer without the trouble (or pain) of holding an election. The practice has such wide cultural appeal that its formal process can involve a coin flip, card draw, roshambo (a.k.a. rock-paper-scissors), or any number of other rituals. Presuming the group can live with any possible outcome of such a process, it has a compelling logic.[37]

Then there is the matter of what to do when deadlocked or tied. A majoritarian group might arrive at this juncture and decide to carry on with the status quo, but what if there *is* no status quo? That happens, for instance, when a group's representative resigns and a replacement is vital for the group's continued functioning. In such cases, a group might do well to follow the practice adopted in more than a dozen U.S. states: Resolve the tie through a game of chance. Thus, as the

Associated Press recounts, "In March 1998, James Farrington won a hand of five-card showdown poker with an ace-high flush to be declared mayor of Estancia [New Mexico] after he and JoAnn Carlson topped a field of five candidates with 68 votes each."[38] If it's good enough for the Land of Enchantment, it's good enough for the rest of us.

Historically, often there was more to random selection than merely a desire to leave things to chance. Early Christians, like many of their contemporaries, used a random selection decision rule as a means of divine discernment. In *Acts*, the Bible tells the story of how the apostles faced the awkward matter of replacing Judas after Jesus' death. They had to choose between two men, Joseph and Matthias. They prayed, "Lord, you know everyone's heart. Show us which of these two you have chosen to take over this apostolic ministry, which Judas left to go where he belongs." The apostles proceeded to "cast lots, and the lot fell to Matthias; so he was added to the eleven apostles."[39] Though the apostles thought they were giving God the decisive ballot, the idea remains the same—turn the decision over to chance.

Though this method boasts efficiency and finality, it comes with liabilities that cause it to be more of an exception to the rules democratic groups employ. The decision has no deliberative quality, though discussion may have winnowed down the set of choices to a smaller pool of ideas or candidates to which none in the group object. It teaches no tangible lessons in democratic process, though it does manifest a truly radical form of egalitarianism. Moreover, it does nothing to strengthen commitment to democracy or to one another. Overreliance on this method, therefore, would likely lead to the desiccation of a group's deliberative norms. That said, as a solution to irresolvable dilemmas or as a means of making trivial decisions quickly, it has no peer.

Vote Counting Variations

Whether groups rely on consensus, majority rule, proportional outcomes, or random chance, they will all have to devise ways of "polling" or registering the views of the membership. Head counting is perhaps the simplest means of polling the members of a group. Other forms of polling include secret or open ballots and preliminary techniques, such as the "straw poll." When a chair in a parliamentary group asks for yeas and nays, she is collecting verbal ballots for and against a proposition. When a facilitator in a consensus group says that he "senses" that the group favors a proposal, he is implicitly asking for group members to cast their ballots, either expressing assent with silent nods or vetoing via verbal objection. All democratic groups use polling techniques, and it is useful to explore the methods available to get beyond mere hand counting.[40]

Polls or ballots on two or more alternatives can be structured in many ways. Consider a school board deciding between two proposed budgets. In its final vote, the board might allow votes for A, B, or abstention. Alternatively, it might require that a member propose one of the two budgets and vote with a yes/no/abstention format. These systems may seem identical, but in some situations they can have different results. If on the first ballot, budget A is rejected, the bylaws of the group may make it impossible (or difficult) to reconsider A. This puts pressure on the board to pass B to avoid the possibility of having no budget for the coming year. If the budgets were considered simultaneously, the vote may have shown a majority favoring A.

In the above structure, abstentions are counted as absent votes. In a forced-choice structure, by contrast, anything but a yes is counted as a *de facto* no. This may seem a minor difference, but it isn't. While serving on the Wisconsin Student Association Senate, I witnessed occasions on which the vast majority of the senators cast abstentions (or failed to vote at all) because they were uninformed, undecided, or uninterested. Under such conditions, a proposal would occasionally pass on something like a 3-1 vote in a senate with twenty-five members present. Had the forced-choice structure been in effect, all votes with fewer than thirteen yeas would fail in that meeting. To its credit, the same senate only used the forced-choice structure for critical issues, such as constitutional amendments and calls for impeachment.

A democratic group can also make polls more sensitive to the full diversity of views. Preferences and judgments, like attitudes in general, are quite complex, and subtle polls can allow members to express shades of agreement and disagreement. When confronted with two choices, a person might be forty percent in favor of one, twenty percent in favor of the other, and forty percent undecided.[41] If given ten votes apiece, a member could vote in accordance with these conflicting sentiments. Alternatively, a ballot might have five or seven choices, ranging from "strong yes" to "strong no," analogous to the seven-point scales used in survey research.

Polls can even distinguish among identical preferences that are based on different reasons. A majority may favor budget A, but not for the same reason. When polls allow members to choose among different rationales as well as different choices (e.g., "Yes because of x" versus "Yes because of y," or simply "Yes because of _____"), groups can receive valuable information. After such a poll, a group might decide to reverse or postpone a decision because there are contradictory reasons for supporting it. If half of a political action group wants to engage in civil disobedience to recruit new members and half wants to protest publicly to test the mettle of the membership, going ahead with the demonstration might prove disastrous, as members would be working at cross-purposes.

Groups can also restructure their polls to take multiple alternatives into account. Some decisions require choosing among multiple proposals, and group members might favor two or three out of ten possible decisions. Groups can choose among multiple alternatives when they need more than one of something (e.g., electing four representatives), but this can also be done when only one proposal or candidate will be selected.[42] To choose among multiple alternatives, members can rank all available choices or give them each ratings ranging from one to three. Members could also have the chance to vote yes or no for each choice, with the final tally adding yes votes and subtracting no votes. In 1985 the Earlham College student government elections used yet another alternative, asking voters to identify both the candidates they preferred, as well as those they found "acceptable."[43] In a simpler approach, the British Columbia Citizens' Assembly also used a multiple-votes approach to ensure that a final tally would show just how large a majority supported the body's final recommendation for a new electoral system.[44]

Polling procedures can also require that the group take more than one vote. This allows members to respond to the information they receive on the first poll. If members are stating both positions and rationales on the first poll, the group might discover that it needs to address some factual or moral question before taking the final poll. In the earlier school board example, a preliminary vote might be taken on the two budgets to make certain that one will pass in the final poll, avoiding the possibility of a deadlock. Preliminary polling techniques such as these assume that a relatively formal method of articulation can help move deliberation forward. An early poll forces members to probe their own views or opinions, and it makes them aware of the views of others.

With any of these polling strategies, it is possible to vote by speaking, raising hands, writing on ballots, or using an electronic voting tool. Most of these techniques allow simultaneous voting, and (unless group members close their eyes) only written or electronic ballots allow secrecy. Democratic groups vary in their use of these different methods, but it might be wise to avoid sequential voting strategies (such as roll-call votes), whereby one-by-one, members state their positions. Research on sequential straw polls shows how the order in which members vote can affect the outcome. If the fifth person in a nine person group has to signal her choice after four "yea" votes have been given, she becomes a bit more likely to go along with the "yeas" than she would be otherwise. To avoid this problem, members can vote secretly or simultaneously, possibly proceeding through a round-robin to elaborate their views after stating their general positions.[45]

Unfortunately, all of these polling techniques are subject to error and abuse. The more complex the method, the more chance there is for confusion, which results in inadequate opportunities to express final preferences. More elaborate polls are also easier to distort, since group members can exaggerate the extremity of their views. Members can vote for their preferred candidate or proposal and vote against all the others—even if they know the others are also fine choices. In multiple polling schemes, members can manipulate the final poll through deceptive votes in preliminary tallies. For instance, a member may want to block a proposal with a veto without having to listen to the counterarguments of other group members. This member can support the proposal during the straw poll, then veto it during the final vote, taken at the end of the group's scheduled meeting time.[46]

The extra time and thought that complex polls require make them appropriate for groups mature enough to present their views honestly in situations with sufficient time to permit reflection. Experimenting with a variety of polling techniques is the best way to determine which combination best suits a group under different circumstances.

Mixing Methods

The spirit of experimentation should also guide a group's efforts to integrate various polling techniques with different decision-making methods. Ideally, groups can find ways to draw on the strengths of each approach and even adapt their procedures to changing memberships, issues, and situations, while keeping in mind the need for bylaws or norms to provide stability.

For example, when I wrote the first edition of this book, I witnessed a hybrid method developed for the Board of Directors for Madison Community Co-ops. That organization allowed board members to vote as favoring, opposing, objecting, or abstaining. An objection blocked consensus, after which the proposal was either tabled or discussed further. Eventually, the objection could be overridden through majority rule. If there was no objection, yeas and nays were counted and the majority decided the verdict. One exception was that any procedural motion, such as a call for recess, was voted on through simple majority rule.

A precursor to the board's procedure is Martha's Rules of Order, which developed at another residential housing cooperative. A group using Martha's Rules tries to work toward a full consensus among group members, but if necessary, the group can override one or two objections to a proposal with a simple majority vote. If three or more group members object, the override requires a two-thirds majority, and the issue gets tabled until the next meeting to allow time for reformulation and compromise. Martha's Rules also formalizes consensus' ability to measure the degree to which an individual supports a proposal. One can say, "I am comfortable with the proposal," or merely, "I can live with the proposal." If there are competing proposals, the distinction between these two degrees of support can be decisive, but usually the distinction merely gauges how enthusiastically the group supports a proposal.[47]

Such methods will not suit all groups at all times. Rather, the point is for each small democratic group to adjust and combine different methods of decision making and polling to meet its needs. Within the boundaries of democratic decision making, a vast number of varieties and combinations of rules exist.

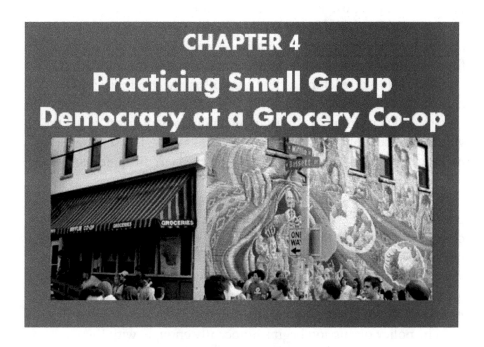

CHAPTER 4
Practicing Small Group Democracy at a Grocery Co-op

"Whatever is, is possible." —T. L. Peacock[1]

At 6:30 PM on a rainy Monday evening, the small room above Mifflin Street Community Co-op fills with greetings and friendly chatter. Each of nine Co-op staff members carries drinks and snacks from the grocery store below. They set their coats on book shelves and file cabinets, then move chairs and floor cushions into a circle that bends its way around desks, boxes, and the odd objects that rest against the walls. When Laura enters, she asks everyone to fill in their slots on the work schedule. She hands the schedule clipboard to Rose, who scribbles down her name a few times and passes it around the circle.

By 6:40 PM the appointed facilitator, Dan, has begun to go down the list of "ongoing" items, and two staff members explain what they have done since the last meeting. Yes, the bicycle rack has been purchased, but it has not yet arrived. Yes, the sign about the ongoing boycott has been posted next to the offending food item.

Dan reads the agenda out loud and asks if anything needs to be changed. A forgotten announcement or two is quickly tacked-on, and the staff turns to new business. Rose briefs the staff on a donation request, and after reaching a clear consensus, the group decides to contribute cheese and crackers to an upcoming community forum. Louis asks what should be done about a person who wants to get the volunteer discount but doesn't work his full hours. The staff agrees to make an exception, due to the person's special circumstances. And so on.

The group takes care of day-to-day business and time flies by, punctuated by the periodic antics of Laura and Sam, who take turns as court jester. Then, in the heart of the meeting, Dan announces that the next agenda item is work schedule policy. The jesters groan and two staff look about the room nervously. Like synchronized swimmers, the group members simultaneously and uncomfortably adjust their sitting positions. There is a five-second pause.

The policy discussion begins innocently enough, with Kate reviewing last week's distribution of work shifts. Louis suggests there was a misunderstanding about who was working on Saturday, and Sam points out that two "shift workers" (part-time, temporary employees) put in a lot of time during the week. Amy expresses concern about overusing shift workers, and other staff members agree. There's a pinch of tension as Ray explains the problem with having too many of one's shifts covered by other staff and shift workers.

Norma correctly discerns that she is the staff member on everyone's mind, and she explains why she had to swap so many shifts. Kate explains why Norma's actions upset her, and Laura, Rose, and Ray nod in agreement. Before too long, all have spoken their minds, a tentative resolution is reached, and the meeting continues. The tension slowly subsides while the discussion turns to three minor business items and the remaining announcements.

By 9:00 PM the last agenda item is done, and the staff makes certain that all work shifts for the following week are covered. Fifteen minutes later, the meeting unofficially adjourns, and the Co-op staff slip into their coats and walk downstairs in pairs. The last person locks the store and leaves at 10:00 PM.[2]

This is a glimpse of a typical staff meeting at Mifflin Street Community Co-op, a worker-managed grocery store that served Madison, Wisconsin for more than a quarter century, from 1969-2006. In that time, it built a reputation as a politically engaged and self-conscious business. It supported and worked with numerous political and community organizations, and it brought its politics to its shelves, providing consumer information and alternative products to its customers.

The "Owner's Manual" for members of the Co-op gave insight into Mifflin's character as a "living, breathing experiment in participatory democracy, community control, and economic alternatives." "Open membership" and "democratic control based on one member-one vote" were its first principles. A pamphlet, available for free at the check-out counter, echoed the language of the Co-op's original bylaws:

> Mifflin Street Community Co-op exists to embody a belief in community self-determination in opposition to the dominant trends in all communities in which control is increasingly concentrated outside the community and operated for profits which are not used for the betterment of the community. Our assets...are committed to this struggle by any means necessary.[3]

The history of Mifflin Co-op reflects a commitment to being more than just a store. The Co-op, including both its storefront and second-floor rooms, served as temporary lodging for the homeless, a community health-care center, a base of operations for organizing community celebrations and demonstrations, an information nexus for political organizers and other co-ops, a shelter from the police, an outlet for alternative products and organic produce, a brick canvas for colorful murals, and a symbol of community identity and determination.[4]

Mifflin Co-op's unique reputation derived more from this remarkable history than the odd brands of food stacked on its shelves or the Marxist posters that adorned its interior walls. What made Mifflin unique was its staff meetings. When I did preliminary research for this book, I heard many first-hand accounts alleging that the Co-op's meetings were as good a model of democratic decision making as I would ever find.[5]

In the fall of 1990, the Mifflin Co-op worker collective gave me permission to study its weekly staff meetings. I chose to focus on those meetings because regularized face-to-face gatherings are the heart of many a group's existence. The life of a small group transcends its meetings, but the times that it meets as a whole have a special importance. As anthropologist Helen Schwartzman argues, a group's meetings reveal the center of its system—the place where shared meanings, power relations, and group norms are developed and validated or challenged. As she puts it, meetings can "make, remake, and sometimes unmake" a group.[6]

I studied the Co-op's staff meetings using a variety of techniques. I started with a wealth of background information, including my previous experiences at Mifflin as both customer and volunteer. (They trusted me to do little more than cut up giant wheels of bulk cheese and repackage it for sale.) I read notes from past staff meetings and learned the history of the Co-op, as recounted by former staff.

Above all else, I relied on the video and audio tapes I made of six consecutive staff meetings, most of which took place in the upstairs room at the Co-op. I set up cameras and microphones in opposite corners of the room and let them run continuously during the meetings.

In addition, I had numerous informal conversations with the staff, and all nine staff members completed a long questionnaire about themselves and the Co-op. I followed up this questionnaire with one-on-one interviews, talking with each staff member for one to two hours. After the last interview, I met with the staff as a whole to elicit their reactions to my preliminary findings. In what follows, I draw on each of these methods of observation to create a multifaceted portrait of Mifflin Co-op's attempt to practice small group democracy.[7]

Group Power

Following the framework outlined in Chapter 2 of this book, the first issue I examined was the extent to which the staff controlled their agenda. Did the staff's decisions have concrete effects, or was the staff merely advisory to some other entity, such as a board?

In the Co-op's bylaws, the staff—sometimes referred to as the "worker collective"—has responsibility for the "day to day affairs of the Co-op and the management of the store." These bylaws give the Board of Directors responsibility for long range planning, budget approval, and the hiring and firing of staff. The Co-op's general membership—mostly customers—elects five board members, and the staff appoints two more. Committees composed of staff, board members, and community members take on other responsibilities, such as personnel review and the development of the budget.

In practice, the staff's weekly meetings are the site of both day-to-day decisions and broader policy development. During the six meetings I observed, the Mifflin staff made several decisions, virtually all of which took effect immediately. The staff made a half-dozen donations, changed store policies, and set work schedules.

Even smaller decisions were made in the store every day through a parallel democratic process involving whoever happened to be at work. As one co-op member said, "Choices about tuna fish or about putting a tax on bananas were informed by the same process seen in staff meetings." More generally, Mifflin's decision-making process was "not just about governance but also about real things in the product line."[8]

My study of the co-op, however, focused on its staff meetings—particularly the most difficult questions raised during those meetings. One such challenge concerned the establishment of "tenure incentives." Retaining long-term staff members enhances the depth of knowledge and quality of work at the Co-op, so the staff proposed giving workers monetary or vacation bonuses for staying with the Co-op longer. In this case, the staff decision was contingent on approval by the Board of Directors. Nevertheless, the Board had previously informed the staff that it would accept whatever the staff decided, so staff deliberations became decisive. The Board often took this approach, so the staff regularly decided long-range Co-op policies.

The staff's power was noticeably constrained, though, by external political and economic forces.[9] As for political sovereignty, the last article of the Mifflin bylaws acknowledges that the Co-op's rules are subject to the laws of local, state, and federal governments. Out of necessity, Co-op activities were sometimes aimed toward complying with health codes and other regulations. Although the Co-op's early years involved acts of civil disobedience, the store's viability required generally obeying existing laws.

Since the Co-op sought to maintain financial stability, its stocking, pricing, and other monetary decisions were constrained by prevailing market forces. The store's comfortable profit margin, however, gave it room for flexibility. The gross receipts from 1990 totaled over $800,000, which allowed the Co-op to maintain and upgrade the store, donate $10,000 to the community, give good wages and full health benefits to the staff, and set aside enough additional capital for investment in the Co-op's future.

Aside from the amount of power held by the staff, it is also necessary to look at the *distribution* of that power. One can crudely assess relative power by noticing the physical location of different group members when important decisions are being made. For example, at a housing board meeting I recently attended, I sat in the outer circle around the board's central table. During the meeting, the board welcomed five new members, all of whom were present and sitting in the outer circle. After a few minutes, it occurred to the new members that they were now equals to those already on the board, so they picked up their chairs and moved to the table. The only remaining difference was that the president of the board had seated himself at the head of the rectangular table.

At Mifflin Co-op, staff members sat in a ragged circle, with no seating distinction among them. It is no coincidence that this geometric shape has become the seating arrangement of choice for egalitarian small groups. In the circle, there is no "head of the table" and there are no outer rings or rows.[10]

Another sign of even power distribution was the fact that staff members all held special assignments, and they had some leeway on issues within their areas of expertise. For instance, Sam was in charge of maintenance, and his views on maintenance issues received greater weight. Also, he was more likely to make minor maintenance decisions on his own or after consulting two or three other staff members. Nonetheless, this system of specialization didn't amount to a formal division of authority, and aside from minor, day-to-day decisions, all staff decisions required staff approval. Even those powers delegated to designated committees could, if necessary, be revoked by the full staff.

Inclusiveness

Though the staff had substantial power, the inclusiveness of its meetings was more ambiguous. Meetings were fully inclusive with regard to the staff: Members had equal authority during meetings, and attendance was always high. Within the slightly larger population of all Co-op employees, however, the meetings were somewhat exclusive.

Recalling the discussion of seating arrangements, it is helpful to note who isn't present in the meeting room when important decisions are being made. The Co-op's shift workers and general membership didn't attend meetings, and their physical absence reflects their lower status in the Co-op. Shift workers received the same hourly wage as staff members and sometimes worked a significant number of hours, but they rarely appeared at staff meetings. These workers were hired part-time, with the understanding that their status was comparable, but not equal, to that of staff members. The shift workers did not have the same "ownership" of the store as did staff.

This inequality, though typical of most businesses, was a controversial issue at Mifflin Co-op. A staff discussion of evaluation policy illustrates the problem that the staff/shift-worker distinction created. Every year the staff evaluates itself and the shift workers, and during one of its Monday night meetings, the staff discussed the possibility of changing this policy.[11]

Rose: Are we going to have the shift workers evaluate each other?

Kate: Well, we want them to, but they don't want to do it.

Rose: Really?

Ray: Scott is opposed to the concept of evaluations.

Kate: He doesn't talk to us about it. He just came up to us and said, 'I refuse to fill out this evaluation.'

Norma: Well, he said that he explained it on his other form.

Kate: I just don't think that's a reasonable situation.

Norma: Well, apparently he thought it was reasonable.

Ray: Those two have a difference of opinion.

Amy: Is Leonard going to evaluate the other shift workers?

Kate: I don't know. He handed in a sealed envelope, and Matthew hasn't handed his back.[12]

As the excerpt shows, the staff took the views of shift workers into account somewhat haphazardly. The shift workers did have the right to attend meetings, and a former shift-worker reported doing so without hesitation. Nonetheless, the shift workers didn't have the same decision-making power; their judgments didn't have to figure into a staff consensus.

Some staff found this system acceptable. They saw the need for two levels of commitment to the Co-op, one for dedicated staff and one for those seeking more temporary employment. Other staff loathed unnecessary hierarchies and viewed this as one of them, yet there was no proposal on the staff's agenda to abolish the distinction between full-time employees and shift workers.

Beyond its employees, the staff tried to include customers and community members in proportion to the impact staff decisions had on those groups. All staff meetings were open to the general public, and non-employees occasionally brought concerns to the Co-op's staff meetings. While those meeting visitors held no decision-making power, they did have the opportunity to raise issues and offer criticisms. Also, those customers who became members of the Co-op through paying an annual fee or doing volunteer work were invited to the annual membership meeting. At those meetings (one of which I attended as a voting member), the membership elected the Mifflin Co-op Board of Directors. In theory, the membership could have a strong influence on the Co-op, but in practice, membership participation was usually low. Less than five percent of the membership attended the annual meeting, and there was little competition for seats on the Board.

Commitment

Since the staff are the people most directly included in the decision-making process, it is essential that they embrace the principles of democracy. Initial evidence of the Co-op's long-term commitment to the democratic process comes from the wording of its bylaws, as updated in 1991. These bylaws distill the Co-op's democratic spirit into written, binding laws, which can be as important to a small group as a constitution is to a nation. The bylaws include a preamble that states the Co-op's broader commitment to democratic participation:

> The cooperative shall function with open, democratic control of its operations exercised jointly by members and the worker collective. Maximum member participation on all levels and continual improvement in the quality of group interactions and communication are to be energetically sought. Community members shall be encouraged to become members of the cooperative, and helped to learn more about the products and operations of the co-op, with an eye toward their future, increased participation.

Staff insisted that these written words hold meaning for them. During interviews, each explained why they valued democracy at the Co-op and beyond. Each had previously worked in undemocratic workplaces, and they valued the power Mifflin granted them over their work environment. They also saw a connection between their appreciation of small group democracy and their commitment to making their society—and their world—more democratic. When asked what democracy meant, each was able to articulate basic principles, such as the importance of placing decision-making power in the hands of the people, ensuring equality of opportunity, allowing freedom of speech, and embracing diversity.[13]

But a democratic group reveals its procedural commitments in its actions more than its rules. Co-op staff showed an active commitment in many ways. Each had participated in more than one workshop on participatory decision making, and all had taken time after meetings to reflect on the strengths and weaknesses of their decision-making processes. Part of the reason they valued their jobs at Mifflin was *because* of its democratic process, and they were willing to expend time and energy on its behalf. In fact, staff permitted my obtrusive observation, completed lengthy questionnaires, and granted in-depth interviews largely because they viewed this project as an opportunity to make their meetings and themselves more democratic.[14]

Relationships

Beyond a shared commitment, small group democracy requires healthy relations among group members. To the extent that Mifflin Co-op staff meetings were democratic, the staff members had to show a measure of congeniality toward one another and regularly affirm each other's individuality, competence, and mutuality.

A starting point for understanding relational communication at Mifflin Co-op is the patterns of talk during Monday night meetings. I looked at what staff said to each other and tried to decode the relational messages their words conveyed. Such interpretation is imperfect, as one can't know precisely the intent or reception of a speaker's words. Nonetheless, I begin with an overview of the staff's relational messages before turning to concrete examples.[15]

I conducted a crude content analysis of the transcripts from the Mifflin Co-op meetings to identify which messages conveyed positive (e.g., affirming, supporting, appreciative) or negative (e.g., critical, dismissive, hostile) relational meanings. Staff members directed most of their positive relational talk toward the group as a whole, or to Ray, Sam, Amy, and Norma. Almost all of the negative messages flew in the direction of Louis and Norma. Ray rarely spoke in negative terms (i.e., invalidation of a member's individuality, denial of mutuality, and hostile comments), whereas Louis, Kate, and Norma sent negative messages more often than the others. Amy, Ray, and Laura received only kind words, whereas Louis and Norma received far more negative than positive messages.

Every staff member except Ray and Norma directed the vast majority of their negative relational talk toward Norma. The affirming talk Norma received came largely from herself, with Ray and Dan each contributing a single affirming comment; the friendly words she received came almost exclusively from Kate. The hostile talk Louis received came from Norma and, to a lesser extent, Kate, and the affirming messages he received came from himself.

In addition, the overall nonverbal communication pattern was positive. If a digital camera had taken still images of the group at regular intervals, the photos would have shown frequent smiles, expressive speakers, and attentive listeners. Staff members usually spoke in steady speeds and at a normal pitch and volume—although lively exchanges or attempts at humor often involved rapid and fluctuating speech. The postures and movements of the staff usually appeared calm and relaxed, revealing their general comfort with the setting and each other.

Staff usually maintained their composure, though their emotions would surface in harsher tones and slightly higher volumes when delivering or receiving angry words. If shouting began, staff quickly intervened, as Rose once did when Louis began to raise his voice. More moderate emotional displays, such as soft crying or a long, frustrated pause in the midst of an impassioned speech, went uninterrupted. The bulk of the tense or hostile nonverbal behaviors was directed toward or sent by Norma and Louis.[16]

A more contextualized look at Mifflin's staff meetings reveals the meaning of these general communication patterns. For the most part, relations among staff were harmonious during meetings. The most prominent recurring form of relational communication was the steady stream of friendly and humorous comments. As one example among many, the staff made light of their decision to donate cheese to an anniversary party for WORT, the community-sponsored radio station in Madison, Wisconsin (that still exists, to this day).

Ray: A block of mild cheddar seems like a nice, solid donation.

Rose: You decide, Kate.

Laura: How exciting.

Ray: Get one of those green [moldy] North Farm ones.

Louis: Yeah, a green and yellow cheese.

The staff also used humor to lighten up discussions of tenure incentives. The tenure incentives plan had been somewhat controversial, because it would create a difference in compensation between new and veteran staff members. Staff couldn't decide on a neutral term to describe the proposed policy ("tenure incentives" is my own invention), so a curious name emerged during one of the staff meetings.

Norma: Okay, the last three items are evaluation schedules, Laura's long-term plans, and turnips for long-term commitment.

Amy: Turnips?

Sam: Mmhmm.

Later that same meeting, Amy joined in the fun: "Okay, we had talked about some kind of plan to encourage people to stay on longer, and we didn't want to call it a reward or an incentive, so it's called 'turnips for a long-term commitment.' We just thought using a vegetable was safe." At the next meeting, staff continued to play with this terminology.

Laura: At any rate, I think we're down to turnips, folks.

Ray: And alternative turnips.

Laura: Yes, like beets and rutabagas.

Louis: Okay, guys.

Laura: Parsnips.

Ray: Long-term benefit alternatives!

These comments served a serious purpose by helping to maintain a friendly group atmosphere during difficult deliberations. In addition, the term "turnip," though thoroughly silly, had a rationale behind it. As Sam recently explained, the staff wanted a tenure incentive policy that defied conventional notions of threat and reward. "A turnip," he said with a smile, "is neither a carrot nor a stick, but it is a root vegetable."[17]

This congenial atmosphere dissipated when the staff discussed whether Norma could take another vacation. This was the only time staff members repeatedly and openly addressed the mutuality and individuality of staff members. Although this discussion was more the exception than the rule at the Co-op's Monday night meetings, it deserves special attention. It created tension for the entire staff, and every staff member brought it up spontaneously during their interviews.

Norma had taken off a lot of time in recent months. She frequently asked staff members and shift workers to cover her shifts to grant her a block of consecutive free days. She had already taken more vacation time than the staff would have liked. The prolonged absence of a staff member put a strain on the rest, so when the staff agreed to give Norma one more vacation during the summer, she promised not to do it again for several months. The understanding was that if Norma violated this agreement, she would have to leave the Co-op.

The issue came up during the first meeting I observed. Norma asked if she could trade two of her shifts to take another vacation. After a few minutes of discussion, Ray expressed his point of view.

Ray: The great thing about the Co-op is that you can take off
        lots of time one stretch at a time, but the people that
        keep working at the Co-op are the ones that suffer. They're

the ones who pick up extra shifts. They're the ones that take over other people's responsibilities, and they just get sick and tired of it.

Sam: And you aren't able to accomplish anything.

Louis: Right, in your own—

Sam: In your own specialty. I get shit done for maintenance.

Amy: If you just add that up and see how many weeks somebody has been gone, it's getting to be almost—

Laura: A full year.

Amy: Yeah, almost a full year. And, it always creates pressure when somebody's gone. It affects everybody.

Later in the meeting, Amy said, "I think that the rest of the staff is trying to stay within the parameters of the vacation policy, but you're looking at it a different way, saying, 'There's a day here, there's a day there, and I don't fit into those parameters but everyone else does.'" After a long pause, Sam said that he agreed: "I guess I feel a similar way. I feel like when people are talking to you about this, I see a lot of nodding and I hear a lot of 'Mmhmm, mmhmm,' but I don't feel like a lot of it's sinking into you about why we feel the way we do. I don't feel like a lot of what we're saying registers."

During the next staff meeting, the staff returned to the issue, and the exchanges between Norma and Kate became particularly heated.

Kate: I've just been doing training for the Board of Directors, and it's become very apparent to me that we have to think of us as being the store. This is a collective, and the Co-op is more than a store. This isn't Food Mart, and we're not hired to just come and do our job. It's an emotional institution, and I think that that's maybe where you've gotten a little sidetracked, Norma.

I think you have done a good job. I definitely have seen improvement, and I appreciate that. And yet I think what Dan is speaking to—this resentment thing—is that you're neglecting the emotional needs of the collective, not necessarily purposely, but for lack of any knowledge of how to do it.

I know I feel tremendously alienated from you, and I don't know that it can be rectified. I don't know how we can get through all of these issues without feeling that bond—that "we're all in this together" sort of feeling. That's what I've felt has been lacking over the last number of months.

And it's not just coming from you. It's coming from all of us, or most of us, too. And that's why when I heard that you were considering whether or not you would resign, I was thinking that might be the easy option. Because then we don't have to try to put it all back together again. I think it's going to be difficult for me, and I know it will be difficult for you—

Norma: I know it will be really difficult, but I've already decided that I'm not going to move on. I don't think that leaving is a solution. I mean, there might be cases where that has to be the solution. But as far as I'm concerned, if we can't get it together here—with our many shared values—then forget Palestine and Israel. Forget it. I just believe that it's possible, and it's worth doing it. I don't want to just bail out.

Kate: But this is not the way to start, and I can tell you that right now. This is not the way to start, and that's what I was feeling last week. If you care about this group at all, don't trade shifts like you did last week. That is not the way to mend the rift that we're feeling in this room right now.

As much as you're trying, I don't think you're seeing the heart of the issue. Or that's how it seems to me. And I know you're trying really hard, but it's just like two ships passing in the night. We're not connecting, and that makes me scared, because connecting takes a lot of time. I don't want to keep spending all this time if the ships are not going to get any closer.

Norma: Well, I'm going to think about that some more, but I've considered it already. I feel like part of the democratic process—part of what has to happen in a collective—is that people have to learn to stand up for themselves when they feel like they're not being treated fairly.[18]

In this excerpt, Kate initially offers encouragement by commending Norma on doing a good job at the Co-op, but Kate may say this only to soften the criticism that follows. Kate explicitly questions Norma's attachment to the Co-op, as well as her awareness of the norms and emotional needs of the collective. Kate portrays Norma and the Co-op as "like two ships passing" and fears that the ships "are not going to get any closer." Kate's feelings are so strong that she considers Norma's resignation the best possible solution, "because then we don't have to try to put it all back together again."

Norma responds to Kate's criticisms by affirming her own mutuality and individuality. Norma admits there is division in the Co-op, but she insists that she is a part of the group and doesn't "want to just bail out." In her view, standing up for personal interests doesn't threaten the cohesion of a democratic group. Seen in this light, her actions don't reflect a separation from the Co-op, but only a legitimate desire to give her personal needs equal priority with those of the collective.[19]

The conflict between Kate and Norma was not resolved in this discussion, nor was it mitigated in subsequent deliberations. Ultimately, Norma went against the wishes of the rest of the group by exchanging two of her shifts with Louis and one of the shift workers.

When I conducted interviews, I found that my own observations paralleled those of the staff, who believed relational talk during meetings generally was respectful and good-natured. As Ray wrote, "Most of the time, things are quite friendly with the staff. The problem comes in with the personality conflicts." Kate concurred: "I feel very unified with most of the collective. The joking and personalness, though time-consuming and distracting, is essential to pulling the group together and making the meetings unintimidating. We learn a lot about each other and can relax into being ourselves."

The one staff member who disagreed was Norma, who felt that the relationships among staff members were not so amicable. In particular, she thought the staff only marginally affirmed her individuality and competence, generally denied her mutuality, and created, at best, a neutral—but not friendly—atmosphere. She believed staff unfairly questioned her prioritization of personal needs, which she believed she should act on regardless of how others talked to her. On the question of competence, she recalled that on one of the anonymous staff evaluations she received, someone had written, "Norma should be more satisfied with where she is in life, i.e. being at work." She felt that this remark questioned her ability to know what's in her own best interests. Finally, she sometimes felt individual staff members were distant and unfriendly towards her. She felt like an outsider.

Because so many of the staff enjoyed their workplace relationships, one might still consider the Co-op's meetings very democratic in this regard. That global assessment, however, must be qualified by the strained relationship between Norma and the rest of the staff. Norma didn't accept the staff's sanguine self-portrayal, largely because they questioned her individuality, denied her mutuality, and directed hostility or resentment toward her. Kate went so far as to ask Norma to leave the Co-op, a request some of the other staff supported.

Was Norma treated unfairly and disrespectfully? Or were the staff trying to maintain reasonable norms by constructively criticizing Norma and openly expressing their emotions? Norma believed that the Co-op went too far, seeking consensus and homogeneity at the cost of her individuality: "I think their ideal Mifflin Co-op would consist of people that agree with them. They hand-pick people with shared values, and I'm just kinda outside of that. Consequently, I don't feel free to be as active. I don't feel like I'm part of a unified whole. I don't feel like I'm a part of the Co-op."

According to Norma, the staff could not accept the fact that she didn't work as many hours at the Co-op as the others. At a meeting held before the six that I videotaped, the staff had agreed that although large differences in work hours ran contrary to Co-op goals, Norma and others could continue working reduced hours under a "grandfather clause." Norma argued that the Co-op was violating that agreement by asking her to heighten her commitment to the Co-op. In her view, the negative messages she received were designed, perhaps unwittingly, to drive her away. Contrary to the spirit of consensus, the staff asked her to bow to the will of the majority.[20]

The rest of the staff argued that Norma had given too much priority to her personal interests and too little to those of the Co-op. Most admitted they had lost respect for Norma as a result, and some acknowledged having strong negative feelings toward her. Nevertheless, it appeared that this hostility was directed toward Norma's behavior with regard to vacation time, not toward Norma as an individual. Remarkably, Norma received almost no negative relational talk during every other discussion. In addition, the staff tempered its negative talk with positive comments. Norma received more negative and positive relational messages than any other staff member.

The conflict between Norma and the staff over vacation time provided a challenging test of the relationships at Mifflin Co-op. The Co-op appears to have passed this test, even in Norma's opinion. Despite her concerns with the meeting process, she insisted that I should put her doubts in perspective:

> I really do think that staff members try to respect the idea that they shouldn't push something through against someone's will. They still really respect the fact that they don't want to be coercive, and they really do want to empathize with what somebody's saying and try to take it seriously, respect it, and integrate it into some arrangement that's agreeable to everybody. And that does work remarkably well.[21]

Relations between Norma and the rest of the staff may have been tense at times, but she remained on the Co-op staff for another two years after the meetings recounted herein.

Opportunities to Speak

Given this relational setting, what was the character of deliberation at Mifflin Co-op? Did staff members always get a chance to talk during meetings? Did they meet their speaking responsibilities? Did they listen to one another? I answer each of these questions, in turn, beginning with how staff safeguarded each other's speaking opportunities.

Opportunities to set the agenda and vote are crucial, because without them, one can't directly influence what it is the group will discuss or what its decisions will be. Of all the forms of communication, these were the easiest to observe at Mifflin Co-op. This fact is, in and of itself, encouraging: if every group member can see how and when the agenda is set and votes are taken, any manipulation of agendas and decisions will be easier to detect.

At Mifflin Co-op, the agenda is set during the week prior to the Monday night meeting. During each workday, staff members can write whatever items occur to them on a scrap of paper tacked or taped onto the basement door. Anything from announcements to serious issues might appear there, and no limits are placed on how much one can put on the written agenda. Then, near the beginning of each meeting, the agenda is briefly reviewed. Items can be removed or postponed, but staff members refrain from using any procedural tricks to sneak items off or onto the agenda. Similarly, the different facilitators moved through the agenda with caution, never rigidly forcing a discussion to close before the group was done deliberating.

Voting was equally straightforward. Under Mifflin's version of consensus, the facilitator's behavior varied greatly depending on the seriousness of the item. When an agenda item required a minor decision, the facilitator would usually intervene as soon as a discussion began to wander. If a staff member made a proposal the group liked, words and nods of agreement would quickly signal consensus. The facilitator would sometimes (but not always) ask if the group had agreed, and the note taker would usually (but not always) make sure the decision was clearly stated.

When an agenda item was more significant, discussion would be relatively open-ended, and the facilitator would often keep a list of speakers. As each person indicated—with a whisper, a hand signal, or a raised eyebrow—his or her desire to speak, the facilitator made a mental note or wrote the person's name on a list. One might get moved up the list if he or she hadn't spoken as much in that meeting, or if the present topic concerned them personally. Sometimes a speaker at the top of the list deferred to another, especially when the speaker thought it would help the flow of discussion. Depending on the issue and the number of people wishing to speak, the facilitator would stop keeping a speakers list and let the discussion proceed on its own.

As the group neared a decision, the facilitator would get a sense of the group's positions by asking every member to state their view. If agreement appeared to exist, the facilitator might ask if anyone disagreed with the apparent consensus. If a concern or objection arose, the group would continue talking, postpone the issue to the next meeting, or drop the issue altogether (though I never saw staff do the latter during the meetings I observed).

A final decision was never made without the awareness and equal participation of all staff. Those unable to attend particular meetings would make certain their views on serious issues were passed along. No important decision was made that contradicted the views of a staff member who was unable to attend that particular meeting.

Agenda setting and voting, though, are just two of the many features of democratic deliberation. It was also important to see whether staff members had equal and adequate opportunities to reformulate the agenda, articulate their views, persuade one another, provide information, and dissent after a decision was reached.

Silence is one of the clearest signs of a speaking opportunity. When a speaker finishes and no one takes the floor for a few seconds, therein lies a chance to speak. Other factors, such as the timing and context of the silence, can make it more or less of an invitation to speak, but for those who rarely interrupt, a pause provides an entry into the discussion. During Mifflin Co-op's staff meetings, such silences occurred somewhat regularly—perhaps every five minutes.

Just as silence signals the existence of an opportunity, speaking constitutes the use of one. The distribution of "speaking turns" shown in Figure 2 provides an indirect accounting of staff members' chances to speak during Co-op meetings. Louis, Dan, and especially Kate spoke most often, and Sam and Rose opened their mouths the fewest number of times.[22]

Figure 2. Number of Times Each Co-op Staff Member Spoke During Recorded Meetings

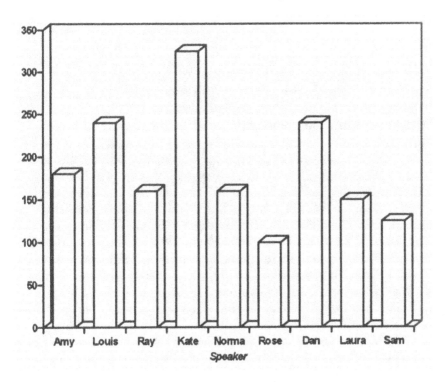

Similarly, an examination of how long each staff member spoke reveals that only Amy, Laura, and Sam held the floor less than the average amount of time. Kate set and reformulated the agenda the most, whereas Rose, Laura, and Sam rarely did so. Louis, Kate, Norma, and Dan articulated their views most often, and Amy, Laura, and Sam did so the least. From one category of talk to the next, there is a rather consistent pattern: Kate spoke the most, while Laura and Sam spoke the least.

One can also look at the number of times during meetings that staff members verbally opened or closed opportunities for others to speak. Speakers can open opportunities by explicitly requesting that another person speak (e.g., "What do you think, Dan?"). Or they can close opportunities by blatantly interrupting another speaker (excepting those instances where the interruption is a short interjection or a word of encouragement).[23] By these calculations, the Co-op staff opened over three hundred opportunities to speak during the transcribed portions of the six videotaped meetings. The people who opened the most opportunities were Kate and Dan, while Louis, Norma, and Sam opened the fewest. Louis cut off others most frequently, whereas Amy and Sam each made only one clear-cut interruption.

Because Kate and Dan tended to speak the most, it is important that they were also the two people who opened the greatest number of speaking opportunities. In effect, they offered chances to speak in proportion to the larger number of opportunities they used themselves. Three of the staff members who spoke least often (Amy, Laura, and Sam) also made the smallest number of blatant interruptions. They might have been too reserved to jump into the deliberations when others were speaking, but perhaps they simply had less desire to speak and felt no need to interrupt a speaker.

Amy, Louis, and Norma received the largest number of personal invitations to speak, whereas Ray received the fewest. The loquacious Kate and Dan were cut off the most, and Rose the least. Kate and Dan were also the only staff members interrupted more times than they were invited to speak. The least vocal staff members, Laura and Sam, didn't receive the most opportunities to speak, but neither were they cut off frequently.

This initial glimpse suggests the need to look closely at the speaking opportunities of Laura and Sam, two of the quietest staff members. To judge the quality of their opportunities, I carefully examine the staff's deliberations of Norma's vacation plans and the proposed tenure incentives plan. I choose these two issues because every staff member had strong opinions about them. Did Laura and Sam get an equal and adequate chance to talk during these important and emotionally charged discussions?

During the first of the two deliberations on Norma's vacation, both Laura and Sam jumped into the conversation and spoke for long periods of time. Neither speaker was interrupted, and both ended with definitive statements, signaling that they had finished their speaking turns. Sam finished by saying, "I don't feel like you're seeing it from our point of view. That's where I'm at." Laura concluded, "I'd prefer to see a full-fledged commitment. And I don't know if you can do that."

During the final discussion of tenure incentives, one hour had passed and neither Laura nor Sam had explicitly endorsed one of the proposals under discussion. At this point, Laura complained that the meeting was going late. "We'd better hurry it up," she insisted. "I don't know what everybody thinks, but personally, I would be in favor of Plan C." She then added, "I'd kinda like to get a sense from the people who haven't been talking so much."

Just after Laura finished speaking, Sam yawned and simply stated, "I think Plan C sounds good to me." Neither Laura nor Sam cared to elaborate, since other advocates of Plan C had already provided numerous arguments for it. It was at this point in the discussion that Laura began a "round robin" that effectively rotated speaking turns to give each member the chance to express preferences and add any final comments. Overall, it appears Laura and Sam were able to speak freely during these crucial staff deliberations. A final decision was not reached until they, and the others, had ample opportunities to participate.[24]

Staff members corroborated this positive portrayal of speaking opportunities.[25] The only exceptions were the accounts given by Louis and Norma. Louis said he wanted more of a chance to persuade and vote on final decisions. Norma also believed she had an insufficient number of voting opportunities. She claimed that relational dynamics among staff made her reluctant to reformulate, persuade, or vote.

The observational evidence from the staff meetings, however, didn't support Louis and Norma's claims. Louis attempted to persuade others more often than all but one other staff member, and he was given the second highest number of personal invitations to present arguments. Louis and Norma expressed their views and interests an average amount of the time, and Norma attempted to reformulate an agenda item or persuade others no less frequently than the average staff member.

As for voting, the staff's consensus method of decision making gave equal opportunities for all staff members to express their views during the final stage of decision making. It was possible, however, that Louis and Norma are more concerned about decisions made outside of staff meetings. Other staff might circumvent formal voting procedures and reach a "mini-consensus" without including Louis or Norma. Since this would have occurred outside regular meetings, this presents a special problem that I will discuss in Chapter 5.

Louis and Norma's claims may need a more subtle understanding. When I asked them why they believed they had fewer speaking opportunities, they expressed personal frustration, rather than a feeling of unfair treatment. "We have equal access to talk," Louis conceded. "In general and in the meetings, we have equal access." In his view, no one at Mifflin "abuses" their opportunities by speaking so often and forcefully that others have little chance to talk. Norma agreed that "every individual is responsible for using their opportunities" and that at the Co-op, "opportunities are equal for everyone. On some level, it's true that I've had the perfect opportunity to speak at all times." Nevertheless, she argued, "there's another level—more of a relationship level. It has to do with how I relate to or fit in with the group the whole time I've been there. It has to do with some things that are unique to me, like my own insecurities." On this "relationship level," Norma emotional conflicts sometimes made Norma reluctant to speak.

Did the negative relational messages directed at Norma during the vacation discussion leave her too upset or intimidated to speak during meetings? The evidence suggests otherwise, since she articulated herself frequently on all issues, including her vacation plans. She began the second vacation discussion with the longest speaking turn in all of the videotaped meetings. This single speaking turn was more than twice the length of the next longest one. Throughout the discussion, she responded to others' comments and forcefully presented her views.

In sum, the opportunities to speak during Mifflin Co-op's Monday night meetings appear to have been more than adequate. The equality of these opportunities is more difficult to gauge: There was undoubtedly an unequal use of opportunities, but this difference in use doesn't necessarily imply an inequality of opportunity. Since everyone had opportunities in abundance, however, the equality of their distribution becomes almost irrelevant.

Speaking Responsibilities

When they used their speaking opportunities, did the Mifflin Co-op staff fulfill their speaking responsibilities, or did they routinely withhold pertinent information or try to manipulate one another? To answer this question, I turn to the series of decisions the Co-op made regarding donations.

During the six meetings I observed, a half dozen staff decisions concerned requests for assistance. As part of its commitment to the community, the Co-op donated some of its inventory and revenue to organizations that sought its aid. Since the amount of food and money requested routinely exceeded the Co-op's donation budget, the staff had to judge the merits of each request. To make such decisions democratically, members needed to provide each other with relevant information to persuade each other with sincere arguments. As the following excerpts show, it appears that the staff members met their responsibilities.

During the first meeting, the staff considered a donation request from the local chapter of the Women's International League for Peace and Freedom (WILPF). To reach a clear decision, staff had to weigh pertinent information and generate persuasive arguments. The following excerpt illustrates both of these.

Dan: The other donation request on the docket for tonight is the folks from Women's International League for Peace and Freedom are organizing an ad [protesting the Persian Gulf

War] to go in the *Isthmus* that reads, "How many lives per gallon?" It only costs $5 to sign on, and after paying for the ad, the $5 goes to further efforts toward organizing for peace in the Persian Gulf.

Sam: Stephen came in from Press House with this originally and showed it to Rose and me, and Rose threw $5 into it. I did it for myself. Rose did it as a representative of DARE, I think. Um—

Dan: Yeah, I think it would be best for Mifflin—

Amy: Yeah.

Sam: Yeah, it's not going in for a while—

Dan: Yeah, it's going in either next weekend or the following weekend, and the due date is tomorrow.

Laura: Yeah, I'm sorry, what was it going into?

Sam: The Isthmus. Is it going to be a full page ad or a half page ad?

Dan: I think it depends on how much money they get.

Kate: Let's do it.

Dan: Okay.

Kate: So, I'll put that down as $5.

Sam: One of the intentions of bringing it to us as a group is they were hoping they could get more than $5. Do we want to just do the five as Mifflin Co-op?

Louis: Can't we give them ten or twenty?

Ray: Can we also give them money from our advertising account?

Amy: We could do that.

Sam: How's the advertising budget doing?

Amy: We have enough money to give it to them.

Sam: What do we want to give them?

Amy: I'm not sure, what do you think?

Kate: Twenty-five?

Sam: What'd you say?

Kate: Twenty.

Amy: How about twenty from advertising and five from staff donations?

Kate: Why so much, though, because if they're gonna get an ad, maybe it would be better for us to wait and give a more concrete type of aid rather than this.

Dan: I agree with that position. My feeling in general on ads is that I'd rather give twenty-five bucks to someone giving a teach-in.

Amy: But didn't they say that after the cost of the ad, the money would be used for other—

Sam: Yeah, but the ad's gonna take a lot of money.

Dan: Yeah, a full page in the Isthmus is like $1600—

Kate: No, really?

Dan: Something ridiculous.

Dan: Anyways, it's a lot.

Laura: [*laughs*] They may not be able to afford a personal ad.

Kate: You know, I think a lot of people will sign on for five bucks.

Louis   Let's decide something and get on with this.

Sam: Maybe ten bucks.

Kate: From marketing or advertising? Or...

Dan: Ten bucks from organizing and—

Kate: Ten from staff?

Laura: Five from staff.

Kate: Five from staff.

Dan: Fifteen total. Sounds good to me.

Kate: Is someone gonna fill that out and send it in?

Sam: I'll do it.

Kate: Okay.

Dan: Okay, donations are done.

These excerpts show the speed and impact of the exchange of information and the presentation of arguments. The discussion of the WILPF request begins with questions and informative answers, as the staff clarifies the nature of the request, the cost of advertising, and the possibility of providing money from two separate budgets. Kate and Dan then put forward an argument for limited funding, a proposal the staff ultimately accepts.

Staff handled other donation requests in a similar manner. Basic information was provided spontaneously or in response to questions. Clear and concise arguments were presented, and then the staff reached a decision. The donation discussions averaged four minutes, with the longest lasting seven. The most striking feature of these discussions, and others like them, was what they don't include. There were no signs of concealed or delayed information, nor did I detect veiled or deceptive arguments. Questions got answers, and staff gave clear rationales for their preferences. Questions were not rebuffed with vague, misleading, or incomplete answers, nor did I see common cues of deceptive discourse, such as incessant appeals to authority, misleading uses of pronouns and syntax, or excessive jargon.[26]

None of the staff members pointed to another as regularly withholding vital information or framing arguments in manipulative ways. The closest thing to an exception was Norma's concern about Kate's privileged position in the information nexus. Because of Kate's strong commitment, high level of involvement, and varied responsibilities, she may have been the most informed staff member. Norma didn't indicate that Kate kept information from the staff, but she was concerned about the timing of the information provided by Kate (and other staff). Norma sometimes learned important facts during meetings, often shortly before the time when a final decision was needed. This gave her insufficient time to process and respond to the information. Norma didn't feel uninformed; rather, she believed the information she received was not timely. I discuss this issue further in Chapter 5, but it should be noted at this point as a possible limitation on small group democracy at Mifflin Co-op.

Listening

Even if staff had ample speaking opportunities that they used regularly and responsibly, democratic deliberation would be impossible if these same people were not able and willing to listen to one another. In particular, any group that aspires to use a democratic process needs to insure that its members have equal and adequate opportunities to comprehend one another. In turn, each member is responsible for carefully considering what others have to say.

Most of the time, Mifflin Co-op staff understood one another, at least during meetings. The staff had developed a language of its own, but every group member knew its nuances. Staff grasped the technical references to the store's unique features or the Co-op's finances, and they laughed together at the inside jokes members cracked during meetings.

Staff also listened to what each other had to say. Side conversations began on a few occasions, but when issues were serious, staff sat (relatively) still and concentrated on the speaker's words. The give-and-take of most discussions showed that staff members were not engaging in what group communication scholar Dean Hewes calls "egocentric" discussion—the artful juxtaposition of unrelated, self-absorbed comments.[27] When addressing minor agenda items, staff quickly integrated each other's different ideas into a final proposal, and during discussions of major issues, staff members would take the time to acknowledge different points of view.

Although Norma and the staff had divergent positions on the vacation issue, they seemed to understand—if not accept—their differences of opinion. By contrast, Louis and the staff sometimes failed to understand the nature of their disagreement with regard to the proposed tenure incentives. Examining this difficulty reveals a great deal about the success and limitations of the democratic process at Mifflin Co-op.

After the initial discussions of the tenure incentives plans, it became apparent that Louis' views differed from those held by the rest of the staff. At various times, Rose, Kate, Dan, and others had raised concerns about providing incentives in the form of increasing annual pay bonuses, but only Louis clearly opposed all three of the proposals for establishing monetary incentives. (The group called these proposals "Plans A, B, and C.") Louis suggested some non-monetary incentive alternatives, but the group didn't clearly understand these. Likewise, Louis didn't appear to understand the purpose of the monetary incentives that other staff endorsed.

Shortly after Amy had described the monetary incentive plans, Louis made his opposition known.

Louis: I think it stinks.

Sam: Why does it stink?

Louis: Just, I don't know, this is bizarre... I guess that's not very descriptive.

Ray: "Stinks," "bizarre"...

Norma: Why, Louis?

Louis: I don't know, it just strikes me as kind of filling our pockets or something.

Kate: [*sarcastically*] That's what we're here on this Earth to do.

All: laughter

Ray: I don't know, I think—

Dan: At least that's what one person thinks.

Louis: I think the percentage—

Amy: Do you understand that—

Louis: I understand that, um—

Amy: It's assuming that the person becomes more valuable, well not "more valuable," but—

Kate: More experienced.

Louis: You said it! There is an assumption that you will become more valuable or more effective in the store. It's an assumption...

Amy: Well, it costs a lot to keep retraining somebody to replace someone.

Louis: Yeah, but it doesn't cost this much more.

Amy: But I don't think the whole thing is just a reward for how valuable this person is, I think—

Louis: It sure comes off that way.

Amy: If I could finish what I'm saying, it's sort of recognizing that this is a very profitable business, and it doesn't need to be some kind of financial sacrifice for people to work here.

Laura: I also wanted to say that just because we work in a co-op doesn't mean that our work should be devalued.

Louis: I never said that.

Laura: But you said that getting money as a compensation for staying "stinks." I just think that if you're going to take this as a serious job—one you can stay at for a very long time and retire from—we need to change policy, because you can't really support yourself in your retirement on the money we make now.

Norma: Do you have an alternative, Louis?

Louis: I think some existing models... I don't know, I would have to look into it. I don't know, but I think there are existing models in the industry that...

Laura: Would you feel more comfortable if it were some kind of retirement package?

Louis: Yeah, that's an idea.

Laura: You know, to me that's a great concern, not that I'm ready for retirement—

Louis: Yeah, okay, the thing that really affected me was that this was thrown at us, and this was the only thing that some of us could come up with. I feel like everybody's adopting it without looking at anything else, and it seemed like we were already passing this before we even got to discuss any other alternatives.

At the next staff meeting, the staff tried to understand and consider the alternatives Louis would prefer.

Ray: So, Louis, not to pick on you or anything...

Louis: This is not a good time to pick on me anyway, so don't waste your time trying to.

All: laughter

Ray: Do you think that the staff should get any benefits aside from the ones we get now? Is any increase in our benefits package excessive in your mind?

Louis: No, not necessarily.

Ray: Okay.

Louis: I really have a problem with this. I think there are other alternative benefits, such as a clothing allowance or paid vacation. I really have problems with percentage numbers because they're based on...I don't know.

Kate: Additional paid vacation is a percentage, too, it's just in a different form. I don't think that it's—

Louis: Right, but it's more tangible in my perspective.

Kate: But you just have different needs from other people. I need money, I don't need vacation. And I think that money—

Dan: That's actually a very interesting point worth pursuing. Should you have a staggered amount of time that you can take off, whether paid or unpaid? That's an idea.

Louis: Yeah, we'll have to remember that. I don't know, I just...It bothers me, and right now I don't really have a clear enough head to continue my opposition to these proposals...

As the discussion continued, confusion increased and staff became exhausted. Louis tried to explain his alternatives and advocate for them, but the others could not understand his position.

Amy: I guess I'm not sure what the difference is between the existing proposals and adding another week's paid vacation after a certain amount of time, because to me—

Louis: It's not that much different, no.

Amy: It's the same thing. It's only that we're calling it something different.

Louis: Yeah.

Amy: And it's figured in the same way, too.

Louis: In a way, yeah. Again—

Amy: Exactly the same way, I don't see a difference.

Louis: Okay, let me clarify it. My objection is to how it's presented. It looks to me as kind of a strange animal when you compare it to everything else that we've done in the Co-op with regard to benefits. It just, just really strikes me as a weird monkey. So, I don't know, maybe we could sit together and come up with a balance of these two ideas, instead of asking me over and over to clarify this—

Ray: It's not at all clear what—

Norma: What your objection is.

Ray: I think Plan C is fine—

Norma: Unless there's an alternative. Oops.

Ray: I've got no problems with it. I mean, I'm being a little harsh but I don't—

Louis: That's not harsh. You're just stating your point—

Ray: My harshness is that I'm losing patience with the discussion. It hasn't been going that long, but I can see it circling for another hour before it comes in for a landing. I don't want to discuss it indefinitely, because I just can't see where... Okay, I don't know what I'm saying, but I don't want to continue without any forward progress.

After repeated attempts at clarification or compromise, Louis and the staff seemed tired of their deliberations. The discussion ended only when Laura insisted there was no point to further discussion.

Laura: It seems like our discussion goes in more and more and more circles, so I'm not sure if more time will yield more circles or if more time will yield an alternative—a truly viable alternative.

Louis: Why assume that it wouldn't?

Laura: Because we've been talking and talking and talking and going in circles to circles to circles. So I can't see where our circles are going to spiral out, you know.

Louis: Well, fine. So go. I mean, I'm not going to block the consensus if you want it. I mean, I'm just giving you an alternative, and I still feel uncomfortable with this plan. If people are so burdened by this process or they feel so certain that this is what they want, then go. I'm not holding you up.

Five minutes later, the group closed the discussion and adopted Plan C. In the end, Louis and the staff didn't understand each other, but they agreed that a decision had to be reached, even if a fully satisfactory consensus was not achieved. Louis had the opportunity to block consensus, but he chose to accept the decision, albeit reluctantly.

These observations parallel the self-analyses provided by the Co-op staff in their interviews. The staff believed they were good listeners:

They claimed to listen carefully to each other and consider what was said, and they reported understanding each other most of the time. Staff said they usually had a chance to get others to clarify themselves, and they used many of these opportunities.

Aside from these general comments, some staff noticed difficulties, such as those that emerged in the tenure incentives discussion. Dan, for instance, acknowledged that "sometimes time constraints make it hard for us to listen to explanations or, conversely, make it hard for others to have the patience to re-explain a point."

Others focused on the general difficulty of understanding Norma and Louis, particularly when discussing vacation policy and the proposed tenure incentives, respectively. Amy wrote,

> I didn't always succeed at understanding others, though I think I tried, especially with Norma and consensus and Louis and the pay raise and tenure incentives discussions. I listened, but didn't understand their points of view. I've spoken to each of them separately, during the week after the meeting, but I still don't fully understand their points.

Ray explained that he also had trouble understanding particular individuals for two reasons: "The people I have trouble understanding are the people I can't communicate well with—the people whose opinions I respect less than others. I try to understand their point, but sometimes I give up." He confided that Norma and Louis were the two people he had the most difficulty understanding.

Laura and Sam had equal difficulty understanding Louis. Laura insisted that even when Laura "asked him to clarify himself, it didn't really help." Sometimes she simply couldn't understand him, no matter how hard she tried. Similarly, Sam said that on the tenure incentives issue, Louis "will never give a concrete reason that any of us can understand. It's just the way he wants to be. He's pretty adamant about that one."

Kate reported some difficulty understanding and seriously considering what Norma and Louis said during meetings. She qualified this generalization, however, with these words:

Some of us could do with better communication skills, but, especially for Louis, it is a deep cultural issue and not easily overcome. I find that one-on-one personal exchanges outside meetings have a lot of influence on how I perceive statements made inside meetings. Since Louis and I are good friends, I have a much better perspective on his somewhat hard to understand statements and views.

Norma and Louis also believed that the staff's inability to understand Louis related to his general communication skills and style. Norma noted, "I think, maybe it's ironic or something, but Louis is the person who feels most like he's not listened to. I also feel that he's the person who has the least developed skills in listening." But Louis attributed the problem to differences in style, not skills. He insisted that Mifflin's meetings were subject to a larger cultural bias: "If you tend not to communicate well, you will be listened to less." Louis saw himself as the victim of such bias, which I discuss in Chapter 5.

In the end, it is difficult to make an unambiguous statement on the character of listening at Mifflin Co-op. Staff members acknowledged difficulty listening to Norma's views on vacation policy and Louis' opposition to the tenure incentives. At the same time, staff made a great effort to understand and consider these two members' views on those issues. The vacation and tenure incentives discussions were by far the longest of those I transcribed, and they were the only ones that spanned more than one meeting. Norma and Louis spoke as much as (or more) than usual during those discussions, while staff members both passively listened and, in the case of Louis, repeatedly asked for clarification and elaboration.

A realistic definition of small group democracy doesn't ask whether a group can always reach understanding. Instead, it asks whether group members are able to listen. Democracy asks that we *try* to appreciate each other's point of view. Although Monday staff meetings at the Co-op didn't always end in mutual understanding, staff made an earnest effort to do so.

Conclusion

When this examination of listening is combined with the other components of small group democracy, the overall portrait of Mifflin Co-op is quite favorable. The staff had power over its meeting agendas, and its meetings were relatively inclusive, although some staff members questioned the distinction between staff and shift workers. Staff were strongly committed to the democratic process and maintained positive member relationships, though the vacation issue created tension that limited the potential for unconstrained deliberation. Staff had adequate (and perhaps equal) opportunities to speak, and although the exchange of information among them was imperfect, they deliberated in a responsible manner. Finally, staff generally understood one another and considered what was said during meetings. In sum, Mifflin Street Community Co-op exemplifies many of the fundamental principles of small group democracy.[28]

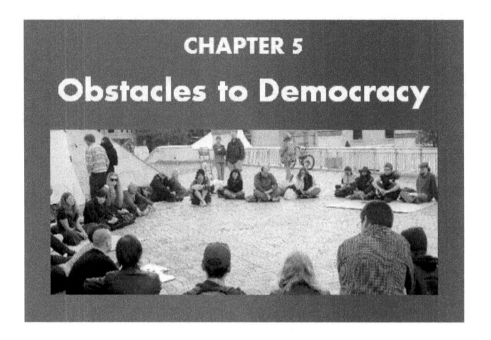

CHAPTER 5

Obstacles to Democracy

If the first half of this book paved a yellow brick road to small group democracy, the second considers the hazards that lie along that path—the clumsy companions and fields of poppies. In this chapter, I return to Mifflin Street Community Co-op to look more closely at where it has fallen short of a fully democratic process. This exceptional group met and surmounted many obstacles in its pursuit of democracy, so the barriers it continued to face are likely to be pervasive and formidable for others.[1]

In my observations and conversations with staff members, certain difficulties kept reappearing: long meetings, unequal involvement in the group and unequal commitment to its goals, cliques and mini-consensus, unequal communication skills, different communication styles, and personal conflicts. This chapter discusses these problems and shows both how they undermine the democratic process and how Mifflin Co-op and other groups can address them.

Long Meetings

Oscar Wilde once grumbled that the only problem with socialism was that it "would take too many evenings." For many groups, the problem isn't the frequency of meetings so much as their duration.[2] The Mifflin Co-op staff admitted that their Co-op proves no exception to this rule. As Ray said, "The democratic process breaks down after two hours, and often...our meetings go more than two hours." Meetings begin at 6:30 PM on Mondays, and after two hours, many staff have grown tired. In Ray's view, the exhaustion makes meetings increasingly disjointed and unproductive. Since members don't grow weary at the same rate, their participation levels also begin to diverge.[3]

Excessive meeting length places two obstacles in the way of a group that seeks to be democratic. Relationships can become strained: Members who grow tired more easily may become angry and bored, as Ray did during the videotaped meetings, and those who are still full of energy may resent those who start to flag. In addition, fatigue makes the distribution of opportunities increasingly unequal, and it may make opportunities entirely inadequate for the group's most weary members.[4]

Though not all staff recognized the effects of long meetings on the democratic process, they generally acknowledged that meeting length had become excessive. They pointed out that sometimes people speak too long, and even before 8:30 PM, people are too easily distracted. As Louis said, "people will sometimes speak more than they really need to. Instead of aiding the discussion, their comments become more disruptive. I try to be very brief and concise in what I have to say. That's partially because I grew up in New York City, and you don't just jabber away—you say what you need to say and get it over with."

Staff considered distraction an even more serious problem. Amy, who could remember well-facilitated meetings from years past, said that rambling discussions were increasingly bothering her. Meetings had become "less democratic, because different people have different levels of distraction. Some people might want to get everything off the track more than other people."

The staff offered a variety of suggestions when asked how they might solve these problems. To prevent excessive talking, Dan suggested that staff should limit the discussion time allotted to each issue. In addition, Ray suggested that before speaking, "We have to self-facilitate to determine whether our comments will be relevant or lead the discussion astray. Self-facilitation aids the democratic process by keeping things focused, streamlined, efficient, but not impersonal. It's important to be efficient so that people don't get burned out."

When self-facilitation fails, Kate believed staff members need to say, "Okay, we've heard your view." Louis agreed, saying that individual members need to gain the confidence "to come forward and say, 'Okay, you're just talking too much.'" This is the facilitator's job, but if "the facilitator's not on top of things," someone else will have to do it.[5]

To reduce the amount of distraction during meetings, Dan suggested the Co-op look for a better meeting time. If meetings were held at a time when people were more alert, members wouldn't be distracted as easily. Regardless of when they meet, Norma added that staff must come to meetings better prepared. For instance, when the Co-op answers donation requests, "If people would prepare more, everything could be cut down by at least a third. If someone would be responsible for summarizing donation requests and making a recommendation, then it could take us three minutes to deal with requests instead of twenty."

During meetings, Laura suggested, staff ought to write down things that come to mind. Otherwise, ideas get forgotten or muddled. Quickly writing down thoughts has the added advantage of making it easier to pay attention. Once the words are written, one's mind is no longer preoccupied with remembering what to say.[6]

Finally, Amy stressed the role of the facilitator. Self-facilitation is important, but the facilitator designated for a given meeting should actively guide the discussion. She believed that the meetings were "straying" more than they used to because they were not as "tightly facilitated." The facilitator must be willing to interrupt speakers who stray from the issue and suggest the direction in which aimless discussions need to go. Otherwise, meetings can drift into the late hours of the night.[7]

Unequal Involvement and Commitment

The Mifflin Co-op staff believed that democracy thrives in an egalitarian setting, and staff currently enjoyed many forms of equality. Every member of the Mifflin workers' collective had the same hourly wage, job benefits, and decision-making power at the Co-op. Staff members were also somewhat equal in their commitment to the Co-op's goals.

Nevertheless, there were noticeable inequalities in staff involvement and commitment to the Co-op. With regard to equal involvement, Louis explained, "We are all equal, and we emphasize the idea that no one has power over other people, [but] by my observation, some people are developing greater power over others at Mifflin...due to their amount of time in the Co-op."

Louis later explained that "some people" referred to Kate. She had worked the longest at the Co-op and had the most experience on almost every subject discussed during meetings. At the time of this study, she also held the broadest range of special responsibilities at the Co-op, and she worked more hours than anyone else.

Like Louis, Norma expressed concern about Kate's exceptional level of involvement in the Co-op. She told a story about how one of her friends visited Mifflin and told Norma, "Kate's the boss." Norma came to agree with that assessment and saw Kate as the top of an unofficial hierarchy:

There is ostensibly no power structure and everything's egalitarian, and that's part of what I was proud to tell my friends and my parents and my family. But it's really not that way, and I'm not sure it ever can be that way. My experience at the Co-op has shown me that. I think that in organizations, people get power even though they don't set out to get power deliberately. There's no malevolence or anything like that.

Regardless of their intentions, if one or two members of a democratic group become relatively powerful in their influence and exceptional in their expertise, this can limit less powerful members' ability to obtain and understand information relevant to group decisions. In addition, the more powerful individuals are more likely to take away others' opportunities to talk by dominating both the establishment and discussion of the agenda. Without seeking to diminish the contributions that such expertise and engagement can bring to the group, it needs to find a way to preserve its democratic character.

It was not always clear exactly when and to what degree unequal involvement undermined the democratic process at Mifflin Co-op. Norma identified Kate as the staff member with disproportionate power, yet Kate dominated neither the agenda-setting process nor staff deliberations. That said, I didn't observe Kate's use of power outside of meetings. When Kate began working at the Co-op, the business was in financial and physical disrepair, a state to which it would return before ultimately closing in 2006. Kate played a central role in revitalizing the Co-op and developing policies that remained in effect for years. On her arrival, Kate was given wide latitude by a grateful staff, and as the Co-op expanded the size of the worker collective from five to nine, Kate willingly yielded more of her authority to the new employees. Even Norma acknowledged that over the years, Kate probably *ceded* more power than the total she possessed at the time of my study.

Staff involvement in the Co-op was not equal, but strict equality of group involvement doesn't exist in any group. What matters is the degree to which some are more involved than others.[8] The dangers posed by unequal involvement increase with the level of disparity, and Mifflin Co-op's relatively minute power differences didn't appear to jeopardize its democratic process.[9]

Unequal commitment, however, posed a more serious problem. Ray described the relationship between commitment and involvement in these terms:

The more that people are involved in the process, the more concerned they are. That, in and of itself, makes for more equality, more of a shared burden, and more shared assumptions of how much work something is. If people are equally committed to the Co-op, then they're equally involved and concerned about the Co-op decisions and their ramifications for themselves and for the store as a whole.

The difference is that a staff member can be marginally involved in the store's day-to-day activities yet remain totally committed to the Co-op's goals. This was the case with Dan, who worked only a few hours at the Co-op every week. As Ray explained, "Dan is as committed to the ideals of the Co-op as much as anyone else, easily. But he's not as involved with the store as anyone else—he's the least involved. He's probably spent more time thinking about philosophical Co-op issues than anyone else. That's where his level of commitment comes in."

Most staff noted an important difference between Dan and Norma. Norma worked the second fewest hours per week and probably had the least commitment to the Co-op. She openly acknowledged that Mifflin Co-op was a lower priority in her life than for other staff.[10] This lower level of commitment led to personal conflicts at work. During one Monday night meeting, Rose expressed this concern to Norma:

> I think what people talk about is feeling like you don't have the store prioritized in the same way that other people do. It's just a matter of where the priority is, and it feels like your relationship with your boyfriend is prioritized over the store. It does conflict with how we see each other's commitment to the store, because I feel like the store is my first commitment. And so it's hard to work with people that have a different commitment than me.

Laura expressed the same feelings to Norma: "A limited commitment makes for odd power plays and strange things. I'd prefer to see a full-fledged commitment, and I don't know if you can do that."

This inequality of commitment obstructs the democratic process by fostering an unfriendly group atmosphere, as illustrated by the hostile exchanges between Norma and the rest of the Mifflin staff. Staff found it somewhat difficult to affirm the legitimacy of Norma's personal interests; instead, they viewed her as somewhat selfish and openly questioned her individual needs and desires. Since Norma didn't share the staff's level of emotional and philosophical commitment to the Co-op, many staff found it difficult to view her as a full member of the group. As Louis put it, staff addressed her as though she were "on probation." In addition, friendly relations between the staff and Norma diminished, since many staff became frustrated with her "lack of commitment."[11]

When asked how they might address these inequalities in involvement and commitment, most staff believed that the inequalities had to be removed, not accommodated. In the case of Kate and Norma, staff suggested that Kate work fewer hours and that Norma either become more committed to the store or quit. What can be done if those individuals don't voluntarily take that advice? Again, the staff identified only one solution: firing. In the case of Norma, a number of staff had not only asked Norma to resign, they had also explored the possibility of firing her. This was something so extraordinary for the Co-op that, at that time, its bylaws contained no dismissal procedure.

Other groups may not wish to take such drastic measures. After all, it is only extreme differences in commitment and involvement that undermine small group democracy. If the inequalities are moderate, a group might find them tolerable, and a group with more extreme imbalances might find ways to mitigate them. If this fails, desperate action may be necessary; however, the inclusiveness criterion cautions against removing members of a democratic group.

Cliques and Mini-consensus

Though my research focused on the weekly meetings at Mifflin Co-op, staff talked with each other in the store throughout the week. Such exchanges were essential for the healthy functioning of the store, but they posed a subtle hazard for the democratic process. For any small group, communicating outside meetings allows individuals to work through issues gradually by exchanging information, developing opinions, and coming to understand other points of view. This can lead to shorter, friendlier meetings when the time comes to make formal decisions together. At the same time, these seemingly innocuous gatherings can result in schisms, as the group divides into factions resembling the social cliques that exist outside the meetings. People may come to meetings with fixed opinions developed beforehand, and they may become reluctant to reiterate their views, which they already explained to many—but not all—group members.

In a group of any significant size, a conversation taking place outside a meeting almost never involves every member. At the Co-op, typical exchanges were informal banter involving two or three staff working in the store or spontaneous conversations between friends at social encounters outside work.[12] Those not present in these casual encounters came to meetings lacking information that had been distributed only informally beforehand.

Norma and Dan typically lacked the information that others had, because they worked at the store least often. Their lack of information sometimes made it difficult for them to comprehend staff deliberations. Dan could usually compensate with his years of experience at the Co-op, but Norma, who was relatively new, had more difficulty.

This led to another problem: When staff members repeatedly requested information during a meeting, other staff could become restless or frustrated. The person requesting information might feel angry because the group didn't provide necessary details beforehand. Norma expressed this sentiment. She resented having to wait until meetings to receive information relevant to the meeting agenda. Other staff sometimes got frustrated when they had to recount (or listen to) information they had already received. For instance, Amy once criticized Rose for failing to obtain and review relevant data before a meeting. In addition, Sam pointed out that even when staff recognized the importance of providing someone with details during a meeting, tension still built up due to the lengthening of the discussions.

In any case, conversations outside meetings can provide more than information to those who take part. Sam said that they also kept staff members up-to-date with each other's feelings, concerns, and ambitions. From passing comments to significant shared experiences, these interactions create "a good bond between us and allow us to understand each other more fully." "We see each other every day, or at least five of us do," he explained, "and with that comes a certain closeness."

Because these informal interactions involve a subgroup of the staff, the rest of the staff can become "outsiders," who lack the sense of mutuality shared by the cohesive subgroup. At Mifflin Co-op, Norma often fell outside of the informal communication network. Norma worked as much as Rose and more than Dan, but Rose and Dan frequently interacted with the other staff members as friends. As Amy described it, there was a certain "resistance" to Norma from the rest of the staff. Even when in the store, Laura explained, some staff tried to avoid Norma.

The formation of cliques or the social exclusion of an individual group member can lead to misunderstandings and hostility. A spirit of comradeship may grow stronger for everyone except the excluded person. In addition, if the members of a subgroup have already defined an issue beforehand, they may try to prevent another member from reformulating this agenda item during the meeting. Louis expressed a concern about this in the case of Kate and Ray. He feared that their pre-meeting discussions of the tenure incentives proposals narrowed the scope of the deliberation during meetings.

By the time a meeting begins, a subgroup may have gone even farther by reaching an agreement just among themselves on an important issue. Such a "mini-consensus" isn't always detrimental to the group. Sometimes staff had to make quick decisions outside meetings, such as when an unexpected delivery arrives. Also, staff regularly designated committees of two or three members to make decisions during the coming week.

A mini-consensus is counterproductive when it is informal and unspoken. In these cases, a subgroup might mistakenly believe that an issue has already been resolved and try to end debate prematurely, thereby closing other group members' opportunities for reformulation, articulation, and persuasion. As Dan said, "If small groups of people achieve consensus on an issue outside of a meeting, [they may] assume it is dealt with, while others have not had a say in the decision."

To address these problems, staff members proposed lessening information inequalities. Norma suggested that instead of "taking it out" on her and Dan for lacking information, the Co-op "could accommodate disparate hours." Clipboards, logbooks, and other forms of written communication would allow her and Dan to keep up-to-date. Others viewed such a system as time-consuming and cumbersome; they placed responsibility for the problem on the staff members who work the fewest hours. Kate, for instance, argued that either Mifflin should hire only full-time staff or part-time staff should be responsible for gathering pertinent information themselves. "We've discussed this a lot over the years," she added, "and it's my main argument for having folks work at least twenty five hours a week, ideally full time, just so this 'information hierarchy' doesn't exist."

Neither of these solutions addresses the problem of subgroup cohesion and mini-consensus. Making every staff member equally involved in the store could mitigate but not resolve such problems. Pairs and subgroups inevitably form bonds distinct from those of the full group, and this becomes a serious problem when personal conflicts result in the conscious exclusion of one or more individuals from the informal interaction network. At the very least, group members can remain aware of this hazard, but groups can also organize fully inclusive social activities to maintain positive relationships among all members.

Communication Skill Deficits

When presented with equal opportunities to talk, in meetings or during information gatherings, people often vary in their ability to use those opportunities effectively. One might expect the members of an egalitarian co-operative to all possess highly developed communication skills. The reality at Mifflin, however, was stark skill differences. Some staff were comfortable and eloquent in group settings, but others were relatively reserved and inarticulate. Some were able and willing to jump into heated debates, whereas others hesitated to enter such discussions. Quieter members could end up feeling intimidated. If not invited into the discussion, they might briefly withdraw.

Sam explained that some staff, usually newer ones, were more subject to patriarchal and hierarchical norms that stunt the development of the skills necessary for democratic decision making: "A lot of people are very used to being led" because "it's easier to be led" than "to be in the forefront."   Amy concurred:

> We come from cultures that are not democratic. We've been raised in families with strict hierarchies, not only between parents and children, but sometimes between siblings, too. Our educations have often been regimented, and we have not been taught that our individual opinions are important to the larger group. Decisions about how our society functions were made long before we were born, and we're made to fit in—not to value the different visions we create. Participating in a democratic experience is rare, but powerful. We all bring the dynamics of our past into the process at Mifflin. We come with unacknowledged personal agendas and different levels of need for hierarchy. We have different levels of personal or political commitment to the worker managed workplace, and we have different levels of desire to take responsibility for it.

"Individual personalities have a great impact," Amy added. "Some of us have little experience expressing our opinions or expecting to have them listened to. Some of us have difficulty expressing our feelings." Kate, one of the more articulate staff members, agreed: "Some people aren't as good at communicating their needs and ideas as others."

Inequalities in speaking skills can result in an inequality of opportunities, with the more skilled among us perceiving and receiving the greater number of opportunities to talk. More agile speakers have more success interrupting, holding the floor, and redefining the discussion. Over time, these individuals become even more skilled through practice, while less skilled group members could become increasingly reticent. Some group members can become accustomed to talking, while others become resigned or accustomed to remaining silent.[13]

To prevent this outcome, the Co-op tried to develop the abilities of those with weaker communication skills by drawing them out and encouraging them to speak their minds during meetings. Louis explained that new members need to become used to being a part of a participatory democracy. The staff tried to empower newcomers by "actually asking people [to speak] and making it a very friendly environment, so that people feel free to discuss things."

This method for empowering new members was similar to the strategy used to develop the skills of long-term members. Kate said that the staff tried to draw out quieter members. She would sometimes ask others for their opinions, or she would nonverbally encourage them through a visual cue, such as well-timed eye contact. As an example, she said that with a glance, she might reassure Sam that he was safe to express emotional displeasure with something Louis had just said.

Staff stressed the mechanisms in place that allowed more reserved members to enter a heated, fast-paced debate. Staff meetings were designed to be informal, with people speaking whenever they wished, but if a member clearly signaled a desire to speak by raising a hand, the facilitator would call on that person when the current speaker finished. Also, Laura pointed to round-robins, whereby group members each gave their opinions in turn. These could be used at any juncture, but they were often used toward the end of an intense discussion. They lowered the heat of a debate and gave members a clear, uninterrupted opportunity to express themselves.[14]

Some of the quieter group members attested to the effectiveness of these empowerment strategies. Louis, for example, believed that his experiences at Mifflin staff meetings have made him "much better at communicating." He now feels more skilled in group settings as well as in one-on-one conversations.

The staff also relies on a self-sufficiency ethic: skilled members are expected to make allowances for the others, but to some extent, other members have to fend for themselves. Sam used Kate as an example:

"There are things Kate does which cause people to feel intimidated. And so far as I'm concerned, that's something that other people need to work out for themselves." He admitted being intimidated by her when he first arrived at the Co-op, but he believed he could only overcome it through personal growth. Norma, who has been most intimidated by Kate, agreed, insisting that she was responsible for getting over her intimidation. At some point, staff argue, the less skilled have to find a way to develop their skills and transcend the feelings of inferiority or intimidation they may feel in the presence of more skilled peers.[15]

Communication Style Clashes

Differences in how we communicate present another challenge for small group democracy. Styles differ from skills in that one style isn't necessarily "better" or "more developed" than another. For the most part, Norma explained, people are just the way they are, and they should not have to change for there to be democracy. People should adapt to, if not appreciate, each other's differences. In Sam's words,

> You have to make allowances for the people you're with. That's part of respecting people, I think. In a totalitarian state where everyone had evolved to be the perfect model of everybody else, you wouldn't have this problem. You also wouldn't have consensus decision making. But everybody's different. Everyone's got their own wealth of experience to draw on and make them who they are. I think that acknowledging and allowing for the individual is fairly critical to democratic group decisions. You need to realize that each person is who they are and that they're going to act and react in different ways.

Amy identified what she considered one of the most prominent differences in communication styles among the various members of the Co-op. She called it the difference between "internal" and "external" cognitive processing:

I definitely internalize things...I don't respond to things as immediately. I think it's more valuable to process things and internalize them—not everything, but certainly many things. But there are different personality types. Some people function better speaking out loud, and some people function better by being in touch with other levels of themselves.

Amy hastened to add that neither of these styles is better. Both are compatible with the democratic process.[16]

Louis described a similar style difference between himself, Amy, Norma, and Sam, on the one hand, and the rest of the staff, on the other. "I would just tend to believe that the one thing we do have in common is that we're perhaps more introverted than other people—more quiet, more self-analyzing." Louis argued that this difference as an inherent problem; instead, the problem derives from a cultural bias in favor of the "extraverted" style of communicating: "I think it's more general than Mifflin. I think it's a cultural bias in our nation that favors extraverts. Extraverts are the people we see as leaders, and we will promote them over the people that are more introverted—those who just do their work and are not outspoken in a positive way."[17]

Differences in group members' evaluations of communication styles can create problems for both democratic speaking and listening. If one of the styles becomes the group norm, those using the unconventional style may have more difficulty receiving and recognizing opportunities to speak. Regardless of whether or not one style dominates, group members who speak in different ways may have difficulty comprehending and considering one another's views.[18]

To a limited extent, Mifflin Co-op tried to address this issue. "We're somewhat conscious of it," Louis acknowledged, "but I think that the cultural bias is so strong that we simply overlook it." Sam agreed that the staff hadn't "made allowances" for these differences and continued to favor the extraverted style. Failing to remedy the cultural bias is, in Louis' opinion, undemocratic:

Democracy means that you make decisions for the whole, with the well-being of all the people involved. And if you overlook someone because he or she doesn't happen to fit in or is unable to speak out, that's not democratic. I think people that are extraverted need to be a little more conscious and realize that other people will not be able to communicate as well or express themselves as well and that because of this, their self-expression is hindered. Because of this unspoken bias, even their self-worth and growth will be hindered.

The solution to this problem lies in the staff members recognizing and accepting these differences as ones of style, not skill. The group can come to understand that there is more than one way to communicate. Ultimately, styles might be combined or synthesized, taking care to treat each equally. Even if such an attempt is unsuccessful, it can build understanding and respect between those members of one style and those of another.

This solution, however, may be easier to propose than implement. Louis was not optimistic: "Try as we may at Mifflin, we are part of this culture, and it's difficult to deal with sensitive issues of this nature. We're trying to work around them and with them, but it's still very cumbersome." Kate expressed a similar view regarding style differences between Louis and Amy and the rest of the staff. "The more we understand each other," Kate said, "the better our democratic process, because then we can accommodate each other's needs better." That said, "It's very difficult to understand someone else's experiences. Our process works on understanding, and I think you can always respect someone else, but you can't always understand them."

Personal Conflicts

Such understanding was even more elusive when it required Mifflin Co-op's staff to transcend the personal conflicts that bedeviled them. Staff endured serious conflicts partly because of a reluctance to confront them. Expressing a typical view, Ray thought that "animosity between some staff people and the lack of respect between them hinders our democratic process. Greater group democracy would come from the resolution of interpersonal conflicts."[19]

Personal conflicts can obstruct democracy by closing opportunities to speak, causing group members to ignore others' views, and undermining mutuality. The conflicts at Mifflin Co-op illustrated each of these problems.

Staff embroiled in unresolved conflicts with each other showed more difficulty speaking, because extreme tension could render apparent opportunities to talk meaningless. As Norma explained, "There are times when because of whatever emotional or interpersonal dynamic was going on at the moment, I felt a reduced opportunity to speak. I feel like there are overriding interpersonal barriers."

When interpersonal conflicts are not addressed, group members lose the mutual respect necessary for seriously considering each other's views. Even if members consciously know they ought to respect a person, anger or resentment can prevent them from doing so. For example, Ray said he generally listened to other staff members,

> but if it's someone I respect less than I should, their comments tend to fly by me. I don't listen to them carefully, or I look for what's behind them. It's not an honest exchange—it's been subverted by things becoming twisted. The truth is key to the democratic process, and the more truthful we can be, the more honest dialogue will occur. If there's not an honest dialogue, then I don't think the democratic process is working.

Similarly, Norma said that she sometimes felt that "there's something simmering behind what [Kate] says, so I don't trust what she says. I feel like it's manipulative sometimes but not always—definitely not always. I just feel really defensive toward her."

If the conflict isn't addressed and respect erodes, interpersonal conflicts can begin to divide the entire Co-op staff. A major contributor to this divisiveness is the gossip that surrounds unresolved conflicts. "There's some kind of taboo," Norma said, "that interferes with the democratic process or there's some sort of pattern of behavior where people aren't good at confronting each other, and they talk behind each other's backs." Laura admitted that she'd resorted to gossiping about Norma with other staff members. In the past, gossip was not uncommon at the Co-op, but after Norma's vacation issues came up, the situation got "ten times worse." Gossip became more frequent, often more malicious. Laura added, "I am just so angry with her, I have lost all respect." The conflict between Laura and Norma lessened their sense of shared group identity. Gossip replaced weakening bonds with strong emotional barriers.

The costs of unresolved conflict are high, but staff were willing to pay this price rather than face their conflicts. The clearest case of this at the Co-op was the clash between Norma and the rest of the staff, especially Kate. During her interview, Norma began to weep as she described how the conflict worsened over time: "Things got worse and worse, in a spiral. People didn't think I was doing a good job, but they didn't confront me about it. I was scared I'd lose my job."

In the opinion of every staff member, the two meetings in which staff explicitly discussed this conflict were among the most stressful they had ever endured. Unfortunately, the meetings didn't offer resolution. Norma reported that after those meetings, many staff wouldn't even talk to her. They avoided her both inside and outside the store. According to Norma, Rose was unwilling to confront her in person but wrote a vicious personal letter regarding the conflict and other issues from the past. Staff members conceded the accuracy of Norma's perception. As Kate put it, some staff simply lacked the emotional energy to do anything more. She admitted the conflict would continue to "smolder" indefinitely.

Conflicts such as this are extremely difficult to solve. As Dan cautioned, "There are times when personality issues preclude people feeling comfortable with doing or saying something…. This probably is true of any grouping of people at any given point in time." It would be hard to "legislate" this problem out of existence, he added. "It's just something that people need to be aware of."

With this caveat in mind, the Mifflin staff offered a number of suggestions for how the Co-op and other small groups could address serious interpersonal conflicts. Staff believed group members must try to maintain their respect for one another in the midst of emotional conflicts. They must resist the temptation to gossip. Staff also advocated preventative medicine—the development of positive relationships before disputes emerge.

Beyond these basic suggestions, staff focused on dealing with the strong emotions that surface when a group confronts a conflict. They acknowledged that anger, frustration, and resentment are part of being human, yet one can try to express these emotions constructively, no matter how awkward and upsetting it might make group meetings. Sam thought that if these emotions were bottled in, it "would just build up stress and tension." Somehow, somewhere, staff members need to vent their emotions.[20]

During meetings, those not involved in the conflict can facilitate the expression of emotions by the persons involved in the conflict. Rose suggested that friendly comments can reduce tension and encourage staff to relax—to take themselves less seriously. In addition, group members can encourage each other to express their feelings. If any members appear frustrated or agitated, others can give verbal or nonverbal support for self-expression. Kate said that she, Laura, and Norma frequently performed this function. She sensed a greater reluctance for male group members to act on those invitations to disclose their emotions.[21]

When those involved in a conflict intended to speak, staff said they should express themselves honestly and respectfully. Kate provided this example of this "reasonable" style of emotional expression: "That makes me really angry, and I'm going to tell you why."[22]

Sam elaborated on this idea:

You can choose your words carefully and think before you speak. Those are things I try to work on most of the time. I'm not that good at it. You can try to phrase what you want to say so that the people you're talking to understand that you're not trying to hurt them with what you're saying—that you're just giving from yourself what you feel you need to give to the group. That's how to avoid compromising democracy because you don't want to hurt somebody.

When one's feelings become too intense to express constructively, Kate recommended neither speaking nor sitting silently. Instead, one should leave the room. During her seven years at Mifflin's weekly meetings, Kate had rarely seen this happen, and she herself had done it only once. During the discussion of Norma's vacation plans, Kate began to confront her, and the two exchanged words for a few minutes. Each took long, uninterrupted speaking turns. Eventually, Kate became so enraged that she decided to leave the room. Her parting words were, "I'm going to have to leave for a while. I'm afraid I'm just..." Then silence. Kate discussed the incident at length during her interview:

> I knew when I left that the things I was saying were deeper than the issue at-hand. I was getting beyond the rational. I wasn't listening well, and I wasn't responding well. It was not productive for me to be involved in the conversation any longer at that point, because I was just going to make it worse. I think everyone knew how upset I was, and it wasn't necessary for me to go on and on, though that's a tendency that I have. So I realized it was important for me to just go and chill-out a little bit. By the time I came back, I had chilled-out a little bit. I was still just as angry, but I wasn't dealing with my anger in the same way. I felt it was more productive.

If a conflict reaches this point, it may be necessary to call on professional counselors or mediators, or at least address the conflict in structured one-on-one conversations outside of meetings. Staff reported success dealing with each other in these ways, and they planned to address all of their serious conflicts in this manner.[23]

Epilogue

During my irregular trips to local grocery stores while living in Madison, Wisconsin, I continued to frequent the Mifflin Street Community Co-op. On one of my last visits before publishing the first edition, I chatted with the staff about this book, and they explained how their meetings had changed since I first studied them. One staffer said I should write an epilogue. Wouldn't it be interesting to see if any of the staff's suggestions had been adopted in the past year? Obviously, I liked the idea, and a recap of the staff's suggestions appear in Table 2.[24]

Table 2. Strategies for Confronting Obstacles to Small Group Democracy

1. Shorten long meetings
   Self-facilitate
   Facilitate others
   Meet when everyone is wide awake
   Come to meetings prepared
   Be attentive during meetings, take notes

2. Equalize involvement and commitment
   Redistribute responsibilities
   Raise the commitment and involvement levels of those least
      engaged
   Change the group membership

3. Avoid cliques and mini-consensus
   Establish a means, such as a logbook, for communicating important
      ideas and information outside meetings
   Make individuals responsible for communicating with others
      outside of meetings

4. Close communication skill gaps
   Encourage and assist the least skilled members in improving their
      abilities
   Implement procedures, such as round robins, that make it easier for
      more hesitant members to speak
   Create a self-sufficiency ethic that spurs members to take
      responsibility for augmenting their speaking abilities

5. Address communication style differences
   Seek to understand and accept differences in communication styles

If possible, blend different styles into a shared group style of talk

6. Mitigate or transcend personal conflicts
   Try to maintain mutual respect
   Resist the temptation to gossip about group members with others in the group
   Build positive emotional bonds among members whenever possible
   Be open and honest with other members
   Help other members work through their conflicts
   If the conflict becomes extreme during a meeting, consider leaving the room and addressing it at a later time, perhaps with a mediator

Since my original observations and interviews, much had changed at the Co-op. The composition of the staff itself had changed: Three new staff members replaced Rose, Laura, and Dan, who left the collective to pursue other occupations. In addition, the number of shift workers was reduced to two, and they worked in the store only on Monday nights, when the rest of the staff met upstairs.

The change in shift-worker policy was designed, in part, to address the inclusiveness problem. Shift workers had begun to cover so many shifts that their hours became closer to those of some regular staff, yet the shift workers lacked formal decision-making power. By limiting the number of shift workers to two and restricting the number of shifts staff could ask shift workers to cover, the difference between the roles of staff and shift workers became clearer.[25]

The Co-op also made an architectural change by adding a new room above the store.[26] The room was used as a lounge, reading room, and meeting space. Previously, the staff had met in the adjoining room upstairs, which was filled with file cabinets, desks, paper, and an odd assortment of quasi-furniture. The staff had also periodically met in staff members' living rooms or in a room on the nearby University of Wisconsin-Madison campus.

The staff found its new meeting room ideal. Like the old room, it provided quick access to records and the store itself, but to open a file drawer or check the computer, a staff member no longer had to disrupt the meeting by stepping over people sitting on the floor. The new room was far more comfortable owing to its spacious layout, its cozy sofa, and new chairs.

Such "comforts" were important to staff. The larger space made it possible to sit in a true circle and see every person in the room. The size of the room also gave staff members the "personal space" that made it more comfortable to sustain eye-contact while speaking directly to even the person sitting beside them. The personal space and good chairs also provided physical comfort. Aching backs and constant shifting had distracted staff members during meetings, so comfortable seating made it easier to concentrate.[27] In sum, if the renovated space made it easier for staff to focus on the meeting agenda and speak their minds, the Co-op took a step toward reducing meeting length and, perhaps, mitigating the tension stemming from personal conflicts.

To further address the problem of long meetings, the staff formalized its agenda-setting process. During the week prior to a meeting, staff members used to scribble on a piece of scrap paper the phrase or half-sentence that described whatever they wished to discuss Monday night. This often resulted in a jumble of incomplete and unorganized agenda items. Under the new system, staff members had the freedom to write down agenda items during the week, but they did so in a more organized manner. They first decided whether their item belonged under scheduling, donations, committee updates, issues, or announcements. This categorical distinction allowed the facilitator to cluster similar items, and it helped focus discussion. Staff members also specified the kind of action their items required: brainstorming, a decision, a discussion, an announcement, or something else. Members then estimated the amount of meeting time their items would take and signed their names beside their items.

Staff had also established a clearer expectation that everyone read the agenda prior to the meeting. Required reading came to include not only the agenda items, but also the "cling-ons," which some staff affectionately called Klingons (after one of the more excitable alien species in the Star Trek universe). These cling-ons included any documents that might clarify an agenda item. One common cling-on was the staff's new donation request form, which was completed by whichever staff member received the request.

Reading the agenda and the cling-ons prior to Monday night would, in theory, provide staff members with knowledge they would otherwise have to obtain during meetings. In the meeting I observed, however, this particular expectation was not always met. Some staff sheepishly asked for details during the meeting that had been available in the cling-ons.

Staff also reported that facilitation and self-facilitation improved somewhat, and my observations confirmed this. Facilitators more regularly tried to gauge total meeting length and pace the meeting accordingly. Facilitators were making a more concerted effort to avoid tangents and steer wayward speakers back on track. As for self-facilitation, staff generally followed the advice of Sam and Kate, who wrote a set of meeting guidelines. Staff concentrated on what each other said, and they (usually) refrained from repeating one another's words, saying "ditto" or "what she said" instead.

One of the most dramatic changes in staff policy came in response to the problem of unequal involvement and commitment. In March, 1991, the Co-op drafted its first dismissal procedure. Under this policy, the staff could "dismiss" (fire) a member of the worker collective due to a "pattern of failure to show up for work," "negligence of individual responsibilities," "consistent substandard job performance," or a "pattern of abusive behavior."

If a dismissal or probation was requested by one of the staff, the request was processed by a staff committee, which then made a recommendation, accompanied by a clear rationale, to the Board of Directors. Designed for dismissing uncommitted and disengaged staff, the policy had not yet been put to use, but its mere existence may serve as a warning to anyone whose involvement might otherwise wane.[28]

Other policy changes made it harder to reduce the number of hours one worked at the store. The new vacation policy specified that staff can take up to four weeks of paid vacation, and vacations must be scheduled in advance. In addition, no staff member could trade more than thirty percent of his or her shifts. It was hoped these policies would prevent misunderstandings and disputes like those that had developed between Norma and the rest of the staff.[29]

The staff communication network also had improved since my initial study. Mifflin Co-op had invented a proto-blog—a written log placed near one of the cash registers, which staff regularly read when beginning a shift. Staff, as well as the two shift workers, wrote in the log any ideas, experiences, or feelings they wished to share. This kept members up-to-date on important events, and it kept them in touch with each other's moods and concerns. An erasable marker board complemented the log by providing a space for information of immediate relevance, from phone messages to notes about food deliveries. Norma and Louis, both of whom raised concerns about cliques and mini-consensus at Mifflin, agreed that the log and marker board improved the flow of ideas and emotions among staff. As an added bonus, these mechanisms absorbed much of the time that was otherwise spent during Monday night meetings to make announcements and present gripes.

Clear differences in communication skills and styles remained, and the three new staff further tested the staff's ability to handle such differences. Nonetheless, the new staff said they felt welcome at the Co-op, and during the meeting, they appeared comfortable. They didn't talk as often as the others, but they always joined in the group laughter and sat in relaxed postures. Most importantly, they spoke when issues of direct concern came up during the meeting. They continued to speak freely even when the meeting turned into an emotionally charged debate on whether certain staff were failing to fulfill work responsibilities and creating uncomfortable work atmospheres.[30]

As this discussion topic suggests, however, interpersonal conflicts remained at the Co-op. Since my original observations, the Co-op had hired a professional mediator to host a retreat at which staff learned about one another's backgrounds, current lives, and future aspirations. Staff told one another the ways they preferred to communicate and how they responded to different kinds of behaviors and messages. Though much remained unresolved after the retreat, staff found the discussions fruitful, because it helped them understand each other's experiences and perspectives.

The staff also wrote a grievance procedure for "any complaint, problem or misunderstanding...which has not been adequately dealt with through the normal staff interaction process." The centerpiece of the policy was finding an ombudsperson acceptable to the entire staff. Initially, this third-party seeks a mutually-acceptable resolution to the problem. If this fails, the ombudsperson then serves as an overseer while the problem is taken to the Personnel Committee and then the Board of Directors, which makes the final decision. If successful, the policy would provide reluctant staff members (or shift workers) with a clear opportunity to air their grievances.

More informally, I witnessed Co-op staff speaking to each other with respect and honesty. Throughout the meeting, staff showed little reluctance to ruffle feathers. Instead, they offered comments such as, "I appreciate your concern," or, "Don't worry. I know that you didn't mean for me to take it that way." Nonetheless, some staff took personal offense at times; through vulgarity, strong words, and staccato hand gestures, some staff expressed anger, frustration, and sadness during the discussion of the store's general work atmosphere.

A few days after the meeting I attended, Kate mused, "What's important is not the existence of conflict, but what you do with it."[31] From this perspective, the conduct and results of the discussion were more noteworthy than the personal conflicts themselves. Every staff member, including the newer ones, spoke directly and held onto their opportunities to speak, even when briefly cut off. Staff spoke with confidence and conviction, and they always took time to clarify themselves and correct misunderstandings. Staff were also careful to speak only for themselves by framing criticisms with "I feel" and "I think," instead of claiming the authority of the group.

The result of the main agenda item at that meeting was a commitment to improve communication about shelf stocking across different work shifts. Staff also reached a better understanding of what behaviors different members perceived as intimidating or hostile. They agreed to change the way they spoke to one another during work shifts, particularly during those times when the store was busiest and staff experienced the greatest stress.

After the staff reached these agreements, the meeting continued as before. Staff relaxed. As I wrote in my notebook, it seemed that the act of meeting together had given the staff a special opportunity to question and rearrange the reality of their workplace. During these special meeting times, staff were free to speak their minds and willing to listen.

It might be impossible for people to relate to one another on a daily basis with such stark honesty and full attentiveness. The physical, mental, and emotional strain would be too great. If, however, a group can set aside two hours each week while following clear rules of conduct, perhaps it is possible for a group of people to relate to one another and make collective decisions in a way that is truly exceptional. It remains a truism that no group can fully overcome the obstacles to small group democracy, but a group might surmount them during brief but brilliant flashes of time.

CHAPTER 6

Pursuing Democracy in Difficult Settings

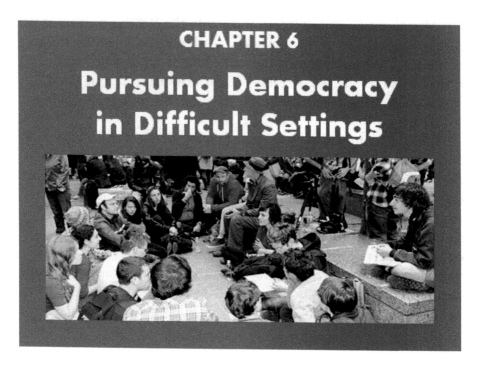

In many ways, the Mifflin Co-op operated in ideal circumstances. It had a stable staff of manageable size, could meet face-to-face as often as necessary, and had a governing board that gave it tremendous latitude. Situated in Madison, Wisconsin, it benefitted from a tolerant legal framework that gave it considerable leeway in its decisions. Even its cultural context—a liberal university town within a historically progressive state—meshed with the Co-op's mission.

Many other groups exist in circumstances quite at odds with their needs and purposes. Democratic groups with rapidly growing memberships can't simply expel members in pursuit of a more manageable size, lest they undermine their inclusiveness. Groups that chafe within external legal constraints may hope to someday change those laws, but in the meantime, they may have to operate within them.

When groups can't change their circumstances, they have to adapt. This chapter looks at how small groups can respond to problems posed by large, geographically dispersed, and unstable memberships, as well as time pressure and economic, political, and social constraints on democratic decision making.

Larger Groups and Organizations

In Chapter 1, I defined small groups as ranging from three to thirty people. Thirty is an approximate upper boundary for "small," but no matter where the line is drawn, it remains arbitrary. Even at just thirty people, though, one has the sense that such a group is "larger" than others, and larger democratic groups encounter challenges that differ in degree and kind from those faced by smaller ones.[1]

As the number of group members increases, it becomes more difficult to maintain an even distribution of final authority. Decision-making hierarchies may begin to separate "lower level" group members from those who make decisions "at the top." In its most benign form, this amounts to a form of representative democracy. At the worst, the group becomes a pint-sized oligarchy or dictatorship.[2]

Whether hierarchies form or not, some members may find themselves in a permanent minority, particularly in groups run by majority rule. In a very small group, each member needs to maintain something of an alliance with every other member, because proposals will often pass or fail by a single vote. In larger groups, close votes become less frequent. After several meetings, some members may be labeled "oddballs" or "outsiders." Even groups using consensus experience this if members of the permanent minority are reluctant to block group decisions.[3]

Even without hierarchies or permanent group minorities, overall member commitment may wane. Larger groups often have more power, because they have more people and resources. However, the larger the group, the lower the average member's political power.[4] As a result, members are likely to have a weaker sense of personal efficacy, feeling relatively ineffective or insignificant. Even if a group increased its power in equal proportion to its increase in size, a group member might still feel a net loss in power due to having a smaller share. This reduced sense of efficacy could result in a lower level of commitment to the process. Just as citizens in large nations easily feel disconnected to the larger political system, so members of larger groups can feel a diminished respect for group decision-making procedures.[5] The fact that larger groups experience less interpersonal trust could further weaken commitment to an intensive deliberative process.[6]

Relational bonds among members may also weaken. It is easier to know ten people than thirty, so larger groups have more difficulty forging a common identity and sense of belonging. As groups grow larger, friendly relations give way to cordiality, as faces and the histories behind them become less familiar. Politeness among strangers may eventually become the norm, but there is also the possibility that such anonymity will make relations cold or hostile, or at least uncooperative.[7]

A group's growing size and its eroding relationships can also contribute to a breakdown in the deliberative process. In larger groups, the equality of chances to speak may remain constant, but the *adequacy* of opportunities diminishes. So long as meeting length remains constant, increases in the number of speakers result in fewer speaking opportunities per person. If members find themselves identifying with different speakers, they may continue to feel that their perspectives are being expressed. Even in these cases, however, the nuances of their own, personal perspectives may be missed by those who speak in their place. Moreover, some members may begin to view themselves as spokespersons and inadvertently silence the members they aim (or claim) to represent. In those cases where clear subgroups don't exist, disagreements may involve such a wide range of perspectives that members find their speaking opportunities altogether inadequate.[8]

The more weakly shared group identity and the cooler atmosphere may make members less interested in considering what others have to say. Even if members try to understand and appreciate each other's views, the task becomes increasingly difficult as the number of viewpoints multiplies. A given member's limited attention and empathy will be divided into smaller and smaller portions per person, and the sheer range of viewpoints can make group deliberation sluggish.[9]

Deliberation in large face-to-face groups is also complicated by the sheer number of people present during a discussion. Larger groups have greater difficulty finding spacious meeting rooms, or comfortable seating arrangements that allow all group members to see and hear one another easily. Speaking itself becomes more challenging for those group members whose apprehension grows as the size of the group changes the setting from a circle of friends to an audience of acquaintances.

Small democratic groups can adapt to size increases in several ways. Large groups often confront potential power imbalances by using formal procedures that protect those group members who hold minority opinions. For instance, groups using majority rule can require significant proposals to pass with a two-thirds majority, as opposed to a simple majority. Experimentation with proportional outcomes might also prove fruitful, especially when group minorities are very small and stable. Groups run by consensus can place more emphasis on the legitimacy of blocking consensus. Such a group doesn't want to encourage stalemates, but it needs to reduce the conformity pressures that build as groups grow in size.[10]

To ensure a sustained commitment to democracy, members can remind themselves of the trade-off between greater group power and reduced individual efficacy. If they recognize the need for a larger group, they may continue to believe that democracy remains the best available means of decision making. Members also need to recognize that although their percentage share of group power has shrunk, their absolute amount of power—as a member of a larger group—may be greater than when the group was smaller. This is especially true for those groups whose very actions require a critical mass of participants, whether raising barns or raising hell.

Instead of relying on spontaneous social interaction, a larger group can make a concerted effort to build strong member relationships. Larger groups have fewer informal "group bonding" activities that involve the entire group, but they can plan social events that aim for maximum attendance to avoid the development of cliques. Groups might also institutionalize some forms of politeness, as parliamentary groups often do by addressing the chair when speaking and referring to one another in a respectful manner.[11] In a more abstract sense, larger groups can appeal to members' shared identification with common group goals and norms, rather than with the individual members, substituting bonds with the group's ideals for bonds among its membership.[12]

One way to secure adequate speaking opportunities is to organize speaking turns before meetings, such that all points of view are presented during deliberation even though people cannot speak as often or as long as they would like. For instance, if five people wish to raise a particular concern, they might discuss or draft their argument beforehand; during the meeting, one or two of them would present their view to the group as a whole.

Such caucusing, however, can exacerbate listening problems. Perhaps the best way of addressing this difficulty is to remind each other of the need to listen attentively. Some groups, such as the Quakers, maintain a slower pace by periodically pausing between speaking turns. This practice makes listening easier, but it also reduces the amount of time available for speaking.

Formal deliberative meeting designs sometimes break up groups into randomly assigned sub-groups, so that a group of twenty-four persons meets as a body of the whole only half of the time. The rest of a meeting day is spent in groups of four-to-six, where each person has ample opportunity to speak. This effectively breaks the group apart, for a time, but if the sub-groups effectively relate their findings back to the larger group, this method can make for richer deliberation.[13]

One final means of addressing the problems faced by larger groups is to move from a direct democracy to a representative form of decision making. A growing group might decide to restructure itself in any number of ways: It could meet once a year to elect a board, break into sections that meet bi-monthly and send representatives to weekly meetings, or split into autonomous committees with distinct jurisdictions. Creative forms of representation can limit the distance between representatives and the general membership, but any such system reduces contact among members and poses the danger of misrepresentation. This particular strategy, however, all but gives up on the aspiration of remaining a small *group*, per se. Rather, at this level of structure the group becomes more of an organization.[14]

One example of a group that struggled to maintain direct, face-to-face participation as it grew in size is the Clamshell Alliance, a political action group most famous for its nonviolent occupation of the Seabrook nuclear power plant. The Clamshells' 1979 Congress of the Alliance drew over one hundred people, and ongoing controversies promised to make deliberation challenging. To ensure a democratic deliberative process despite the Congress' size, the organizers repeatedly split into small groups, which drafted, debated, and revised proposals. When the group met as a whole, a team of facilitators made deliberation possible. One person served as the presiding clerk, responsible for coordinating the meeting. Another was assistant clerk, keeping track of which person was next on the list of speakers. Yet another took responsibility for writing on a blackboard the names of people who signaled their wish to speak. Any members wishing to make procedural motions wrote a note or spoke with the two "process people," who jointly decided which motions to pass on to the clerk. Finally, a timekeeper intervened if the group strayed too far from its schedule, and a "vibes watcher" monitored the group atmosphere. Numerous participants found this elaborate procedure effective, and it serves as an example of how small groups can find innovative ways of adapting their decision-making process accommodate large memberships.[15]

A present-day group with digital technology at hand could translate many aspects of this process into software that helps the group manage the flow of speaking turns, ideas, proposals, critiques, and votes. A variety of companies have developed electronic technology to help face-to-face groups work through complex agendas more efficiently. Hand-held "clickers" get used to record votes automatically, with the results projected on a single screen for all to see, and these devices can record far more nuanced opinions than simple "yea" or "nay" votes.[16] Wall-mounted monitors can also replace the sheets of paper and the semi-legible handwriting that causes group members to squint. All this is for the greater good, so long as the digital technology does not end up excluding some members who cannot adapt to these devices rapidly enough to participate in the group as equals.[17]

Geographically Dispersed Groups

Some groups are not only large but also geographically dispersed. Unable to meet as a whole regularly, they forego meetings or gather online, through synchronous web-chats, online forums, or conference calls, or they correspond via asynchronous emails or bulletin boards.[18] In the first edition of this book, I guessed that geographically dispersed groups would become increasingly common, but in the twenty years since, they have advanced to the point of becoming normal, if not the norm.

To see the primacy of the face-to-face encounter, one need only consider how difficult it has been for teleconferencing to supplant in-person interaction, even after the ascendance of the Internet. Civic associations, private organizations, professional associations, religious societies and all other manner of decision-making bodies will spend fortunes and endure the inefficiencies of road and air travel to arrange for co-presence, rather than simply logging into a shared online space. Even in the digital age, during which some groups certainly choose to meet online, the face-to-face meeting remains a preferred medium for group interaction.[19]

I focus on those decision-making groups that *must* meet online because they are unable to meet regularly face-to-face. What are the challenges that such groups face if they wish to function democratically, and how can they address those difficulties? Though there are also advantages to meeting online,[20] there are also common problems geographic dispersion can cause for groups that aspire to deliberate democratically.[21]

When group members can't meet regularly in person, there is a danger that group power will concentrate in the hands of one or two members. Whether intentionally or accidentally, a member may begin to make decisions for the group and wield ever-increasing influence over other members. The one or two powerful members may derive their power from their central location in a communication network, such as the individual who convenes online meetings.

The most powerful members can gain additional power by taking advantage of group members who consider themselves outsiders. These peripheral members, who almost never meet directly with the group, may voluntarily yield their votes or influence to other members. A powerful member could accumulate actual or *de facto* proxy votes and gain a disproportionate amount of influence during group meetings.

Such differentiation can occur in face-to-face groups, as well, but the online setting makes passivity or withdrawal less obvious than in-person meetings, where one's silence is more noticeable. On a conference call, for example, one can't always know who is present and who is absent. Each caller may offer a brief hello when joining the call, but at any given moment, some of those not speaking may have dropped out of the call, hit the mute button to type on their keyboard, or wandered off to feed the cat.

The more distant or less involved group members in geographically dispersed groups face another problem: Powerful members might make and implement decisions long before other members learn of them. This problem is most prominent for those groups that have a central physical location, such as a headquarters or place where the group does its work (philanthropy, commerce, politics, etc.). If only some members reside or work regularly at that location, this affords them a degree of short-term autonomy that may strengthen their position against the wishes of more peripheral members. Distant members may gladly grant short-term flexibility to the more centrally located members, but this can grow into a gathering of authority that leads to significant decisions being taken without consulting or informing the group.

Regardless of the character of group power, members' commitment to democratic procedures may lessen if they rarely deliberate as a whole, a temptation that arises from the lack of regularized co-presence. If the group's decision-making process becomes indirect or non-existent, the function and importance of deliberation will become less apparent. Similarly, mutuality and congeniality may not develop as readily in a group that never meets as a whole. Though studies have confirmed that online groups can develop strong relational bonds, working together online can lead groups to foreground immediate analytic tasks over the less obvious need for relational maintenance.[22] Groups that maintain anonymity face a special hazard, in that mutuality and respect tend to erode when members can't hold another accountable for what they say online.[23] "Flaming" occurs online so frequently precisely because the individual operating the flame-thrower has no fear of getting burned,[24] though the worst incidents occur in open online settings outside the boundaries of small group interactions.

Fortunately, groups that must do the bulk of their meetings online can address each of these problems. One way to mitigate the unequal distribution of power is to institutionalize regular group communication, ensuring that no members fall out of touch and none take too much initiative. The temptation to meet sporadically is just that—a temptation that modern technology can overcome through even media such as Google+ Hangout that make videoconferencing easy, provided one has adequate Internet access. Also, online groups can rotate formal responsibilities, such as that of meeting facilitator, agenda organizer, etc. To the extent that any of these jobs require facility with digital technology, it is important the group agree on an interface with which all members have familiarity.[25]

If members' commitment to the democratic process wanes, the group might need to reexamine its reasons for choosing to make its decisions democratically (see Chapter 1). An explicit discussion of the group's purposes and principles might lead the group to commit to more regular meetings and other shared activities that make the group itself feel more "real" to the members.[26]

To maintain a sense of mutuality and congeniality, members can seek alternatives to the easy social cues of face-to-face interactions. Video-chats can provide some intimacy, especially when each group member participates from within his or her home or another setting that provides modest visual insight into that person's life. (On the Internet, everyone can bring their dog to work.) Just as groups that meet in person devote some time to play and socializing, so can online groups seek out shared experiences online and develop a powerful sense of co-presence.[27] The only caution is, once again, to do those activities as a complete group, lest cliques form for that sub-group that takes the extra time to socialize, play online games together, and so on.

Beyond merely inventing substitutes for in-person interaction, groups should also take advantage of the benefits of "impersonal" means of communication. Just as "many people have the experience of expressing something in a letter that they were unable to say face-to-face," so can online groups find exceptional opportunities for sharing and friendship when geographically dispersed.[28] Online groups can bring together members with deeply personal shared concerns, as in the case of consciousness-raising groups or those designed to offer social support. Intimacy may come more easily for some people in online settings, and that can have powerful positive effects on the group members.[29] That, in turn, could nurture the relational health of democratic groups.

As for the perils of anonymity, online groups that choose to (or must) keep identities private can still socially sanction those who disrespect other group members. In some cases, however, such punishment only spurs further online vitriol (a.k.a. "e-bile"), as is the case when Internet "trolls" feed on even negative attention.[30] In those cases, the group might reconstitute itself online in a more secure setting that the offending person can't access. In effect, this sacrifices some inclusion in pursuit of other democratic objectives.

Even deliberation itself may function well in the right online settings, provided that it creates opportunities for rich interaction among the full membership.[31] Some experiments in online deliberation have yielded unsatisfying outcomes, wherein a small sub-set of the group does the bulk of the talk and leads groups to relatively unreflective judgments or takes over the decision-making task entirely.[32] Others have shown that, for instance among the online editing groups that form in Wikipedia, group discussions can achieve high levels of analytic rigor.[33]

To aid online group deliberation (or enhance face-to-face meetings), specialized digital technology has developed called *group decision support systems* (GDSS). Also known as *groupware*, these systems typically display group-level information, such as the total pool of ideas generated, the solutions currently under consideration, and vote tallies. GDSS can integrate members' quantitative weightings of evaluation criteria with ratings of ideas and alternatives, such that a group can quickly assess member preferences and attitudes on agenda item before recording a final decision. Such technology can improve overall group performance, but more often than not, face-to-face groups outperform the deliberation of computer-mediated ones.[34]

The average online group, which has nothing more at its disposal than a simple discussion board, web-chat, or similar interface, must make do with what's available. As existing technologies become commonplace for a wider range of users, more and more groups will be able to rely on them for effective group deliberation.[35]

Unstable Memberships

Whether dispersed geographically or centrally located, every group has members joining and departing. This is particularly true of groups influenced by external cycles, such as the semi-annual turnover at a housing co-op or the semester-by-semester changes in campus organizations. Membership changes are usually addressed without much difficulty, but some groups have membership compositions one might call "unstable." These groups are always in flux, with people joining and leaving every month or every week and no member lasting more than a period of months.[36]

In these groups, inclusiveness becomes a potential issue. The group has to ask itself why people are coming and going. Is the scope of the group's power changing in step with the changing membership? Is the group constantly pushing people out who really belong? Are members leaving because they find the group unproductive or unsatisfying? There is even the danger of a vicious cycle: The group's unstable membership might make it ineffective and frustrating, causing members to leave, exacerbating its instability.

Commitment can be a problem for these groups, because they have a disproportionate number of new members at any point in time. Unless new members already have a commitment to the democratic process, they may not develop one before they leave. In larger co-operative houses, for example, a few people may move in and out on a month-to-month basis, making it hard to establish democratic norms in monthly meetings. Again, an ever-worsening cycle could emerge, whereby the unstable membership makes it hard to teach democratic norms that, as a result, become weaker over time.[37]

For similar reasons, instability can jeopardize a sense of mutuality. Group members may be cordial to each other, but a group in flux can't readily form a strong common identity. As instability increases, the group's members have increasing difficulty thinking of one another as essential parts of a shared group identity.

Similarly, it may be difficult for members to understand one another in unstable groups, as no common language will evolve. In particular, if a core of members remains while the rest of the membership changes, the new and old members may have difficulty communicating effectively. The old members may be reluctant to repeat things they have said in the past, and the new members will not understand the group language that developed before they joined. Accurate communication will take more time and energy, so either comprehension or speaking opportunities will diminish.

Small democratic groups with unstable memberships can confront these difficulties in several ways. To address the problem of inclusiveness, the group will have to reach out to those who have left the group and try to understand why they left. If they felt pushed out, the group might need to consider restructuring itself to accommodate them. Otherwise, the scope of the group's agenda might have to change in response to the changing needs and power of the membership.

As for commitment, the group might have to institutionalize itself more than other groups, safeguarding democratic norms and procedures that would otherwise be washed away by the changing tides of membership. The group could also require new members to undergo a period of training before joining the group. If too demanding, however, this requirement could turn away potential members.

Perhaps the group can maintain a common identity by looking beyond its current membership. For instance, if the group is a community action planning committee, it may have five to fifteen members at any given time but identify itself with a relatively stable geographic area or transcendent core value. Thus, the membership identifies with something larger and more enduring than the group itself.[38] In addition, group members can try to maintain a more personal group identity by engaging in "ice-breaker" activities at meetings.[39]

Similarly, the group members might communicate better if they speak in the vernacular of the larger community. The group could consciously avoid developing its own language, relying instead on an imperfect but common vocabulary and dialect. However, since the larger society is always the site for struggles among competing forms of discourse, the most common way of speaking likely favors a particular speech community, such as the middle class.[40]

Time Pressure

Just as all groups have changing memberships, all face time pressures. It is the nature of human existence that we have limited time and can only be in one place at any given time. Some groups regularly face severe time constraints, and most will, at one time or another, have to make a decision too quickly. Therefore, it is important to understand the problems this creates.

It is impossible to define what constitutes "severe" time pressure in terms of hours or days. For groups accustomed to extended timelines, making a decision in one month may strain their capacities. For other groups, a month is a luxury, with fifteen minutes constituting a challenging time constraint. The seriousness of a deadline depends not only on the absolute amount of time available, but it also depends on the procedures the group uses, the nature of the issue, and the group's experience with working under pressure.

When time constraints are severe for a group, members may exaggerate the need to end deliberation, then quickly delegate authority to an individual or ad hoc committee. If these delegates are responsible for reaching irrevocable decisions on the group's behalf, the group has temporarily yielded its final authority. There may be times when this must be done, but it is important to circumscribe the delegates' authority and give them principles on which to act.

It is also impossible to provide members with equal and adequate opportunities to speak when time runs short. If deliberation is rushed, members may have little chance to present their views, short of voting or responding to a call for consensus. Differences in speaking skills and styles are exacerbated, as the quicker and less reflective speakers will have greater speaking opportunities. The intense pressure to reach a decision may be felt most by those holding a minority opinion, or those who can't easily articulate an opinion. This is especially true when, as a deadline approaches, a majority becomes impatient with dissenters.[41]

Democratic groups can take measures to alleviate strain that time pressure places on group power and deliberation. Most of all, they can resist the temptation to give one or two members full responsibility for what is actually a group problem. Even if selected individuals have the group's confidence, they can't discern the group's will by themselves. At the very least, the group can establish a broadly defined policy and let a delegate or committee work out the details.

As for deliberation, groups can reduce meeting time by talking in subgroups beforehand—not to reach a pre-meeting mini-consensus but to talk through concerns so that they can be articulated efficiently. Groups under tight deadlines may not be able to do this, but they can at least take extra caution to avoid repeating one another's words. The group might aid this process by encouraging members to gesture quietly when they hear something with which they agree.

Finally, there is sometimes a solution to time-pressure that groups overlook entirely. Some time constraints come from forces outside the group, such as a foundation's deadline for drafting a grant proposal. Other pressures, though, come from within the group itself, and some of these are either arbitrary or reflect an overemphasis on speed. One of the virtues of Hermann Hesse's famous character, Siddhartha, was his ability "to wait."[42] Habitual impatience, as opposed to situational necessity, sometimes causes groups to set unnecessarily tight schedules, and such a habit isn't conducive to democratic deliberation. To be resolved effectively, decisively, and democratically, some issues take more time than a group originally designates. Mifflin Co-op, for instance, set aside a great deal of time for discussing its tenure incentives policy, yet the group had to struggle to meet its original deadline. When it appeared that its first consensus might have been premature, the Co-op found a way to extend deliberation.

Economic, Political, and Social Constraints

The final and most important situational constraint on small group democracy is the ubiquitous influence of the political, economic, and cultural forces that transcend the group. All small groups are under these "external" constraints. Even the most sophisticated groups can't entirely escape the power inherent in language and social norms, and political and economic power networks extend into even the most isolated small groups.[43]

Some groups, though, face particularly severe external constraints—ones that are painfully apparent whenever the group tries to reach and implement important decisions. For instance, groups actively involved in a competitive economic system may have difficulty when democratic values conflict with the pursuit of profits. The long success of Mifflin Co-op for over a quarter-century shows that this isn't an impossible situation, but its ultimate demise discourages undue optimism. Small democratic groups dependent on outside financial resources have the same problems, because a person or organization outside of the group limits their autonomy.[44] Similarly, groups politically subordinate to a larger organization, such as a union or national association, can have their agenda dictated to them by those at higher levels of authority. Even if the group has a great deal of power today, its autonomy could be compromised tomorrow. This specter of powerlessness can distort group decisions by causing group members to accept proposals that run counter to their own interests.

External forces can also make power unequal within the group. If one member sits on a board with authority over the group, this member may have an inordinate influence. Even if group bylaws make member authority officially equal, this external power imbalance can generate in-group inequalities. Social stereotypes can also distort the distribution of power within the group by causing the group to discriminate in favor of dominant social groups when making committee appointments or delegating tasks.[45]

Both overt and subtle power dynamics can distort member relationships and deliberation due to members' differences in class, ethnicity, culture, gender, sexual orientation, and so on.[46] Sex stereotypes and socialization create patterns of individual and group behavior contrary to small group democracy.[47] Even among university students—a group one might expect to be less sexist than the overall population, studies have shown males to have greater confidence in their ability to persuade and more willingness to use controlling behaviors in mixed-sex groups.[48] In such groups, women adapt to men's nonverbal and verbal communicative styles more than vice versa.[49] As Shirley Ardener argues, patriarchal social relations are designed to "mute" women in mixed-sex social situations. In this view, women may not actually be silent. On the contrary, "They may speak a great deal. The important issue is whether they are able to say all that they would wish to say, where and when they wish to say it. Must they, for instance, re-encode their thoughts to make them understood in the public domain?"[50] Even when females adapt to the "male" speaking style, other group members sometimes (but not always) continue to rate their speech less favorably than that of males.[51]

Charles Derber argues that patriarchy and other "stratification systems" tend to create "distinctions of social worth that are communicated, learned, and enforced in ordinary face-to-face processes." Social conventions dictate that women remain nurturing and attentive, whereas men are socialized to be controlling and demanding of attention. The pressures exerted by conventions such as these go against democratic principles, such as the equality of speaking opportunities and mutual consideration.[52]

The problems presented by external power relations must be addressed if groups wish to sustain democratic norms. Groups whose agendas are directly controlled by external forces or entities must start with what they have and work toward greater autonomy over time, until they have what they deem sufficient for their purposes. Strategies include breaking away from superiors and using persuasion to gain more power incrementally.

Also, groups must confront inequalities among members that derive from external power imbalances. If dominant members are unwilling to relinquish their status, the group ought to seriously consider removing them. Otherwise, the group can consciously work on undoing the influence of the social and cultural inequalities that manifest themselves within the group.[53]

When working to reduce these internal constraints on the democratic process, the group would do well to consider shifting its focus from deliberation on policy to dialogue oriented toward greater mutual understanding.[54] For a time, this forces a democratic group to worry less about its decision-making tasks and focus instead on better understanding and appreciating its members, their personal histories, life aspirations, and ways of seeing the world. Dialogue won't bring the group to a consensus on any particular issue, but it *can* help the group develop a greater capacity to deliberate on such issues democratically in the future.

CHAPTER 7
Democracy in Daily Life

"There is a world of difference between accepting the democratic ideal for society at large and being willing to accept it as a guide for one's own everyday conduct." —Bruno Lasker[1]

Democratic principles can shape formal group decision making processes, but they also can shape how we live every day. A democratic society is just that—a social world infused with democracy not just in its governance but in the lives its people lead. Theorists and activists alike have called for democratizing the economy, or workplaces in particular, but here I want draw out the implications of small group democracy for three aspects of daily life. Informal conversations, close personal relationships, and the way we raise our children each shape democratic society. They help to define how we relate to intimates and strangers alike, and they teach the next generation lessons that will shape their sense of what it means to work together. For a democratic society to thrive, each of these must have a vitality that daily reinforces principles of equal power, inclusion, commitment, connection, and deliberation.[2]

Conversation

It is in conversations that we decide how to view or "name" ourselves and our world. A long and heartfelt talk with a spouse, sibling, or friend can change a person forever, and conversations can become turning points in our lives. Even a spontaneous exchange with a stranger on a train can change the course of events.[3] The serendipity engine known as the Internet now makes such chance encounters no longer subject to chance. Via social media, anyone can now find in minutes another person who would be happy to chat about anything on one's mind.

This influence we have on one another constitutes a form of power, and in *democratic* conversations, participants jointly develop the conversation. No single speaker dominates its topic or direction. Democratic conversation also has an open and inclusive character. Particular conversations may involve only two or three participants, democratic conversationalists seek to maintain a diverse network of conversation partners. Democratic conversants sometimes ask, "Who isn't present?" Or, "Is anyone here being ignored?"[4]

Fully democratic conversations also embody the relational and deliberative features of small group democracy, albeit with greater emphasis on free flowing exchange than on closure.[5] Conversational partners respect and appreciate one another, safeguard speaking and listening opportunities, argue responsibly, and listen carefully.

These idealized conversational norms may sound familiar, because according to linguists, these rules define the conversational ideal in Western cultures.[6] For everyday conversation to function, we must begin with the assumption that each speaker speaks truthfully, clearly, and with relevant information of one kind or another.[7] We follow these norms instinctively, and we respond strongly to their violation.[8]

Competitive Narcissism

Unfortunately, the democratic conversational ideal stands at considerable distance from the more typical exchange. Regardless of the topic or the conversation partners, competitiveness, individualism, and narcissism predominate in conversations in the United States, as demonstrated by Charles Derber in *The Pursuit of Attention*:

> Everyone is in a competitive position in a conversation because the amount of attention received depends on the relative success of one's own initiatives to attract and hold the common focus. Commonly focused attention...is limited and can become "scarce" if the amount any person seeks is greater than that available. Under conditions of unusual scarcity, the competitive features become more visible and pronounced.... However, in most settings the competition remains disguised because [participants] are expected to be more subtle and discreet.[9]

In three quarters of the conversations Derber recorded, there was "significant inequality in the distribution of attention...with one person described as clearly dominant in over fifty percent of the conversations." Sometimes a participant became virtually "invisible" by failing to obtain "even the minimum attention required to feel that his or her presence has been acknowledged and established."[10]

The opposite of the invisible participant is the "conversational narcissist." Whereas democratic conversationalists occasionally shift the conversation's topic, narcissists quickly shift the topic to themselves after dispensing with the requirements of politeness. Narcissists use supportive responses sparingly, and they sometimes use purposefully flawed timing to disrupt the flow of conversation. When they respond supportively, they typically use the weak forms of support, such as background acknowledgements (e.g., "Mmhmm," "Yeah"), instead of questions or statements that would better sustain the conversation's focus on the speaker and the speaker's topic.

Conversational narcissism may be more of a relational dynamic than a personality trait, with all people showing varying degrees of narcissism depending on the setting, circumstances, and conversational partners.[11] Men, for example, have been found to be more likely to draw attention to themselves than women, such as when using humor to differentiate themselves favorably from others, as compared to women's tendency to seek laughter than builds cohesion.[12]

Bonding and Arguing

Speaking of which, the accumulation of social cohesion and trust counts as one of the important features of conversation. Democratic conversations build social capital, which better prepares a society for the challenge of self-government.[13] A problem arises, however, when we limit ourselves to conversation partners who share our background and point of view.

After political scientist Katherine Cramer spent three years with citizens who regularly talked politics with a group of their peers, she concluded that "when most people talk informally about politics, they aren't doing it to solve the world's problems." Instead, such conversations "are a way of sharing time, figuring out the world together, and feeling like part of a community."[14]

Often, political conversations reinforce borders between social groups rather than bridging them. A systematic survey of political interactions and media use found that the setting in which participants were least likely to hear different views was in talking with a "primary discussant," typically the friend or relative with whom one talks politics most often.[15]

The fact remains, however, that conversations do occur across party lines, and even among like-minded conversants, considerable persuasion takes place. When done in the spirit of democratic conversation, these exchanges can cause people to become more knowledgeable about candidates and issues or even change their electoral choices.[16]

Multiply those effects across the many connections in one's political conversation network, and the power of conversation becomes more obvious. Even when one nudge is not enough, when one gets strong signals from different corners of one's social network, the individual nudges add up to a powerful push.[17]

The fact that so many of these exchanges occur online might cause worry, given the frequency of hostile online exchanges. Studies of discussion online, however, suggest that the Internet gives as much cause for hope here as despair. In particular, when one more carefully parses politeness from civility, online conversation tends to sacrifice courtesy in service of pointed political disagreement. So long as one does not cross over into outright disrespect, a bit of brusqueness might be a small price to pay for a frank exchange across ideological lines.[18] Moreover, some online conversants will simply shrink away from opportunities to talk politics in face-to-face settings, and a rough exchange online might be better than none at all.[19]

Reclaiming Conversations

Though typical conversations often lack the idealized qualities of democratic exchanges, they remain an important means of building up the skills of citizenship. There remains a special place in democracy for private exchanges of ideas, aspirations, and fears outside of the pressure of more public settings.[20] Regular interpersonal exchanges can help to fuel political engagement more generally,[21] and even imperfect discussion networks and conventional media use can, in turn, spur more deliberative conversation.[22]

If left to their own devices, everyday citizens can produce spontaneously conversations that have features evoking the democratic ideal. This was what sociologist William Gamson found when he studied how small groups of friends and acquaintances talk about politics. He transcribed thirty-seven discussions involving nearly two hundred diverse working-class participants, then reached a conclusion far more optimistic than did Katherine Cramer in the aforementioned study. Gamson wrote, "Listening to their conversations over a period of an hour or more, one is struck by the deliberative quality of their construction of meaning about these complex issues." Talking among their peers, people "achieve considerable coherence in spite of a great many handicaps, some flowing from limitations in the media discourse that they find available and others from their own lack of experience with the task."[23]

When it comes to political conversations, we might do well to leave well enough alone. Imposing strict standards for discourse might do more to stifle sincere exchanges than to stimulate democratic ones,[24] and one can even turn people away from political participation with too forceful a push into more deliberative talk.[25]

Even if we let go of prescribing conversational norms for others, we can each choose to change the way we talk to others, as I pledged to do when I wrote the first edition of this book. Two decades later, I continue to find that when I make a conscious effort to keep my conversations respectful, whether they are political or not, other participants usually follow suit. When I converse with those who disagree with me, I find that others welcome honest cross-partisan exchanges. Earnest efforts to make conversations more democratic and deliberative can produce immediate and gratifying results.

Love and Marriage

Democracy invites civil conversation, but it also welcomes the heartfelt embrace. If this seems too far a leap, consider that "eros" has a central role to play in democracy. Educational philosopher Kerry Burch reminds us that eros, which denotes a blend of connection and passion, plays a central role in any democracy that aspires to do more than count the raised hands of disconnected private individuals. Just as small democratic groups need to temper individuality with mutuality, so does a democratic society need to both secure individualism and ensure strong bonds of love. A civic education in democratic eros serves to "educate" our desires. The goal is not an "unmoored eros, unmediated by critical reflection," but instead a "sensuous rationality" that can lead us to discover, together, a common good.[26]

Some of the earliest American theorists of deliberative democracy, such as Jane Mansbridge and Benjamin Barber, likewise stress the importance of friendship and mutual bonds in any democracy that hopes to break free of the restraints of strict liberal individualism.[27] If, as some argue, societies form partly from the accretion of experience in smaller groups, or "tiny publics" as sociologist Gary Fine calls them,[28] it may be just as true that dyadic bonds between romantic partners may also provide the reflective eros that fuels a more mature and deliberative democracy. Thus, to push the envelope slightly, I focus not on friendship but on romantic relations.

Democratic Romance

Democracy concerns decision making, and intimate relationships often require making choices. Thus, as political theorist Carole Pateman explains, to carry the logic of democratic society through to our romantic relationships, "Democratic ideals and politics have to be put into practice in the kitchen, the nursery and the bedroom."[29]

Couples make daily decisions about cooking, child care, and sex, but weightier decisions can involve relational commitments, careers, family planning, and more. The foremost feature of a democratic partnership or marriage is an egalitarian power distribution. Decisions that have serious consequences for both partners are reached through consensus, and if a decision requires great sacrifice by one partner (e.g., one has to move to follow the other's career), the other partner can make an equally significant concession.

Aside from equal power relations, the hallmark of democratic relationships is, once again, *eros*, or love. Psychologist Erich Fromm revered human affection and caring as much as democracy, and his classic work, *The Art of Loving*, promotes a conception of love that is both romantic and democratic. For Fromm, love is expansive and inclusive. People who love "only one other person and [are] indifferent to the rest" have not love, "but a symbiotic attachment, or an enlarged egotism." Fromm explains,

> One can often find two people "in love" with each other who feel no love for anybody else. Their love is, in fact, an egotism a' deux; they are two people who identify themselves with each other, and who solve the problem of separateness by enlarging the single individual into two.[30]

The partners in a fully democratic relationship don't withdraw from friends and family. Instead, they allow their private love to radiate more publicly to the others around them, strengthening their connections with the larger world.

The other distinguishing feature of a democratic relationship is an artful balance between separate and shared identities. "Mature love," wrote Fromm, "is union under the condition of preserving one's integrity, one's individuality...In love the paradox occurs that two beings become one and yet remain two."[31] Just as the members of a democratic group simultaneously affirm one another's individuality and mutuality, so do the partners in a democratic relationship cherish both their joint existence and their individual lives.

Existing relationships regularly deviate from this democratic ideal in every respect. In particular, long-term heterosexual partnerships or marriages have a tradition of male domination, exclusivity, and disrespect towards women. Although numerous exceptions exist, husbands often regard their wives as less than equal partners when making important decisions, and a patriarchal legal structure has reinforced and legitimated this attitude. One of the most blatant examples is the historical absence of laws protecting wives from spousal rape. Even though there have been some legal advances in recent years, these changes are only partial and underlying sexist attitudes too often remain unchanged. One need only listen to the words of Alaska Senator Paul Fischer, who insisted in 1985, "I don't know how you can have a sexual act and call it forcible rape in a marriage situation."[32]

As Fromm lamented, close relationships often lead to a withdrawal from larger social networks. Research on communication networks confirms this commonsense view.[33] An exception is that husbands have tended to seek political conversation partners outside of the marriage, because they devalue their spouse's political knowledge.[34] This move includes a person outside the relationship, but only at the cost of excluding the wife.

Patriarchal social norms in Western cultures discount women's competence not only as discussion partners, but also as autonomous individuals capable of making their own decisions. As Pateman explains, society portrays women as "beings who, in their personal lives, always consent, and whose explicit refusal of consent can be disregarded and reinterpreted as agreement." Pateman ties this denial of women's competence to a rejection of their individuality:

> Women find that their speech is persistently and systematically invalidated. Such invalidation would be incomprehensible if the two sexes actually shared the same status as "individuals." No person with a secure, recognized standing as an "individual" could be seen as someone who consistently said the opposite of what they meant and who, therefore, could justifiably have their words reinterpreted by others.[35]

All friendly and romantic relationships can involve unequal power, exclusivity, and disrespect for one or both partners' competence and individuality, but patriarchal cultural traditions exacerbate these problems in intimate heterosexual relationships. As Fromm observed in 1956, "Love is by necessity a marginal phenomenon in present-day Western society."[36]

In spite of such patriarchal underpinnings in modern society, most people can point to friends or neighbors who have forged democratic partnerships and marriages. These couples offer the hope that daily resistance to undemocratic habits and traditions can prove successful. These couples also show how constant personal struggle can benefit society by providing lessons and role models for others:

> Every woman's assertion of a degree of autonomy, or of a recognition of her needs, or of a restructuring of the division of labor and the decision-making process in the household today represents not only a change in her personal condition but also in the social position and role definitions of all women. Every man's recognition of the legitimacy of such claims, every change individual men make in the exercise of their traditional dominance, similarly contributes to the social reconstitution of sexual power relations.[37]

Such gender equality forges not only more democratic relationships but also a more equal public sphere, in which men become more likely to support the political participation of women as vice versa.[38] One of the quiet accomplishments of the feminist movement of the late 20th century may well be the signs of heightened gender equality in younger generations across the world—part of a cultural transformation that should improve the prospects for democratic relationships and governments alike.[39] Even college-aged women who wrestle with traditional gender roles during heterosexual courtship still hope to move into egalitarian marriages.[40]

Legalizing Love

And what of those who do not follow the heteronormative convention? They might aspire just as often toward a democratic intimate relationship, but in many cases, they have not had the option of state-sanctioned matrimony. Even as I write, this is changing in state after state within the U.S., and more than a dozen countries have legalized same-sex marriage. Even so, a greater number of countries offer imprisonment (or worse) to those in such relationships, and a majority of U.S. states give limited or no recognition to same-sex marriages, or even civil unions.[41]

When people have the opportunity to vote on whether to recognize same-sex unions, more often than not they choose to deny this minority the same rights accorded to heterosexual couples.[42] Exceptions exist and may become more frequent, but one could conclude that "democracy" is hostile to the rights of gay, lesbian, and transgender individuals. This denial of civil liberties and equal treatment under the law will, in time, go down as a regrettably myopic choice from a public accustomed to viewing only hetero-normative relationships as worth of respect.[43]

What I wish to argue here, however, is that the recognition of same-sex relationships constitutes more than a question of minority rights. The democratic *eros* demands it as a means of broadening the connections among the members of the demos. Those who seek out same-sex relationships should be able to do so openly, so that their love becomes more of a beacon than an inward force. To compel privacy in one's closest relationships engenders paralytic stress in many individuals and encourages the withdrawal from the wider society of which Fromm warned.[44]

Moreover, the act of *recognizing* same-sex love draws those giving the recognition into another kind of public relationship. The more open we become to recognizing the bonds of love that form around us, the better prepared we are for a democratic society in which we balance our individual needs with a concern for others. The public embrace of same-sex marriage—beyond merely legalizing same sex unions—then becomes a welcoming of wider, stronger, and more diverse connections among all members of society.

From Children to Citizens

Small group interactions that mix children and adults represent another special form of relationship in a democratic society. Minimum age requirements for voting (and seeking elected office) reflect the fact that children and adults tend to have markedly different levels of political maturity.[45] Ideally, children and young adults learn the fundamental principles of small group democracy and civic engagement before reaching the legal voting age, and the most straightforward path to democratic political socialization runs through our schools and families.[46]

Democratic Schools

Many educational reformers have envisioned and created democratic classrooms and schools. Their view of democratic education incorporates all of the features of small group democracy, at least by degrees. Democratic schools give substantial power to students, make themselves inclusive, and instill a commitment to democratic values. A democratic education also develops children's autonomy, self-esteem, mutual respect, group identity, and friendliness, and it teaches children the skills and habits of deliberation and cooperative decision making. These ideas are discussed at length in the writings of educators and philosophers, such as John Dewey and Polly Greenberg.[47]

At the very least, a school can design its curriculum to provide a civic education that prepares students for life as democratic citizens. This pushes civics education beyond the conventional standards, which ask that students learn basic facts about their country's constitution, political history, and electoral and legal processes. Such general political knowledge has a strong relationship with political engagement, but it offers no insight into how to deliberate in small democratic groups.[48]

Education scholar Walter Parker has helped lead the charge to infuse classrooms with more activities that teach students how to think through controversial issues together to reach a more informed and reflective judgment about the common good.[49] One tool he recommends provides the following structure for students to guide them through research, debate, and deliberation:

1. Students are assigned to teams.

2. Teams are divided into pairs, and each pair is assigned a position and told to prepare a presentation of its position and reasons to the opposite pair.

3. Pairs study the issue and prepare the presentation.

4. Pairs present to one another, listening carefully to the reasons given.

5. Pairs feed back what they have heard to the satisfaction of the other pair.

6. Genuine discussion: Students are told they can drop the assigned positions and see if their team can reach a decision on the question or, if not, then clarify the disagreement.[50]

Parker rightly emphasizes the final step, where students can step out of their assigned position on the issue and discover their own individual views, or even a view their whole group can embrace.

As an instructor, one can go a step farther and make the classroom itself more democratic by ceding a measure of one's power to the students. When I taught from the first edition of this book in courses on small group communication, I always gave students the opportunity to adjust the syllabus at the start of the semester: They would usually decide to make group projects worth more points and the first exam worth fewer, but a spirited debate always preceded their vote. Since I earned royalties from using my own book (roughly $30 per class), I also gave them the authority to allocate that money. More often than not, they chose a charitable cause and also "taxed" themselves an extra dollar or two each.

University of Iowa professor Rahima Wade took the experiment much farther in a graduate seminar she taught in 1996 at the University of Iowa. She gave the students control over the grading structure, let them personalize the readings, and even the structure of the class sessions themselves. Wade struggled to maintain a measure of control while still empowering the students. By the end of her experiment, both she and the students found that the course had been remarkably democratic, yet not *wholly* democratic. As one student wrote,

> Free rein of minds within certain limits can bring about participation, and that is what democratic education is all about. Maybe part of the reason the class did not develop to its full democratic potential is because you didn't let it. To truly be democratic is really risky. You have to let people be themselves. The whole definition of democracy is struggle. I think the confrontational nature of democracy kind of shocked you, but at least it was interesting.[51]

As Wade and I both conceded in our experiments, wholesale equalization of power is often unworkable. Nonetheless, even in social work settings where adults work with youth who demonstrate serious behavioral problems, the democratic model might improve educational outcomes. Erik Laursen and Thomas Tate, the co-directors of the Academy for Positive

Peer Culture in Richmond, Virginia, adapted the first edition of *Democracy in Small Groups* for their group work to contrast coercive and democratic teaching/mentoring in groups. In a traditional group, the adult commands and the youth submissively receive instruction to modify their inadequate behavior. In a democratic group, the adult facilitates in a relationship of mutual interdependence with youth who contribute to their own learning, to help themselves and others and become more socially interested and involved.[52] The point is not to cede the role of adult to the youth but to work within the constraints of a professional social-work relationship to accord students respect.

A handful of schools have gone farther and built remarkably egalitarian decision making structures. One example is the Meeting School, whose experience might inspire others to explore the possibilities of democratic education. When my brother taught at this Quaker boarding high school in New Hampshire during the early 1990s, many of its important decisions were reached during weekly community gatherings. These three-hour meetings involved students and faculty (who also did the administrative work), and all participated as equals in a consensus method of decision making. By meeting together, students and faculty reached numerous decisions, ranging from the abolishment of student curfews to the use of a cut Christmas tree. Although consensus provided a safeguard against hasty policy changes, students are given the power to shape the school rules that govern their daily lives.[53]

Consensus and democracy didn't always work to the satisfaction of the faculty and students at the Meeting School. Even as students obtained ever-greater power, they remained reluctant to deal with many important issues. Faculty, who retained final authority over hiring, firing, expulsion, and the annual budget, also had to address administrative and community concerns that the students chose to ignore. Students also neglected to participate fully in the committees that manage policy minutiae, and even when participating in meetings, students would sometimes show apathy, impatience, frustration, and an incomplete understanding of consensus. Such shortcomings are to be expected. So long as they don't threaten the existence of the system itself, they can be as valuable for the students as they are frustrating.

What counts is that students learn about the process and come to appreciate its virtues.

Even a principal at a public school can infuse a more democratic process into the curriculum. One such leader, at Park Forest Elementary School in State College, Pennsylvania, spurred active student engagement all the way from kindergarten through fifth grade. With a quarter of the students receiving free or reduced-cost lunches, the school is not an especially privileged one, yet starting in 2009, principal Donnan Stoicovy implemented a system that balances conventional educational goals with democratic aspirations. Using a mix of "all school gatherings" and ongoing "small school gatherings" (groups of 12-15 children each), students develop more reflective opinions and influence select school policies. An independent study found that this program has inspired many of the Park Forest students, though it has not won over all the teachers, some of whom feel that the democratic process is, ironically, an imposition.[54]

Democratic Families

In comparison to schools, the family has received relatively less attention in the literature on democracy. In the writings of some classical philosophers, such as John Stewart Mill, one occasionally finds the claim that when "justly constituted," the family is the "real school of the virtues of freedom." The implications of such statements, however, were rarely drawn out in such works. More often, the family was ignored altogether or assumed consistent with democratic principles.[55]

Since the first edition of *Democracy in Small Groups*, however, the concept of democratic parenting has become so commonplace that even empirical research has begun to emerge on the subject.[56] A study of more than a thousand Finnish adolescents, for example, found that their democratic parenting strategies tended to inculcate democratic values in their children.[57] Secondary benefits of democratic parenting range from reduced substance abuse during adulthood to a better sense of self-worth and heightened classroom engagement for African-

American youth whose parents raise their children's awareness of racial barriers in the midst of a democratic home environment.[58]

Though it has its advantages (and some philosophers view democratic parenting as a responsibility of citizenship on par with other forms of civil service) many family structures instill patently undemocratic dispositions in children.[59] This more autocratic approach stands as a basic assumption in many conservative political philosophies.[60] Thus, democratic parenting should not be taken for granted, and its basic features bear elaboration.

Democratic relations between children and parents share many of the features of small group democracy.[61] The ultimate in family democracy, writes therapist Cameron W. Meredith, "is when the family begins to function as a democratic group and is truly a microcosm of our dream of a larger democratic society." An example is "a family council with regular meetings, rotating chairperson, and council minutes, but families need not be that structured to reach decisions democratically." The essential features of this example are equal power among participants and the inclusion of as many family members as is appropriate in a given situation.[62]

In all other respects, the task of democratic families parallels that of democratic educators. The family needs to provide a space in which children can become committed to the democratic process, develop healthy relationships with parents and peers, and learn how to speak and listen in a deliberative manner.[63]

It can be difficult for parents to pursue this ideal in their daily interactions with their children. Parents have to draw a delicate line between limiting children's choices and letting children make decisions for themselves. Some parents prohibit drug abuse or smoking, because these behaviors pose clear dangers to children's health. It isn't as easy to establish and enforce rules about playing with war toys, overusing Nintendo, and watching too much television. In these cases, it isn't as clear that the cost of parental intervention—in terms of the child's reduced autonomy—outweighs the cost of the child's behavior. After all, many of today's parents laugh at the extreme restrictions previous generations of parents placed on romance, radios, and the reading of comics and other "unsuitable" books.

To resolve such dilemmas, some parents strike a middle ground by refusing to pay for war toys or video games, but allowing their children to spend their own money and use other children's toys. In effect, the parents veto the use of family funds for these activities, while allowing their children the autonomy to engage in them through the use of their own personal resources—friends and allowances.

As in other democratic relationships, another problematic issue for families is the tension between individuality and mutuality. This is particularly true of patriarchal families, where the mother is the sole caretaker and gender roles are rigidly reinforced. In The Reproduction of Motherhood, Nancy Chodorow explains how the "sexual and familial division of labor" makes women "more involved in interpersonal, affective relationships than men" and "produces in daughters and sons a division of psychological capacities which leads them to reproduce this sexual and familial division of labor." Sacrificing their individual identities, daughters learn to over-identify with others, whereas sons develop an isolated sense of self at the cost of mutuality.[64]

The solution, Chodorow argues, is for fathers to fulfill a greater proportion of primary parenting responsibilities:

> Children could be dependent from the outset on people of both genders and establish an individuated sense of self in relation to both...This would reduce men's need to guard their masculinity and their control of social and cultural spheres which treat and define women as secondary and powerless, and would help women to develop the autonomy which too much embeddedness in relationship has often taken from them.[65]

Shared parenting sews the seeds of a democratic adulthood by developing a stronger sense of individuality in girls and mutuality in boys.

Parents also pass on to children their orientations toward political discussion. In a study of married couples and their grade school children, Steven Chaffee and his colleagues distinguished two ways in which parents speak to their children. Some parents simply stress the need to follow social and parental rules, whereas other parents openly discuss the reasons behind these rules. The authors found that children from families with the more deliberative orientation developed higher levels of political knowledge and involvement; a deliberative child is more likely to become a deliberative adult.[66]

Having extolled the virtues of democratic parenting, I have to take a step back to acknowledge the reality of the parental relationship, particularly with regard to younger children. Israeli sociologist Shlomit Oryan introduced me to the idea that the admonition to parent democratically presents parents with an unsolvable problem, if one takes the idea of democracy seriously. Oryan studied parent education programs, such as Parent Effectiveness Training, in the United States and Israel, and she found that both the instruction manuals and the classes taught parents how to manipulate their children and enforce parental power, rather than acknowledging the inherent power imbalance. Thus, Oryan concluded that the guardianship model provides a more honest parenting model, whereby parents gradually enable children more autonomy and increasingly forceful participation in more family decision making.[67]

Such distinctions between democratic and guardian models of authority may seem semantic, but in cases like this, precise meanings matter. Children learn more about small group democracy when parents articulate each element clearly and honestly. In that way, children can sense the growing scope of their power and the increased importance of deliberative norms and democratic relationships. Their commitment to the process will grow as they see that they walk a path toward equal power as full citizens, rather than wearing blinders that hide parental authority from their view.

Social Butterflies

People who, in the name of democracy, change the way they talk, relate to one another, and raise their children are welcoming profound changes into their lives. Such changes might seem insignificant, but these personal acts are the building blocks of larger social habits and expectations. As Richard Flacks explains in *Making History*, the minor victories we can win in our everyday lives are all imperceptible ripples in time: "Historical action is not necessarily noted or recorded, nor is it always embodied in the kinds of public happenings that are taught as history in schools. A historical act may appear as exceedingly mundane behavior." Something as small as a phone conversation, a lover's quarrel, or a mother-daughter picnic "can initiate a chain of actions and events that fundamentally reshape the lives of millions."[68]

This view appears naive only if one stubbornly overlooks the ways in which people influence one another every day. Research on political conversations shows that people regularly change each other's minds and voting decisions. When friends and acquaintances influence each other, there is an "explosive potential," whereby Person A changes the votes of Persons B and C, then Persons B and C change the votes of Persons D, E, F, and G, and so on.[69] Through social media, the speed of these influence cascades can be even greater, even if the intensity of individual interactions might be somewhat diminished.[70]

Just as we change one another's votes, so do we influence the way we act in the other parts of our lives. Initially, we might change our daily lives for purely personal reasons. Even if unintended, these decisions have a profound effect on the ever-changing social world. The changes in our own lives affect people close to us, and these friends and family may, in turn, change the lives of others. In the words of Czechoslovakian poet Vaclev Havel, "Everything in the world is so mysteriously and comprehensively interconnected that a slight, seemingly insignificant wave of a butterfly's wing...can unleash a typhoon thousands of miles away."[71]

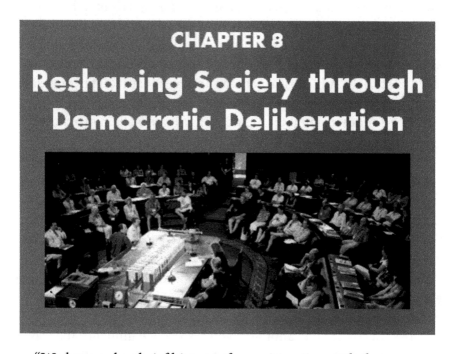

CHAPTER 8

Reshaping Society through Democratic Deliberation

"We have only a brief history of experimenting with the adaptations of democracy to the large-scale nation-state. There is plenty of room for innovations." —James Fishkin[1]

No system, large or small, can reach the democratic ideal, but one can pursue the modest goal of making existing systems more democratic or one can imagine replacing those systems with ones that land closer to the mark. This is the task for advocates of democracy in any country, including the United States. I begin this final chapter by explaining the special place group deliberation has in modern society, then I consider two different political reform strategies—one that intervenes to improve existing institutions and a second that restructures society more fundamentally. One strategy is more reformist and the other more radical, but both draw on the principles and strengths of small group democracy.

Finding a Place for Small Groups in the Public Sphere

In the two decades since the first edition of *Democracy in Small Groups* appeared, two distinct movements have brought groups to the forefront. These movements emphasize the power of groups to reshape both our social relationships and our collective decision making.[2] The first emphasizes the importance of group bonding, particularly in face-to-face settings, and the second stresses the deliberative quality of small democratic groups.

The Role of Small Groups in Society

Sociologist Robert Wuthnow, who directs the Center for the Study of Religion at Princeton University, was among the first to discern a "small-group movement." He conducted the first national survey of group participation in the United States and found that "four out of every ten Americans belong to a small group that meets regularly and provides caring and support for its members." These include emotional support groups, religious study groups, youth groups, singles groups, discussion groups, community athletic clubs, hobby and game clubs, and local political and civic groups.[3]

Wuthnow views this movement toward ever-stronger small-group ties as an antidote to the breakdown of traditional bonds in modern American society:

> Providing people with a stronger sense of community has been a key aim of the small-group movement from its inception . . . Community is sputtering to a halt, leaving many people stranded and alone. Families are breaking down. Neighbors have become churlish or indifferent. The solution is thus to start intentional groups of like-minded individuals who can regain a sense of community.[4]

This new wave of small groups gives its members limited obligations: Members come when they have time, stay as long as they like, and offer only as much energy to the group as they care to give.

This arrangement reflects "the fluidity of our lives by allowing us to bond easily but to break our attachments with equivalent ease."[5]

This movement to small groups has drawn the most attention from religious leaders, who have turned to such groups as a way of rekindling the commitment of the faithful. A 2001 U.S. Congregational Life Survey confirmed that participation within small groups devoted to prayer, discussion, or Bible study can increase both attendance and charitable giving, whether these groups offer respite from the anonymity of a mega-church or simply complement the regular activities of a more modest-sized congregation.[6]

German political and social theorist Jürgen Habermas provides a larger critical perspective on this yearning for community. Though some of Habermas' recent writings have stressed the special role religion plays in modern society,[7] his body of work sweeps more widely across modern philosophy and social science. Small social groups and affiliations fill out our "lifeworlds"—the network of human relationships we form to ensure a degree of shared social norms, mutual understanding, and sense of the common good.[8]

Democratic small-groups, in particular, serve these ends. Their emphasis on shared power, inclusion, and commitment provide the building blocks for an interconnected and interdependent community in which people resolve to find common purpose. Democratic relationships can foster the kind of mutual respect that people crave from their group associations, without sacrificing altogether one's individual identity. Small group deliberation also provides lessons in how to persuade and how to listen—skills that atrophy in a society that reduces politics to the aggregation of unreflective private interests.

The Rise of Deliberative Democracy

Appropriately enough, it was Habermas' work that also gave rise to a vast literature on deliberative democracy. Habermas argues that a healthy democratic society makes its decisions based on the weight of arguments, rather than in deference to authority, economic power, or social conventions. Each participant in such an "ideal speech situation" can challenge any empirical or moral claim, and the hope is that participants can thereby arrive at a mutual understanding—a kind of near-unanimity or large supermajority. By contrast, social influence occurs naturally within larger institutions and systems that overwhelm the lifeworld and leave ever-fewer opportunities to negotiate our identities, purposes, and plans, even in our day-to-day lives.[9]

In response to the need for a more robust democratic society, a movement has emerged to transform modern democracy. The earliest theories of democracy saw the need for the masses to sanction an elite that governed wisely. More popular conceptions of democracy stressed the need for broader participation.[10] Deliberative democrats seek to complement widespread participation with robust forms of public debate, dialogue, and deliberation both within and beyond government. Figure 3 shows that the amount of peer-reviewed theory and research on deliberative democracy has exploded since 1990, and this includes scholarship in every conceivable field within the humanities and social sciences, though the strongest concentration comes within the fields of political science and communication.[11]

Figure 3. The Growth of Peer-Reviewed Scholarship on Deliberative Democracy[12]

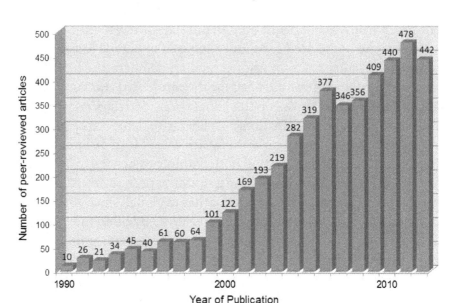

Public affairs scholar Tina Nabatchi and her colleagues edited a recent collection of essays summarizing the wave of scholarship and reform. Nabatchi explains that recent expressions of the deliberative ideal "have appeared in new constitutions, civic reform programs, and the resolutions of transnational movements and organizations, such as the United Nations Millennium Declaration." Studying, promoting, or designing deliberative civic engagement opportunities has become the chief cause of many nonprofits and colleges and universities, with a handful of public officials across the globe taking up the cause.[13]

One of the aspirations of the deliberative democracy movement is to bridge conflicting worldviews and partisan political commitments. Without denying the place of strategic political action, advocates of deliberation contend that we can often overcome the most severe schisms that prevent the public from speaking with a stronger, more unified voice on problems of common concern.

At the very least, we can become more adept at working together even amidst differences—a vision of society far removed from the partisanship that has caused paralysis in the federal government during the Obama administration. The United States Senate, which at one time had the reputation as the world's "greatest deliberative body," has started to earn a reputation closer to that of the U.S. Congress. After interviews with ten current and former Senators, a 2012 Reuters news analysis concluded that the Senate has lost its way:

> Faced with pressing issues like a ballooning national debt, an ailing healthcare system and the threat of climate change, the Senate now consumes its time with contentious debate that usually ends with no action…. The chamber has been paralyzed by routine budget bills. Judicial nominations languish, even when they have bipartisan support. And some of the Senate's most dramatic moments, broadcast on national television, are little more than calculated brinkmanship to stir up voters.[14]

As a counterpoint to such legislative karaoke,[15] deliberative democrats have devised a wide range of projects and designs for bringing together citizens, communities, and policymakers, and most of these have small-group interaction at their core. To demonstrate the potential power of such interventions, I will review some of the most promising reforms.

Deliberative Interventions in Mass Democracy

On the historical timeline, existing systems of representative government are new and underdeveloped. Many of the institutions we take for granted now, from the secret ballot to the direct election of U.S. senators to the inclusion of women and minorities in the electorate, have come about only in the past century. New reforms have appeared in countries and cities across the globe, and some of these prominently feature the small democratic group.[16] In this chapter, I review two kinds of reforms—those that bring together small random samples of the public and those that seek to engage larger numbers of citizens in deliberation.

Random Sampling to Create Specialized Deliberative Bodies

The jury system stands as one of the oldest and most overlooked deliberative citizen bodies. Though not as ancient as the Greek assembly, the jury's use extends back centuries and continues into the present day in the United States and countries across the globe. The jury's reputation for both deliberative quality and lighting a civic spark for its participants has led some nations, such as Japan, to install a quasi-jury system into a legal branch that otherwise relies on judges.[17]

Deliberative reformers have drawn on the jury's method of random selection (coupled with better monetary compensation) to design a variety of alternative ways of making public decisions.[18] Most directly, the Citizens' Jury process has convened one or two dozen citizens at a time to study complex public policy issues over the course of a week, then produce recommendations. Such juries have tackled issues from climate change to traffic congestion to health care, and they have convened in countries across the globe.[19] Larger scale processes, known as Deliberative Polls, have used random sampling to convene hundreds of citizens to see whether study and discussion on broad policy questions causes shifts in the aggregated judgment of a cross-section of the public.[20]

Though some Citizens' Juries and Deliberative Polls have exercised a measure of power, there are three other random-sample institutions that have wielded considerable authority from the outset. Established by the provincial government, the British Columbia Citizens' Assembly was charged with drafting a concrete proposal for revising the voting system in British Columbia. It brought together eighty women and eighty men to weigh a range of alternatives, which the Assembly members discussed both in small groups and in large plenary sessions. After a series of weekend deliberations and town meetings, the Assembly recommended a single transferable vote system for use in provincial elections. That's where its authority ended, and although the assembly's proposal won majority support when put to a province-wide vote, it failed to reach the 60 percent threshold required for passage. Nonetheless, it demonstrated the capacity for a random sample of the public to craft legislation on a controversial political issue.

An alternative use of the random sample has citizens not drafting laws but critiquing them. First established in 2009, the Oregon Citizens' Initiative Review (CIR) aims to improve the quality of public reflection and deliberation that takes place during initiative elections. Like many other U.S. states, Oregon created its initiative process during the Progressive Era to let voters weigh in on the passage of state laws or amendments to their state constitutions. Ballot initiatives and referenda (often called simply "ballot measures") were meant to make the government more accountable by circumventing the corrupting powers of entrenched parties and special interest groups.[21] Many voters, however, lack the time, resources, and in-depth knowledge about each proposition in question and instead rely on interest group campaigns and political elites to form their preferences.[22]

Built on the Citizens' Jury model, each CIR brings together twenty-four registered Oregon voters for five days to study and deliberate on a specific statewide initiative. At the end of their deliberations, each CIR panel writes a page long analysis about their assigned initiative for the official Oregon State Voters' Pamphlet, which the Secretary of State delivers along with mail-in ballots to every registered voter in the state. I helped evaluate this process when it was used in 2010 and 2012, and it has set a high bar for small group deliberation, while also reaching a majority of Oregon voters and making them more knowledgeable and reflective about their voting choices.[23]

As a final example, voters in California passed ballot measures of their own to establish a Citizens Redistricting Commission, which draws more loosely on the principle of random selection.[24] Thousands of Californians volunteered to go into the applicant pool for this Commission, and a panel of auditors winnowed those down to sixty people, equally divided between Democrats, Republicans, and non-aligned voters (including both independents and third-party members). Legislative leaders from both major parties then reduced the pool to an equally balanced set of thirty-six, from which the State Auditor randomly drew three Democrats, three Republicans, and two non-aligned voters. Those eight commissioners then selected the final six members from the list.

In 2011, this citizen-based commission produced its first districts with the necessary cross-partisan supermajorities, including majority votes of 13-1 and 12-2. The net result was a competitive set of districts that faithfully followed the redistricting criteria, even if the boundaries upset Republicans, who brought three unsuccessful challenges to the State Supreme Court.[25]

The point of such examples is not that any one of them represents the single-best approach to wedding small group democracy with larger political systems. Rather, the three examples show the range of ideas already implemented to give deliberative bodies of everyday citizens power not just within the judicial branch but also in legislative politics.

Engaging the Mass Public in Deliberative Forums

For some deliberative democrats, however, random sampling misses the opportunity to engage the wider public. Though specialized deliberative bodies have a role to play, one must also find methods that can bring together an entire community, or even perhaps a nation.

For example, the most widely adopted public discussion program in the United States is the National Issues Forums (NIF). Developed at the Kettering Foundation, thousands of individuals across the country have received training in the NIF method of convening and moderating forums, and millions of Americans have taken part in these (as have citizens in numerous other countries that have adapted the NIF model). The Forums promote the idea that citizens must make "hard choices" and take responsibility for the "public judgments" they discover through deliberation. A typical NIF issue booklet advances three or four solutions to a vexing public problem, and each choice usually has elements that will appeal across the political spectrum. When this works as intended, NIF deliberation reveals to participants that values-based "conflict is not only among us, it is within us."[26]

I discovered NIF while working on my Master's thesis, and I chose to write my doctoral dissertation on these forums. Through that research, I discovered that NIF does realize some of its aims, such as broadening participants' outlooks and causing them to arrive at more well-conceived judgments on public issues, though participants may end up taking more ideologically consistent stances on a given issue. In addition, NIF appears to teach participants new ways of participating in groups and talking about politics. It may not make participants into ideal deliberators, but it does appear to reduce the likelihood that they will be domineering or unwilling to listen when talking about politics with fellow citizens.[27]

A vast array of deliberative alternatives have proliferated in the more than thirty years since the NIF first arrived in 1981. Among those still in wide use in the United States, the most prominent are the study circles convened by Everyday Democracy and the Twenty-First Century Town Meetings organized by AmericaSpeaks. These processes have managed to bring together hundreds or thousands of people to engage difficult community and national issues, from public schools to the national debt.[28] Some of these have a more dialogic emphasis, wherein the goal becomes mutual understanding rather than decision making or even the formation of a policy judgment. Dialogic approaches go by names such as World Cafes, Conversation Cafes, Appreciative Inquiry, Sustained Dialogue, and Compassionate Listening.[29]

The most ambitious idea as-yet-untried for deliberative civic engagement may be Deliberation Day, an idea hatched by two influential democratic theorists, Bruce Ackerman and James Fishkin. They propose that every two-to-four years, the United States should hold a national holiday two weeks before the election for face-to-face citizen deliberation on competing parties and candidates. Participants would be paid a $150 stipend and fed holiday-caliber food to meet together for a full day. Citizens would gather together at a local deliberation site, where they would get to watch, via satellite, a real random sample of the nation's citizenry interact with national candidates in a town hall format. Afterward, they would develop questions of their own in small discussion groups. Forming a local assembly, citizens would then put those questions to local party officials. Though Deliberation Day comes with a price tag—roughly one or two millions dollars every four years —it could be well worth the expense if it resulted in better public deliberation and more reflective voting.[30]

If the idea of gathering masses of people together to judge candidates sounds chaotic, consider that this happens regularly in those states that use a caucus process during Presidential elections. Those events are more commonly excuses for party-mobilization than for deliberation, let alone cross-party conversations, but the point is that processes like Deliberation Day do resonate more than one might realize with existing political institutions.[31]

Newly arrived in the United States is a process imported from Brazil that combines the mass-mobilization politics of the caucus with a real local decision-making task. The process of Participatory Budgeting now allocates small portions of city budgets in Chicago and New York, and it has been linked to the city-wide budgeting process in Vallejo, California. As practiced in the United States, this two-tier process begins with the identification and elaboration of potential public works projects, then it convenes a show-and-tell event where local residents can get to know each proposal. An open vote, in which all city residents can participate, determines which projects get funded. In some cases, the participatory process even continues through the project implementation and evaluation phases.[32] Intensive deliberation may have to be reverse-engineered into Participatory Budgeting, but there is no reason this can't be done.

Integrating Different Levels of Deliberation

The most ambitious institutional changes go far beyond budgeting via deliberative public meetings. In the first edition of this book, I proposed a fourth branch of government that involved community-level forums, a legislative body made up of delegates from those forums,
and representative random sample bodies both large and small. The gist of the proposal was to give lay citizens a voice in the legislative process by drafting bills for consideration in Congress, as well as resolving issues that Congress sought to avoid.[33]

Were I to amend that proposal today, I would further empower citizen bodies to act in the event of a political impasse by forming a commission that could hammer out necessary legislation that Congress could only stop by forging a majority to oppose it. This was the logic that made the Base Realignment and Closure Commissions effective in the late 1980s and early 1990s, when members of Congress knew that after the end of the Cold War, they would have to close bases popular in selected representatives' hometowns. Only by making passage the default did the well-reasoned lists of base closures make its way through Congress without amendment.[34]

Other proposals to infuse citizen deliberation into mass politics include legal scholar Ethan Leib's proposal of a popular legislative branch, chosen by random lot, to complement representative institutions. He writes,

This branch would replace the initiative and the referendum; its institution would be established to address many of the shortcomings of those forms of direct democracy. Its functions could be brought about through national or state constitutional amendments, and its findings would enact laws . . . that could be repealed or vetoed by the relevant . . . executive or legislative branch (with a supermajority), or could be challenged in the judicial branch.[35]

Democratic theorist Kevin O'Leary proposes establishing an even larger complementary legislative branch, which would consist of 43,500 citizens chosen by lot.[36] He proposes a People's House built on the same 435-district model as the House of Representatives but with one hundred deliberating citizens in each district. This networked body could introduce bills each session, pull dying bills out of committee for a floor vote, and reject legislation by majority vote (overridden by a three-fifths vote in the House or Senate). A steering committee consisting of one representative from each district would set the body's agenda.

The idea of *replacing* a legislative body with a randomly-selected group of citizens has also gained some renewed interest. Two

University of Wisconsin-Madison professors have suggested that the House of Lords transform itself into a popular Assembly of citizens, which would "provide a check on the failures of electoral democracy and, simultaneously, deepen the democratic character of the legislative process." Members would serve staggered terms of three years each, with the random selection stratified to ensure even demographic representation. Assembly members would be paid enough to create a strong incentive to participate, and (as with the jury) the Assembly's employers would be barred from penalizing them for missing work. Finally, the Assembly would have roughly the same powers as the existing House of Lords: It could slow up legislation, send it back for reconsideration, or even block some legislation from passing.[37]

Given the limited effectiveness and staggering low public approval of the U.S. Congress, one wonders if the time has finally come to replace that body with a random sample.[38] Reelection rates are so high in that body that the very idea of accountability is open to question, so could it be any worse to bring in one-term citizens in their stead? Surveys of the American public have found that at the national level, lay citizens are far more likely to place their trust in a representative cross-section of their peers than in an elected body.[39]

My only caution would be to ensure that the small group features of such bodies, such as the committees that review legislation, play at least as important a function as they do today. It is in those smaller settings where researchers have found the last glimmers of deliberation in the federal legislature.[40]

Restructuring Society

All of the foregoing political reforms seek to inspire the public to become more engaged in public life. Skeptics of institutional tinkering argue that more fundamental changes will be necessary to empower citizens. In this view, a first step toward improved deliberation on a national scale involves serious socioeconomic reform. As political theorists Joshua Cohen and Joel Rogers insist, "Since the absence of material deprivation is a precondition for free and unconstrained deliberation, a basic level of material satisfaction...would be required for all members of the political order." In additional to ensuring full employment, it is necessary to reduce "the labor time necessary to secure an acceptable level of material well-being for all." This, in turn, would "enhance the conditions of individual autonomy and social deliberation by increasing the availability of free time..."[41]

To make political opportunities meaningful, however, reforms would have to go even farther. Equal access to elementary and adult education would further balance many inequalities in political skills and information. These reforms might even reduce the amount of political apathy, and an increasing number of people, with more free time and political aptitude, would involve themselves in the political process.[42] In addition, an economic system that tolerates extreme inequalities cannot secure political equality, unless laws manage to reform the campaign finance system to separate money from political voice, at least by degrees. The Citizens United decision by the U.S. Supreme Court has taken the country in the opposite direction, but other nations (and local/state governments in the United States) have shown the viability of an array of different campaign finance systems.[43]

Those structural reforms, however, make more equal a national citizenry without infusing small democratic principles into the process. For some, it might be enough to couple socioeconomic and campaign reforms with the new deliberative institutions described earlier in this chapter. Other critics, however, propose a more fundamental political move toward decentralized political system.

From the decentralization perspective, the small democratic group is more than an inspiring ideal for large-scale democracy. Instead, small and medium sized groups are a *model* for democratic institutions. Equal power, inclusiveness, commitment, democratic relationships, and genuine deliberation are only realized when a demos constitutes a community of manageable size. Anarchist C. George Benello went so far as to argue that "democratic decision making requires face-to-face groups."[44]

To show how a decentralization might move society closer to the principles of small group democracy, Table 3 contrasts highly centralized and decentralized systems in relation to four questions.

Through what process are political boundaries drawn or redrawn? What criteria will be used to establish those divisions? How is decision-making authority distributed among the different levels of government? Through what process do citizens participate in deliberation and decision making at the different levels of government?

Table 3. Centralized versus Decentralized Political Systems

Centralized Systems

Federalism

   Divisions: historical; corresponding to military conquests, economic exchanges, political redistricting and negotiation

   Levels: local, state, national, international

   Power center: state and national

   Politics: primarily representative (all levels); also direct (local, state) and indirect representative and ad hoc (international)

Global Citizenship

   Divisions: historical

   Levels: local, state, national, international

   Power center: national and international

   Politics: primarily direct (all levels); also representative (all levels)

Decentralized Systems

Bioregionalism

   Divisions: redrawn by residents; corresponding to ecosystems and cultures

Levels: local, regional, interregional
Power center: local, regional
Politics: primarily direct and
   representative (local and regional);
   also ad hoc (interregional)

Confederalism
   Divisions: historical localities
      subdivided by residents;
      corresponding to smaller, existing
      communities
   Levels: municipality, regional,
      interregional
   Power center: municipality
   Politics: primarily direct (community);
      also representative (regional) and ad
      hoc (regional, interregional)

Council Democracy
   Divisions: historical
   Levels: local, state, national,
      international
   Power center: local and county
   Politics: primarily indirect
      representative (state through
      international); also representative
      (local) and direct (local, state)

Demarchy
   Divisions: redrawn entirely by citizens
      according to different public
      activities, as opposed to geography
   Levels: local activity, regional activity
   Power center: local and regional

Politics: primarily representative by
  lottery among volunteers (local,
  regional); also ad hoc (regional)

The federalist system relies on existing, historical divisions between nations and regions. Although some activity takes place on local and international levels, power is centralized in nations and states. Elections at local, state, and federal levels send representatives to councils and assemblies, where most decisions are made. In addition, some local and state governments permit direct forms of political participation, such as referenda, initiatives, and recall elections. International decisions are reached through assemblies of appointed representatives (e.g., the United Nations, European Economic Community) and ad hoc negotiations and agreements (e.g., the General Agreement on Tariffs and Trade).[45]

An alternative centralized model, which I call global citizenship, relies on existing divisions and governmental levels, but it increases the concentration of power by giving substantial authority to an international body. Under this scheme, the nature of political participation also changes, as citizens directly vote on many decisions at all levels. Taking advantage of innovations in telecommunication in the Internet age, the global citizen model uses online networking and face-to-face videoconferencing to cross geographic boundaries. This system continues to rely on weakened versions of traditional representative assemblies, and it creates an additional elected parliament at the international level.[46]

The four other systems in Figure 3 adhere to the decentralist principle: "decentralize all functions to their lowest possible level."[47] Most recently, the advocates of "slow democracy" have argued that the modern emphasis on locally sourcing our food, energy, and culture augurs for more local governance. Pushing meaningful political decisions down to the local level might yield a more slow-moving—or even piecemeal—politics, but doing so better meets both participatory and deliberative democratic aspirations.[48]

The bioregionalist approach begins by redrawing political boundaries to reflect existing ecosystems and cultural communities.

This, in turn, makes local and regional governance more meaningful and efficient. The sizes of locales and bioregions depend on their unique features, and although political systems within these regions might also vary, bioregionalists emphasize the importance of direct democracy within local communities.[49]

Like bioregionalism, confederalism begins by redrawing political borders, with a focus on subdividing counties and cities into smaller municipalities. Ten neighborhoods of 500 adults each constitute a municipality, and one hundred municipalities constitute a region or mini-nation of 500,000 people.[50] Most political activity takes place within municipalities, where citizens are directly involved in decision making and administration. Citizens within each municipality elect regional representatives, and interregional decisions are reached through *ad hoc* negotiations among these representatives and their appointees.[51]

Council democracy also bases itself on local initiative. Such a system might use existing political boundaries, but it would redirect many political decisions to local councils. The council system might use local and state referenda and initiatives, but reliance on a tiered system of representation is its distinctive feature. 10,000 citizens in a given locality elect representatives to their town council. These local officials select a council member to represent them at the state council, then the state council sends a member to the national council, which selects a representative for the international council. If the state, national, and international councils consist of 100 members each, this four-tiered system can represent up to 10 billion people.[52]

Demarchy may be the most distinctive form of decentralized government, because it assumes a need to redistribute power both vertically and horizontally. In this view, power is unnecessarily centralized at higher levels of government, but it is also too centralized within each level of government. Power should be located at the most appropriate agency/association and level of government. Thus, the regional transit authority should be independent of the local hospital board, with no city council controlling either one. The members of councils concerned with welfare, education, police, and other issues would all be selected through a lottery among volunteers. These lotteries would be designed to represent the interests of only those people directly affected by a given council's activities.[53]

Whereas centralized governments place far less emphasis on citizen deliberation, let alone in small groups, the bioregional and confederalist systems give a great deal of power to small-scale citizen assemblies. These schemes also increase the potential for citizen deliberation during elections, because local and regional officials are elected by small communities or municipalities. The council model utilizes higher levels of government, but its tiered system relies on face-to-face relations and group decision making at each level. Demarchy also relies on small representative councils representing more narrowly targeted constituencies.

In light of these advantages, decentralists argue that a radical restructuring of government provides the most promising route toward democracy. Many of the ideas proposed by bioregionalists and demarchists, in particular, remain untested, but economic decentralization has already shown its potential in many instances. For example, the highly participatory People's Campaign in Kerala, India, proved itself an effective means of publicly engaging previously marginalized social groups and improving economic development policy decision making.[54] Cross-national studies have also shown the potential for decentralization to reduce corruption in the provision of government services—a finding that holds up using a wide range of corruption indices.[55]

More important than the mechanics of decentralization may be the impetus for it. In cases like India, as well as for Participatory Budgeting in Brazil, a political commitment to grassroots democracy spurred the movement of power to the local community.[56] In many other cases, by contrast, the devolution of power reflects a more technical, partisan, or tactical move by elites, which makes the fruits of the decentralization scheme more suspect.[57] The bottom line is that the movement of power from central to local government does not *in and of itself* ensure a more deliberative or democratic politics.

Getting from Here to There

There are many shapes a more democratic government might take, and one might wonder how to get from here to there. Envisioning a possible future makes its eventual existence more likely, but good ideas don't lead to democratic social change unless accompanied by a sound political strategy.[58]

A fully elaborated strategy is beyond the scope of this book, but I wish to make one final point with regard to political action. Whether change comes through mainstream politics, third-party campaigns, union organizing, or community action, small democratic groups will play a vital role. In their book *Free Spaces*, University of Minnesota professors Sara Evans and Harry Boyte show that democratic social movements in the United States have arisen from small, voluntary groups that have distinctly democratic features. Interconnected small groups contributed to the African-American resistance to slavery, the civil rights struggle, American working class protest, the suffragist and ERA movements, and the populist movement of the 1880s.[59] Participants in these groups have a remarkable experience:

> [They] discover in themselves and their traditions new resources, potentials, resonances. They repair capacities to work together for collective problem solving. They find out new political facts about the world. They build networks and seek contacts with other groups of the powerless to forge a more heterogeneous group identity. And this whole process in turn helps to clarify basic power relations in society. In sum, people deepen the meaning of what they are doing, from understanding politics merely as a protest against threat to coming to see the need for a struggle for new conceptions of rights and participation and power.[60]

When connected with participation in larger movements directed at fundamental social change, membership in small groups can transform individuals and even a whole society.[61] An enduring spirit of civic activism in the United States and across the globe provides a wellspring of opportunities for joining such groups. Small group democracies will never receive the attention given to national political systems, and in the foreseeable future, elites, the media, and the public will probably continue to ignore the actions of small, seemingly insignificant groups of citizens. Nonetheless, small group democracies can shape the course of history, because these microscopic societies forever change their members—the same individuals who constitute the larger social world.

Small Group Exercises

These discussion questions and exercises are for groups seeking to understand themselves and become more democratic. They concern issues central to small group democracy: power, inclusiveness, commitment, competence, individuality and mutuality, congeniality, speaking opportunities and responsibilities, and listening.

Most of the questions and activities are geared toward groups of three to twenty people, but all can be adapted for larger groups: exercises and discussions can be streamlined, and large groups can do many of them by breaking into small groups. All of the exercises can be tailored to the unique purposes and features of the group.[1]

Power

Discussion Questions

1. What is power? What are the different forms that power takes in the world and within our group?

2. What kind of power do we want our group to exercise? What do we hope to achieve by working together?

3. Do any external forces prevent us from realizing our goals? What, if anything, can we do to change this?

4. How should we handle the power we have? How should we distribute our group power among ourselves? If we want an equal distribution, how equal need it be?

5. Does our current distribution of power align with this ideal? If not, how did it become out of synch? What can we do to reach a better balance of power?

Group Activity

Every group member rates themselves and the other members of the group on a one-hundred point scale according to how much power each person appears to have. A score of one hundred signifies virtual omnipotence, whereas zero corresponds to powerlessness.[2]

If group members insist on viewing power as a zero-sum equation (i.e., when you gain power, I lose power), they can work with percentages. The combination of each group member's power score equals 100%. Otherwise, the group can rate group members independently; two or more group members could have over fifty points each.

Once every group member has rated both themselves and the rest of the group, compare scores. If the group is small, one person can quickly write the scores on the board in a matrix (rows for who did the ratings, columns for who's being rated). Comparisons could prove revealing. One person may be rated most or least powerful by all group members—or by all but themselves. Variations in ratings might reveal misunderstandings or complementary perspectives on power within the group. Group members might also find it useful to discuss what kinds of power they believe they and others possess.

Inclusiveness

Discussion Questions

1. When we formed our group, whose lives did we hope to change? What role do those people play in our decision-making process?

2. Has anyone besides the current membership expressed interest in joining our group? Why have they not joined? Is there anything we do that might discourage people from joining us?

3. Who has left our group? Why did they leave?

4. How large can our group become before becoming "too big"?

5. Do we want anyone else to join our group or talk with us about group business on a regular basis? What can we do to encourage those people to join or maintain contact with our group?

Group Activity

As a group, brainstorm to identify the different kinds of people that your group affects when it makes and implements its decisions. Consolidate this list into a dozen or so kinds of people, then mark each according to the impact your group has on them (1 = profound, 2 = significant, 3 = small).

Draw three concentric circles. The inner circle represents full power within your group's decision-making process. The second circle represents having influence on the group, and the third circle symbolizes being disconnected from the group. Locate each of the people your group affects within one of these circles.

A highly inclusive group would have "1"s in the inner circle, "2"s in the middle circle, and "3"s in the outer circle. There might even be "2"s in the inner circle and "3"s in the middle circle. A highly exclusive group would place none other than the group members themselves in the inner circle. Where does your group fall on this spectrum? Why?

Commitment to the Democratic Process

Discussion Questions

Talking about a commitment to democracy makes more sense after clarifying what exactly constitutes a democratic process. For this reason, the first two questions might help a group develop its own definition of small group democracy.

1. What does democracy mean to us? What would a fully democratic group look like?

2. What are some of the most effective or satisfying small groups to which we have belonged? What features of these groups were democratic or undemocratic?

3. What are the different things we value in our group? What are our goals? How does democracy relate to our other goals? Do any take precedence over ensuring a democratic process?

4. What would each of us do if our group used a democratic process to reach a decision we strongly disliked? If this has happened before, what did we do?

5. Are our democratic principles embodied in our group's meetings? If not, how committed are we toward making our meetings more democratic?

6. Are our democratic principles embodied in our group's written procedures or bylaws? If not, what can we do to put our principles in writing?

Group Activity

Write on a chalkboard all of the words and phrases group members associate with democracy (e.g., "free speech," "equality"). Then cluster these ideas into categories and try to coherently organize them. Use these as a basis for defining the democratic process. (Alternatively, groups might wish to focus on what democracy means *in small groups,* in particular.)

The list of terms and ideas may produce some contradictions. Clarify the meaning of the conflicting ideas (e.g., majority rule vs. consensus) and make certain that the apparent tension between them isn't superficial. Discuss any possibilities for integrating or reconciling the two opposing principles.

The list should also produce some principles or procedures that all group members agree are a part of democracy. Clarify the degree to which the group agrees and build a definition of democracy that all members can accept.

Competence

Discussion Questions

1. Who do we think is incapable of deciding what's in their own best interests? (If group members can't think of any people, ask the group to consider conditions such as infancy, insanity, senility, and ignorance.)

2. In general, how much confidence do we have in one another? In what situations are we most willing to trust each other's judgment? When are we most likely to doubt one another's judgment?

3. Are we, as individuals, the best judges of what's in our own personal interests? Under what circumstances would we prefer that someone else decide something for us?

4. Do we think we are the best judges of what's in the interest of our group? Under what circumstances would we prefer that someone outside the group make the decision for us?

5. What information or resources do we need to act as competent judges of our own best interests? What do we need to be good judges of what is in the group's best interests?

Group Activity

Each group member writes his or her name on a slip of paper and places it in a hat (or other receptacle, if no hats are available). Each member then writes an action, trivial or serious, that requires a decision (e.g., what school to attend, where to go to lunch, whether to marry, what movie to watch) and places these slips of paper into another hat.[3]

Stir the contents of both hats, then each group member picks a name and an action and tries to make the decision for the other person. People should draw again if they draw their own name.

After each decision, the person deciding can say how it would feel to make that decision for the other person. What information would they need? Have they ever played such a role?

The group members who had decisions made for them can also share their feelings. What would it feel like to have that other person make the decision on their behalf? Have others, in their past, made such decisions for them?

Individuality and Mutuality

Discussion Questions

1. When we are together as a group, do we still maintain our identities as individuals?

2. When we are by ourselves, do we still sometimes view ourselves as part of the group?

3. At what times have we most clearly identified ourselves as separate individuals? When have we viewed ourselves as independent of our association with the group?

4. At what times have we felt most strongly connected to our group? When do we mention our group membership when describing ourselves to other people?

5. During group meetings, when is it most important to be treated as an individual? When would it be inappropriate for others to stress our group identity?

6. When is it most important to draw upon our identity as a group member? When would it be inappropriate to focus upon our separate, individual identities?

Group Activity

Be forewarned: This exercise can be very revealing, but it may bring up strong emotions. Before embarking on it, make sure the group can handle it.

On a piece of paper, write the name of each group member in a pattern that forms a circle. Make a photocopy of this circle for each group member, then have each draw straight lines connecting every pair of group members that has a strong bond. (In newer groups, draw lines for any moderately strong bonds, such as a budding friendship or regular friendly interaction.)

After drawing the lines, place arrowheads on them, indicating which of these people seeks the other one out. (Arrows point toward the person sought.) There might be a one-way relation between two group members, or the relationship may be reciprocal.

Compare members' different drawings, discussing noteworthy similarities and differences in the patterns of lines and arrows. Discuss why some people have more or fewer lines connected to their name. Discuss why some group members have more arrows pointing towards them, and why some have more arrows pointing away from them.

Congeniality

Discussion Questions

1. Is it important to us that we create a comfortable or friendly group atmosphere?

2. What makes us feel at ease in a group? What does a congeniality norm require of us?

3. What do we do to make each other feel welcome? How do we show our affection for one another as group members?

4. In what ways do we express hostility toward one another? Do we ever intimidate each other?

5. How can we show anger or frustration without making others feel defensive or hurt? Is it possible to be friendly while expressing "negative" emotions?

6. How do we treat the people we consider friends? How is this different from how we treat each other? Why is it different?

Group Activity

If the group has built up enough mutual trust to discuss strong emotions openly, it can be fruitful to examine those directly. Each member shares with the others one group experience they have had that made them feel good (e.g., comfortable, happy) and one that made them feel bad (e.g., uncomfortable, angry, intimidated). It is preferable if these experiences occurred in the group doing the exercise. Be sure to budget enough time for this exercise, as relating difficult emotional experiences can take longer than one might expect.

Speaking Opportunities

Discussion Questions

1. What rules does our group have to regulate speaking turns? (For example, only one person can talk at a time, or one can only speak when called on by the facilitator.) Do we follow these rules? Do these rules make us feel constrained, or do they make it easier for us to speak up during meetings?

2. Do we all have ample opportunities to set the meeting agenda? Do we all get a chance to redefine the issues on the agenda by amending them or reframing them?

3. When we have bits of information, personal views, or arguments that we wish to share with the group, do we present them? If not, why not?

4. Do we all get a chance to vote during meetings? If we still disagree after taking a vote, is there a way we can reiterate our views?

5. What does it mean to "talk too much"? Do any of us do this? What do we do when we think someone else in the group is dominating the discussion?

6. What does it mean to "talk too little"? Do any of us do this? What do we do when someone is the group falls silent?

7. How do we respond to silence during meetings? Does someone always quickly take the floor when there is a pause? Is there space in our meetings for quiet contemplation?

8. How can a more reserved speaker join a heated discussion? If it is difficult to do so in our group, how can we ensure that a reticent speaker has access to the floor?

Group Activity

Sit in a circle with two chairs in the middle, facing each other. Go around the circle, placing people in the middle in pairs until everyone has done so once. When a pair sits in the middle, both people begin talking and try to hold the floor as long as possible. Some pairs may wish to play in a "no holds barred style," unrelentingly talking over one another for a minute. Others can try to gain and regain the floor using more subtle tactics.

After each pair returns to the circle, discuss the tactics used to hold the floor. Which of these are appropriate, and which are rude? How does the group enforce speaking norms? Should the group create new norms to make it easier for more reticent speakers to gain and hold the floor?

Next, get out a clock or timer that counts in seconds that every group member can see. A group member begins speaking to the group on a current issue. Each group member holds a notepad and listens attentively, then writes down on the paper the time when they believe that the speaker should stop talking. At the same time, each writes down what it was that made them believe it was time to stop talking. A volunteer walks around the group to determine when everyone has written a stop time. Once done, compare the times written down and the reasons for wishing the speaker to stop.

After testing members' patience with speakers, the group can explore its feelings about silence. A group member makes a brief comment on a current issue, followed by total silence. Each group member writes when it feels necessary for someone to speak. Also, each member notes what he or she did during the silence. Were they thinking? What distracted them? When did the silence become uncomfortable or cease to be productive?

Speaking Responsibilities

Discussion Questions

1. What kind of information can we justifiably withhold from one another?

2. If a decision requires specialized information that only one or two group members possess, in what cases should the information be shared with others before making a decision? How detailed does this shared information need to be?

3. What effort do we make to ensure that our decisions are well-informed? Do we always conduct as much research as necessary before making a decision? Do we check the accuracy of our assumptions before resolving an issue?

4. When we are trying to persuade other group members, what responsibilities do we have to them? What kinds of argument are unethical? What responsibility does a speaker have to acknowledge any weaknesses they see in their own arguments?

5. What role can emotion play in the persuasion process? Is it acceptable for a group to be swayed by emotions? What can a speaker appeal to the group's feelings? Is it okay to appeal to some emotions, but not others (e.g., hope vs. fear)? What does it mean to "manipulate" a person's judgment on an issue?

Group Activity

Make a list of past decisions the group has reached and/or future issues the group may need to discuss. Identify the kinds of information that the group needed/would need to make informed decisions. Discuss how the group can ensure that it obtains the information it needs (e.g., we have a lawyer on retainer if we are sued, or one of us should learn more about noncompetitive children's games before we decide what activities to sponsor at the community fair).

Each group member shares a time that he or she felt moved by another member's argument. Identify what made the speaker effective and consider when these speaking strategies might be unethical. Each group member can also share a time he or she felt manipulated, inside or outside the group. What strategies made the speaker (or advertisement, etc.) manipulative or unethical?

Listening

Discussion Questions

1. When do we have the greatest difficulty understanding each other? Do we speak too soft or too loud? Do others sometimes speak in words or styles that we can't understand?

2. When do we have trouble expressing ourselves clearly?

3. Do we carefully consider what others say? What speaking behaviors make it harder for us to listen to a person?

4. How do we show a speaker that we are listening? Do we nod or make eye contact? Do we ask for clarification or elaboration if we are unable to follow what a speaker is saying? When have we sensed there was too little time to make sure we understood each other?

5. When we sense a need to speak, are we still able to listen attentively to those who are currently speaking?

6. How do we feel when others listen to us? How do we react when we sense that others are not listening carefully to what we have to say?

Group Activity

Every group member thinks of something that might be hard to express to the rest of the group (e.g., a moving personal experience or a highly technical concept). Members then take turns trying to express their idea or experience in a way others can comprehend. No one can interrupt the speaker. The group discusses what each person did to try to make themselves clear.

Next, every group member thinks of something they would like others to hear about—an idea or an experience they have in mind. Members then take turns telling others about their idea or experience, without worrying about how best to express themselves. Listeners can interrupt the speaker only if they believe it is necessary to improve their comprehension. Members make a concerted effort to listen and to show the speaker that they are listening.

Discuss what it felt like to be heard and what signs made it clear that others were listening. Did anything make it difficult to understand the speaker?

AUTHOR NOTE

John Gastil (Ph.D., University of Wisconsin-Madison, 2004) is a professor at Pennsylvania State University in communication arts and sciences and political science. He also directs the McCourtney Institute for Democracy. His research specializes in political deliberation and group decision making. His work on the Citizens' Initiative Review has helped evaluate an exciting new form of public deliberation that should improve initiative elections. The Jury and Democracy Project has investigated, and hopefully helped vindicate, the jury system as a valuable civic educational institution. He has assisted with the Cultural Cognition Project in demonstrating the ways in which our deeper values bias how we learn about issues and form opinions. He has written overviews of his two main fields of research: Political Communication and Deliberation uses the idea of public deliberation as a way to organize the wider study of political communication, and The Group in Society presents a system-level theory that integrates research on group communication and behavior. For an introduction to his work, listen to a forty-five minute interview on ABC Radio (Australia), from a program that intersperses discussion and music.

ACKNOWLEDGEMENT IN THE FIRST EDITION

The word 'democracy' has been...used and betrayed by state, party, sect, and interest. Yet it still has honest lovers, who detect in it something that has mysteriously remained immaculate and true. —Charles Lummis[4]

I gratefully acknowledge the assistance of all of those who helped make this book possible. For critiquing my initial ideas on democratic deliberation, I thank the students in my small group communication courses, program officers at the Kettering Foundation, Todd Wynward, Perry Deess, Lea Haravon, Harry Boyte, Richard Merelman, C. David Mortensen, and Kenneth Sharpe.

Fortunately, this book bears little resemblance to my original manuscript, owing to timely feedback from Murray Edelman, Raymond Gastil, Len Krimerman, Jane Mansbridge, Roger Smith, and Phil Weiser. Readers should personally thank Barbara Hirshkowitz of New Society Publishers, who did everything in her power to make this book both intelligent and intelligible. Following protocol, I absolve reviewers of responsibility for all heresies and omissions herein.

My parents, however, are complicit in this project. I thank them for dragging me to Quaker Meeting (before I was old enough to stay home), exposing me to politics at an early and impressionable age, and inspiring me to follow my dreams. Although they surely think I've gone too far, I couldn't have gotten where I am without them.

Most of all, I thank the current and former staff of Mifflin Street Community Co-op. They courageously revealed the inner life of their workplace and gave freely of their time, filling out questionnaires, participating in lengthy interviews, and making themselves available for endless questioning by the author. When they agreed to let video cameras into their meeting room, they insisted that I pursue publication. Without their gentle prodding, this book wouldn't have been written.

John Gastil
Madison, Wisconsin
February, 1993

Photo Credits

Cover: "Steelworkers' meeting." Factory worker training meeting in an eco-design stainless steel company in Rio de Janeiro, Brazil. Photo courtesy Alex Rio Brazil. Metaphorically, the group depicted perhaps is one that could be more democratic in many respects, though the company may have some democratic features already. I chose to use it because, as Alex said on seeing its use, "the photo was made for it."

Preface: "Uncle Ray." I took this photo while visiting Uncle Ray's old haunts, including the childhood home in Alpine, California in 2008. The trip was a chance to learn more about his life growing up in San Diego County with my father, Russell Gordon Gastil, but it also gave me the opportunity to see first-hand what a comedian Ray was. For someone so serious about democratic reform and the preservation of Enlightenment values, he was quite the jester.

Chapter 1: "Beer summit." On July 24, President Barack Obama shared a drink with Harvard University professor Henry Louis Gates, Jr. and Cambridge Police Sgt. James Crowley to mend fences after an ugly incident from two weeks earlier, during which Gates was arrested after a witness had reported him as a suspected burglar. Pete Souza captured this photo on behalf of the White House.

Chapter 2: "Quaker meeting." This uncredited photo shows a Quaker Meeting for Worship taking place at Candler's Cannon Chapel at Emory University.

Chapter 3: "Conference discussion." This photo was taken at the 2006 National Conference on Dialogue and Deliberation in San Francisco, CA. It features Brian Sullivan of CivicEvolution.Org and other attendees. The photo was provided by Sandy Hierbacher of the National Coalition for Dialogue and Deliberation.

Chapter 4: Photo of Mifflin Co-op during the 2007 Mifflin Street Block Party. Photo taken by Grandmasterka (a.k.a. The Moose) and provided through the Widimedia Commons. The mural was created by Olilvia Gude and Jon Pounds in 1987, who used to piece to experiment with a collaborative design process for community art. More details appear in Gude's "Art Journal" entry on the project.

Chapter 5: "Anger during a protest." David Shankbone took this photo when Mahmoud Ahmadinejad spoke at Columbia University in September, 2007. Though those pictured aren't part of a small group, the image effectively shows the level of anger that can arise in political organizations, sometimes leading to their division or dissolution.

Chapter 6: "Occupy." This is another photo by prolific public artist David Shankbone, who took this picture during a meeting that occurred during Occupy Wall Street. The upload came on September 18, 2011, and innumerable meetings large and small happened during the Occupy gatherings in New York and cities across the world.

Chapter 7: "Parent education." This photo shows an instructor teaching infant massage as part of the Navy New Parent Support Home Visitation Program. Mass Communication Specialist 1st Class Jason Swink took the photo for the U.S. Navy.

Chapter 8: "Citizens' Parliament." This photo shows the full assembly of participants in the Australian Citizens' Parliament in Canberra in February, 2009. The photo comes courtesy Kaye Shumack, John Pacitto, and newDemocracy foundation.

Small group exercises: "Research workshop." I took this photo during the August, 2013 workshop on the Oregon Citizens' Initiative Review, held in State College, Pennsylvania. Pictured left-to-right are Lauren Archer, Mark Major, Robin Stryker, Jeremy Johnson, Robert Richards (face obscured), and Mark Hlavacek.

Endnotes

Chapter 1

[1] Quote from an interview conducted with Norm Stockwell on September 21, 2014. Though the co-op members have pseudonyms when the book was first published, Norm asked that his real name be used for this second edition. And yes, it has been pointed out previously that Norm had an ideal last name for someone working at a grocery co-op.

[2] The closest thing to an exception was the campaign of Dede Feldman. She had to win a tough primary to get into the New Mexico senate, but she managed to do so with a very classy campaign. She's since retired from the senate and has written a wonderful memoir on the challenge of governing effectively, let alone deliberating, in the legislature. See Dede Feldman, *Inside the New Mexico Senate: Boots, Suits, and Citizens* (University of New Mexico Press, 2014). Though retired from politics, she has an active blog on New Mexico politics and more.

[3] The Kettering Foundation continues to thrive and has shaped many people's understanding of what democracy can mean. I ended up writing my Ph.D. dissertation on the National Issues Forums. Articles that came from that dissertation include a solo piece, "Adult Civic Education Through the National Issues Forums: Developing Democratic Habits and Dispositions Through Public Deliberation," *Adult Education Quarterly* 54 (2004), pp. 308–28, and two with my doctoral advisor, Jim Dillard: "Increasing Political Sophistication Through Public Deliberation," *Political Communication* 16 (1999), pp. 3–23; and "The Aims, Methods, and Effects of Deliberative Civic Education through the National Issues Forums," *Communication Education* 48 (1999), pp. 179–92.

[4] James S. Fishkin, *The Voice of the People: Public Opinion and Democracy* (Yale University Press, 1997).

[5] William M. Keith, *Democracy as Discussion: Civic Education and the American Forum Movement* (Lexington Books, 2007).

[6] Jane J. Mansbridge, *Beyond Adversary Democracy* (University of Chicago Press, 1983).

[7] Lynn Heidmann, "Board May Stop Cooperating with Mifflin Street Co-op," *The Badger Herald* (October 24, 2006). For a history of the co-op, see Michael Bodden, *People's History: A History of the Mifflin Street Community Co-op* (Unpublished, 1992). A health advocacy organization, ABC for Health, Inc., currently operates out of the co-op's historic building. Former co-op Norm Stockwell provided a succinct explanation for the store's demise in an interview conducted on September 21, 2014: "Staff turnover became more rapid in the years after I left. Costs at the co-op rose due to the benefits structure. Staff could work part-time for full benefits, while the cost of benefits nationwide was skyrocketing. The co-op was also unable to redefine its

outreach strategy to attract and welcome the new residents of downtown condos, many of whom were Madison progressives. The small size of the store made product line expansion difficult, and the lack of parking made it hard to entice customers from farther away to get to the store and stock up, the way they could at larger stores. Finally, there were payroll tax liabilities that accumulated and resulted in a huge tax bill, which forced the co-op to sell the building and close the store."

[8] As reliable a list as any may be that of the National Cooperative Grocers Association.

[9] Some have argued that Occupy relied on structureless or "horizontal" decision making. The analysis provided by Marianne Maeckelbergh in "Occupy the US: Musings on Horizontal Decision-Making and Bureaucracy," *STIR* (Spring 2012), suggests how participating in the Occupy process might transform the participants themselves, something witnessed in even more conventional democratic social movements; see Sara M. Evans and Harry C. Boyte, *Free Spaces: The Sources of Democratic Change in America* (University of Chicago Press, 1992). A more straightforward description of the Occupy process is as a variation of consensus; see the Wikipedia entry on "General assembly (Occupy movement)." For a variety of perspectives on Occupy, focused on the city of Portland, see Renee Guarriello Heath, Courtney Vail Fletcher, and Ricardo Munoz (eds.), *Understanding Occupy from Wall Street to Portland: Applied studies in communication Theory* (Lexington Books, 2013).

[10] The library is available at http://tinyurl.com/dsg2nded.

[1] More in-depth analysis of democracy in schools and families appears in Chapter 7. Portions of this chapter are reprinted with the permission of Plenum Publications from John Gastil, "A Definition and Illustration of Democratic Leadership," *Human Relations* 47 (1994), pp. 953–975.

[2] In a small way, the 1993 publication of *Democracy in Small Groups* helped advance the concept of the democratic group. This idea found its way into textbooks, such as Mary Ann Renz and John B. Greg's *Effective Small Group Communication in Theory and Practice* (Allyn and Bacon, 2000), and I elaborated on the idea in my own book on group behavior, *The Group in Society* (Sage, 2010). Democratic group process also got discussed among civic reformers, such as Matt Leighninger, "The Recent Evolution of Democracy," *National Civic Review* 94:1 (2005), pp. 17–28, and public participation scholars, such as Marian Barnes, "Researching Public Participation," *Local Government Studies* 25:4 (1999), pp. 60–75. Interest in group democracy has also received a boost from online technologies, which provide new opportunities for deepening small group democracy: see Beth Simone Noveck, "A Democracy of Groups," *First Monday* 10:11 (2005), and Laura W. Black, Howard T. Welser, Dan Cosley, and Jocelyn M. DeGroot, "Self-governance through Group Discussion in Wikipedia: Measuring Deliberation in Online Groups," *Small Group Research* 42 (2011), pp. 595–634. Working with two doctoral students, I articulated a group-centered conception of democratic deliberation in Stephanie Burkhalter, John Gastil,

and Todd Kelshaw, "A Conceptual Definition and Theoretical Model of Public Deliberation in Small Face-to-face Groups," *Communication Theory* 12 (2002), pp. 398–422. I discuss this work on deliberative democracy in more detail during the final chapter of this book.

[3] Hanna F. Pitkin and Sara M. Shumer, "On Participation," *Democracy* 2 (1982), p. 43.

[4] Some have argued that people don't seek out greater democratic engagement but would prefer, instead, a more passive role. This argument appears in John R. Hibbing and Elizabeth Theiss-Morse, *Stealth Democracy: Americans' Beliefs About How Government Should Work* (Cambridge University Press, 2002). For a reply to this and other doubts about the value of democratic deliberation, see Loren Collingwood and Justin Reedy, "Listening and Responding to Criticisms of Deliberative Civic Engagement," in Tina Nabatchi, Michael Weiksner, John Gastil, and Matt Leighninger (eds.), *Democracy in Motion: Evaluating the Practice and Impact of Deliberative Civic Engagement* (Oxford University Press, 2012), pp. 233–261.

[5] In *Democracy from the Heart: Spiritual Values, Decentralism, and Democratic Idealism in the Movement of the 1960s* (Communitas Press, 1991), Gregory N. Calvert makes this argument with regard to the New Left of the 1960s. Similarly, John Burnheim, in *Is Democracy Possible?: The Alternative to Electoral Politics* (University of California Press, 1989), argues that "the lack of any clear and plausible view of how a socialist society might work is...the main obstacle to significant radical activity" (p. 13). Marxists, in particular, have been hamstrung by their failure to articulate an adequate theory of democracy (pp. 189–190).

[6] Charles Douglas Lummis, "The Radicalism of Democracy," *Democracy* 2 (1982), pp. 9-10. In arguing that no national political system should be called a democracy, I follow Robert A. Dahl's usage of the term in *Democracy and Its Critics* (Yale University Press, 1989). Dahl created the neologism "polyarchy" to describe certain forms of representative government. Democracy remains a noble ideal that ought to be pursued, but large-scale systems can only approach it, never fully reaching it. When generally defined, "democracy" is broad enough "to allow ample scope for the more elaborated and specific definitions"—such as the one I propose for small group democracy; see Anthony Arblaster, *Democracy: Third Edition* (McGraw-Hill International, 2002), p. 9. For attempts to cluster different definitions used by politicians, activists, and scholars into different "types" of democracy, see David Held, *Models of Democracy* (Stanford University Press, 2006). For a critical history of the term in Western political theory, see John Hoffman, *Marxism, Revolution, and Democracy* (B. R. Gruner Publishing Co., 1983), chap. 3. Given these diffuse meanings, one might argue that the term ought to be scrapped altogether. In response, I take the position of Samuel Bowles and Herbert Gintis, who also choose to work with the term. Their choice to do so "reflects a recognition of both the hegemony of liberal democratic discourse as the virtually exclusive medium of political communication in the advanced capitalist nations and the profoundly

contradictory, malleable, and potentially radical nature of this discourse" (*Democracy and Capitalism: Property, Community, and the Contradictions of Modern Social Thought*, Routledge, 2012, p. 209).

[7] For an eloquent conception of democracy as a means of bridging cultural divides, see W. Barnett Pearce and Stephen W. Littlejohn, *Moral Conflict: When Social Worlds Collide* (Sage, 1997).

[8] The idea of democracy having this dual character of conflict and consensus comes across eloquently in Jane J. Mansbridge, *Beyond Adversary Democracy* (University of Chicago Press, 1983).

[9] As just one example, Mahatma Gandhi connected democracy with many other moral principles, prominently including nonviolence. See the discussions by S. M. Tewari and G. Ramachandran in Krishna Kumar (ed.), *Democracy and Nonviolence* (Gandhi Peace Foundation, 1968). One might claim that such a broad use of the term "democracy" simply associates it with everything "good." Democracy and the ideas historically associated with it have always had their critics in the Western world, however. What is taken for granted today was unpopular or highly controversial in previous years. See Michael Levin, *The Spectre of Democracy: The Rise of Modern Democracy as Seen by Its Critics* (Macmillan, 1992). In any case, many authors have argued that a fully adequate definition of democracy has an ethical dimension. On the relationship between empirical and moral definitions, see Dahl, *Democracy and Its Critics*, pp. 6–8; on the inseparability of democracy and ethics, see Claes G. Ryn, *Democracy and the Ethical Life: A Philosophy of Politics and Community*, 2nd ed. (Catholic University of America Press, 1990), especially Chapter 1.

[10] Chapter 8 of this book will elaborate on some of the ways to enhance the deliberative quality of mass society. The "Real Utopias" project advocates advancing democracy and other values well beyond current achievements. For an overview, see Erik Olin Wright, "Transforming Capitalism through Real Utopias," *American Sociological Review* 78 (2013), pp. 1–25. On deliberative democracy, see Archon Fung and Erik Olin Wright (eds.), *Deepening Democracy: Institutional Innovations in Empowered Participatory Governance* (Verso, 2003).

[11] Examples of work drawing on the concept include: Stephanie J. Coopman, "Democracy, Performance, and Outcomes in Interdisciplinary Health Care Teams," *Journal of Business Communication* 38 (2001), pp. 261–284; Victor W. Pickard, "Assessing the Radical Democracy of Indymedia: Discursive, Technical, and Institutional Constructions," *Critical Studies in Media Communication* 23 (2006), pp. 19–38; and Raymond J. Pingree, "Decision Structure and the Problem of Scale in Deliberation," *Communication Theory* 16, (2006), pp. 198–222.

[12] This definition is based on that of Arthur D. Jensen and Joseph C. Chilberg, *Small Group Communication* (Wadsworth, 1991), pp. 8–16. Instead of discussing the full range of group activities, I focus on group meetings. Anthropologist Helen Schwartzman, in *The Meeting: Gatherings in Organizations and Communities* (Springer, 1989), provides an excellent definition of what constitutes a meeting. In

her view, a meeting is "a communicative event involving three or more people who agree to assemble for a purpose ostensibly related to the functioning of an organization or group.... A meeting is characterized by multiparty talk that is episodic in nature, and participants either develop or use specific conventions (e.g. *Robert's Rules of Order*) for regulating talk" (p. 7).

[13] Hereafter, I use the terms "group" and "small group" interchangeably. Kirkpatrick Sale, in *Human Scale* (New Society Publishers, 2007), suggests that the ideal size for "small" face-to-face groups is somewhere between 7 and 20 people, but other factors, such as cohesiveness and familiarity, shape how "large" a group feels to its members. I discuss this in detail in *Group in Society*, pp. 5-6.

[14] For a more detailed discussion, see my essay, "A Definition and Illustration of Democratic Leadership." Sources for the decision tree include Dahl, Democracy and Its Critics, pp. 85, 97–98, 100; Franklyn S. Haiman, *Group Leadership and Democratic Action* (Houghton-Mifflin, 1951); Ronald A. Heifetz and Riley M. Sinder, "Political Leadership: Managing the Public's Problem Solving," in Robert Reich (ed.), *The Power of Public Ideas* (Harvard University Press, 1990), 179–204; Norman R. F. Maier, *Principles of Human Relations* (John Wiley & Sons, 1952); Marshall Sashkin, "Participative Management Is an Ethical Imperative," *Organizational Dynamics* 12 (1984), pp. 5–22; Victor H. Vroom and Arthur G. Jago, *The New Leadership* (Prentice Hall, 1988).

[15] The question in the oval parallels an ongoing philosophical debate about whether public policy should respond to people's raw preferences or their informed judgments. This is a classic problem in Western political theory. For example, Mill forced utilitarians to grapple with the question of "lower" and "higher" pleasures. See John S. Mill, *Utilitarianism and Other Writings* (Meridian, 1962). Numerous philosophers have sided with the view that a person's existing preferences must be distinguished from what might be called potential preferences, enlightened judgments, or fundamental interests. See Benjamin Barber, "Opinion Polls: Public Judgment or Private Prejudice," *The Responsive Community* 2:2 (1992), pp. 4–6; Bowles and Gintis, *Democracy and Capitalism*, chap. 5; Bernard Manin, "On Legitimacy and Political Deliberation," trans. Elly Stein and Jane Mansbridge, *Political Theory* 15 (1987), pp. 338–368; Claus Offe and Ulrich K. Preuss, "Democratic Institutions and Moral Resources," in David Held (ed.), *Political Theory Today* (Stanford University Press, 1991), pp. 143–171; Daniel Yankelovich, *Coming to Public Judgment* (Syracuse University Press, 1991). The distinction between unreflective interests and considered judgment is fundamental to deliberative democratic theory; see, for example, Amy Gutmann and Dennis Thompson. *Why Deliberative Democracy?* (Princeton University Press, 2009).

[16] See Chapter 5 in the Second Treatise of John Locke, Two Treatises of Government (Cambridge University Press, 1960).

[17] There is much debate about the ethical imperative of democracy in the workplace. For recent advocacy, see Tom Malleson, "Making the Case for Workplace

Democracy: Exit and Voice as Mechanisms of Freedom in Social Life," *Polity* 45 (2013), pp. 604-629. Also see Peter Bachrach and Aryeh Botwinick, *Power and Empowerment: A Radical Theory of Participatory Democracy* (Temple University Press, 1992); Robert N. Bellah et al., *The Good Society* (Random House, 1992); Carole Pateman, *Participation and Democratic Theory* (Cambridge University Press, 1970); Sashkin, "Participative Management." For a series of individual case studies and an excellent list of resources and writings, see Len Krimerman and Frank Lindenfeld, *When Workers Decide: Workplace Democracy Takes Root in North America* (New Society Publishers, 1992). On the ethics of democracy and the economy, see Bowles and Gintis, *Democracy and Capitalism*; Joshua Cohen and Joel Rogers, *On Democracy* (Penguin Books, 1983); Barry Schwartz, *The Battle for Human Nature* (W. W. Norton, 1987).

[18] The musical example is inspired by Robert Nozick's idiosyncratic hypotheticals in *Anarchy, State, and Utopia* (Basic Books, 2013). Among other things, his work addresses consent and obligation, two issues related to inclusiveness.

[19] The experimental literature on the relative "productivity" of democratic groups has focused on the effects of member participation and democratic leadership styles, and the results have been, on balance, favorable to the view that democratic processes increase productivity and satisfaction for all but the most mundane tasks. For reviews, see Bernard M. Bass and Ralph M. Stogdill's *Handbook of Leadership* (Simon and Schuster, 1990); John Gastil, "A Meta-analytic Review of the Productivity and Satisfaction of Democratic and Autocratic Leadership," *Small Group Research* 25 (1994), pp. 384–410; Rob Foels, James E. Driskell, Brian Mullen, and Eduardo Salas, "The Effects of Democratic Leadership on Group Member Satisfaction: An Integration," *Small Group Research* 31 (2000), pp. 676–701; Katherine I. Miller and Peter R. Monge, "Participation, Satisfaction, and Productivity: A Meta-analytic Review," *Academy of Management Journal* 29 (1986), pp. 727–753; George Strauss, "Worker Participation in Management: An International Perspective," *Research in Organizational Behavior* 4 (1982), pp. 173–265; John Simmons and William Mares, *Working Together* (Alfred A. Knopf, 1983). For a more recent (unpublished) study along these same lines, see Philip Mellizo, Jeffrey P. Carpenter, and Peter Hans Matthews, *Workplace Democracy in the Lab* (SSRN Scholarly Paper) (Social Science Research Network, January 1, 2011), http://papers.ssrn.com/abstract=1755998. More generally, recent research has dispelled the "camel committees" myth that individuals are usually better than groups at making efficient, high-quality decisions. One of the most widely cited works on the subject emphasizes the power of diversity in groups: Scott Page, *The Difference: How the Power of Diversity Creates Better Groups, Firms, Schools, and Societies* (Princeton University Press, 2008). The most recent popular account of this research is James Surowiecki's *The Wisdom of Crowds* (Random House, 2005). One particularly rigorous study on this question found that groups outperformed the most proficient individual group member 97% of the time; Larry K. Michaelsen, Warren E. Watson, and Robert H. Black, "A Realistic Test of

Individual Versus Group Consensus Decision Making," *Journal of Applied Psychology* 74 (1989), pp. 834–839. See also Vroom and Jago, *The New Leadership*; Richard H. G. Field, Peter C. Read, and Jordan J. Louviere, "The Effect of Situation Attributes on Decision Method Choice in the Vroom-Jago Model of Participation in Decision Making," *Leadership Quarterly* 1 (1990), pp. 165–176; Warren Watson, Larry K. Michaelsen, and Walt Sharp, "Member Competence, Group Interaction, and Group Decision Making: A Longitudinal Study," *Journal of Applied Psychology* 76 (1991), pp. 803–809.

[20] For an excellent critique of guardianship, see Dahl, *Democracy and Its Critics*. A proponent of guardianship might argue that although group members are capable of representing themselves, a democratic process wouldn't give equal consideration to each member's interests. Dahl argues, however, that it would be necessary to "demonstrate that the democratic process fails to give equal consideration to the interests of some who are subject to its laws; that the quasi guardians will do so; and that the injury inflicted on the right to equal consideration outweighs the injury done to the right of a people to govern itself" (p. 192).

[21] Some of the dangers of legal guardianship for persons deemed incompetent are discussed by Madelyn A. Iris, "Threats to Autonomy in Guardianship Decision Making," *Generations* 14 (1990), pp. 39–41.

[22] Groups in such situations can still choose to retain ultimate authority, weakening the position of the guardian.

[23] On preparing students for democratic self-government, see Walter Parker, *Teaching Democracy: Unity and Diversity in Public Life* (Teachers College Press, 2003).

[24] Many democratic theorists and activists have stressed this point. As John Dewey argued, "The foundation of democracy is faith in the capacities of human nature; faith in human intelligence, and in the power of pooled and cooperative experience. It is not belief that these things are complete, but that if given a show they will grow and be able to generate progressively the knowledge and wisdom needed to guide collective action"; quoted in David Fott, "John Dewey and the Philosophical Foundations of Democracy," *Social Science Journal* 28 (1991), p. 33. On the educational effects of participation, see Mark Warren, "Democratic Theory and Self-Transformation," *American Political Science Review* 86 (1992), pp. 8–23. For a recent review of research on this, see Heather Pincock, "Does Deliberation Make Better Citizens?" in Tina Nabatchi, John Gastil, Michael Weiksner, and Matt Leighninger (eds.), *Democracy in Motion: Evaluating the Practice and Impact of Deliberative Civic Engagement* (Oxford University Press, 2012), pp. 135–162.

[25] Surowiecki popularized the idea of the group's power in *The Wisdom of Crowds*. The importance of the group in modern society also gets elaboration in Gary Alan Fine, *Tiny Publics: A Theory of Group Action and Culture* (Russell Sage Foundation, 2012) and the last chapter of my book, *The Group in Society*.

Chapter 2

[1] Mary Parker Follett, *Creative Experience* (Longmans, Green, and Co., 1924), pp. 225–226.

[2] To the best of my knowledge, no published work before 1993 had attempted to provide a detailed definition of democracy in small-scale systems. On the optimistic presumption that any work since would have cited *Democracy in Small Groups*, it appears none of the more than 150 or so works by other authors who have cited it have proposed an alternative definition. Many democratic theorists ignore small group democracy altogether by defining democracy in a way that limits it to large-scale, representative political systems; for example, see Larry Diamond (ed.), *The Democratic Revolution: Struggles for Freedom and Pluralism in the Developing World* (Freedom House, 1992), p. 26; Milton Fisk, *The State and Justice: An Essay in Political Theory* (Cambridge University Press, 1989), p. 166. Sidney Verba's *Small Groups and Political Behavior* (Princeton University Press, 1972) is one of the only modern works focusing on democracy and the small group, but his purpose was to understand the small group's role in large-scale democracy—not the small group as a democracy in and of itself. The most theoretical work to date on the subject may be Jane Mansbridge's *Beyond Adversary Democracy* (University of Chicago Press, 1983), which elaborates and illustrates the "unitary" model of democracy through case studies of small democratic groups. One might argue that Jean Jacques Rousseau, in *The Social Contract and Discourses* (E.P. Dutton & Co, 1950 [1762]), presents a theory of small-scale democracy, but he discusses medium social scales (i.e., 1,000 to 10,000 people) and fails to address in detail the features of face-to-face deliberation. Moreover, Rousseau's theory of deliberation is seriously flawed; see Bernard Manin, "On Legitimacy and Political Deliberation," trans. Elly Stein and Jane Mansbridge, *Political Theory* 15 (1987), pp. 338–368. For a more favorable recounting of Rousseau, see Regarding Rousseau's theory of deliberation, see Joshua Cohen, *Rousseau: A free community of equals* (Oxford: Oxford University Press, 2010).

[3] I discuss the writings underlying this definition in greater detail in "A Definition of Small Group Democracy," *Small Group Research* 23 (1992), pp. 278–301; portions of this chapter are reprinted from that article with the permission of Sage Publications. Even more details comes from my thesis, "Democratic Deliberation: A Redefinition of the Democratic Process and a Study of Staff Meetings at a Co-Operative Workplace," *Masters Abstracts* 30-04M (1992), 1114 (University Microfilms No. 1348177). Testing a cynical theory of a fellow graduate student, I slipped a twenty

dollar bill into the pages of the thesis that resides at the University of Wisconsin-Madison library. It may still be there, though I've since heard that this was such a common practice that a local Madison resident regularly checked the shelves for new theses to extract the cash. I prefer to think that the prize went to the person with the thankless task of digitizing old theses like mine, which surely are no longer kept in paper format. Compared to my thesis, this book has a clearer conception of the nature of power, inclusiveness, commitment, and deliberation, and I have highlighted the importance of obtaining adequate information during group discussions. Elsewhere, I have elaborated on deliberation, in particular, and proposed more sophisticated ways of measuring it; see Laura Black, Stephanie Burkhalter, John Gastil, and Jennifer Stromer-Galley, "Methods for Analyzing and Measuring Group Deliberation," in Lance Holbert (ed.), *Sourcebook of Political Communication Research: Methods, Measures, and Analytical Techniques* (Routledge, 2010), pp. 323–345.

[4] I have had the pleasure of working with numerous colleagues on two edited volumes that foreground the small group in the theory and practice of public deliberation. See Tina Nabatchi, John Gastil, Michael Weiksner, and Matt Leighninger (eds.), *Democracy in Motion: Evaluating the Practice and Impact of Deliberative Civic Engagement* (Oxford University Press, 2012), and John Gastil and Peter Levine (eds.), *The Deliberative Democracy Handbook: Strategies for Effective Civic Engagement in the Twenty-First Century* (Jossey-Bass, 2005).

[5] For example, see Joshua Cohen, "Deliberation and Democratic Legitimacy," in Alan Hamlin and Philip Pettit (eds.), *The Good Polity* (Basil Blackwell, 1989), p. 22. Quentin Skinner identified one of the most important reasons for defining democracy as an ideal: Calling a political system a democracy "serves to commend the recently prevailing values and practices of a political system like that of the United States, and it constitutes a form of argument against those who have sought to question the democratic character of those values and practices." The quote comes from his wonderfully-named essay, "The Empirical Theorists of Democracy and Their Critics: A Plague on Both Their Houses," *Political Theory* 1 (1973), pp. 303–304. The use of the term "democracy" to describe existing institutions can cause the term to lose legitimacy in step with the institutions. Thus, critic Manning Marable can proclaim that "American democracy has failed," simultaneously rejecting the system and the term "democracy." Fortunately, Marable and other critics often reject a brand of democracy, and suggest another form of democracy as an alternative; see Marable's *The Crisis of Color and Democracy: Essays on Race, Class, and Power* (Common Courage Press, 1992). This form of criticism preserves the value of the word but complicates its meaning. Once again, the problem stems from using the term to refer to an existing institution, rather than an ideal. For criticism of the "idealist" approach I embrace, see Samuel Huntington's contribution to the movement "to make democracy less of a 'hurrah' word and more of a commonsense word;" *The Third Wave: Democratization in the Late Twentieth Century* (University

of Oklahoma Press, 1993), p. 7. Anne Norton, author most recently of *On the Muslim Question* (Princeton University Press, 2013), also argued against complicating the meaning of democracy in remarks given at Penn State in October, 2013. In her view, it is more important to focus on the core meanings of freedom, political equality, and self-government than to infuse the term with complex meanings regarding relationships, deliberation, and so on. I take the contrary view because I believe people's appetite for democracy only grows when they reflect on and come to appreciate its nuances. This is not merely the satisfaction the wine connoisseur gains from a more refined palate; rather, it is a deeper understanding of what democracy requires to function effectively, which makes one a more effective critic of the deficiencies of contemporary political practices.

[6] I call this definition "comprehensive" because it includes elements that one does not find in my own definitions of "democratic deliberation." Since writing this book in 1993, my writing has tended to focus on the latter term, which defines a process whereby a group can deliberate in a way that is democratic. This is also the preferred term of the Center for Democratic Deliberation, in which I participate as a faculty member in Communication Arts and Sciences at Pennsylvania State University. When I write about deliberation, one can still see elements of this definition, such as mutuality/respect, speaking responsibilities and listening. This definition placed relatively little emphasis on the rigor of the analysis that takes place, because I was more concerned with ensuring a group was democratic than making certain its pre-vote discussions were maximally deliberative. I considered revising this definition in writing the second edition, but I've opted to keep it intact, because I think it complements more than contradicts my conception of democratic deliberation, which is meant to apply not just to groups but to all social scales. I articulate the latter term most fully in *Political Communication and Deliberation* (Sage, 2008). A shorter version of that same definition appears in John Gastil and Laura Black, "Public Deliberation as the Organizing Principle of Political Communication Research," *Journal of Public Deliberation* 4:1 (2007), art. 3.

[7] Robert Dahl, *Democracy and Its Critics* (Yale University Press, 1989), p. 113. Dahl's work had as much influence on my theory of small group democracy as anyone's. For a lovely overview of his career, see Margaret Levi's interview with him in "A Conversation with Robert A. Dahl," *Annual Review of Political Science* 12 (2009), pp. 1–9, which can be seen as a video interview online.

[8] As Anthony Arblaster writes in *Democracy, 2nd Ed.* (Open University Press, 1994), "Accessibility and a readiness to listen are not...incompatible with a fundamentally authoritarian structure of power and government. Nor is making a show of consultation and participation, when what is being looked for is essentially a ratification of decisions already taken...Democracy involves debate and discussion, but these are not enough if they remain inconclusive and ineffective in determining actual policies" (pp. 94–95). For an example of groups with the trappings of democracy but no real power, see William Graebner, "The Small Group in

Democratic Social Engineering, 1900–1950," *Journal of Social Issues* 42 (1986), pp. 137–154.

[9] This definition borrows from a discussion of power by Douglas W. Rae. In further agreement with Rae, I would add that power is the "knowing capacity" to influence; one must be aware of one's causal role to say that one's influence constitutes "power." See "Knowing Power: A Working Paper," in Ian Shapiro and Grant Reeher (eds.), *Power, Inequality, and Democratic Politics* (Westview Press, 1988), pp. 17–49. Note that if "power" includes forms of influence over emotions and beliefs, the term has wide applicability. Therapy and consciousness raising groups, for instance, are powerful even if they focus on changing how people think and feel, more than how people behave. The distinction may be largely academic, however, since people who change their emotional and cognitive perception of the world are likely to behave differently as a consequence. Moreover, research on emotion and cognition shows how intertwined the two are, as in this study of their relative contributions to the moral judgments people make: Jean Decety, Kalina J. Michalska, and Katherine D. Kinzler, "The Contribution of Emotion and Cognition to Moral Sensitivity: A Neurodevelopmental Study," *Cerebral Cortex* 22 (2012), 209–220.

[10] I thank Gail Pietrzyk for permitting me to use an adaptation of her piano metaphor. A more mathematical definition of group power is provided by Andrew King in *Power and Communication* (Waveland Press, 1987); he argues that group power can be defined as the product of a group's mass (number of people and amount of resources) and its unity or cohesion.

[11] Catharine A. MacKinnon, *Toward a Feminist Theory of the State* (Harvard University Press, 1989), p. 102; see also chap. 5. For more on women's consciousness raising groups, see Sara M. Evans and Harry C. Boyte, *Free Spaces* (University of Chicago Press, 1992), chap. 3; Virginia Sapiro, "The Women's Movement and the Creation of Gender Consciousness: Social Movements as Socialization Agents," in Orit Ichilov (ed.), *Political Socialization, Citizenship Education, and Democracy* (Teachers College Press, 1990), pp. 266–280. For a case study of a consciousness-raising group in the gay community, see James W. Chesebro, John F. Cragan, and Patricia McCullough, "The Small Group Techniques of the Radical Revolutionary: A Synthetic Study of Consciousness Raising," *Speech Monographs* 40 (1973), pp. 136–146. Paulo Freire's writings on liberatory education in Latin America provide a more general conception of consciousness raising in small groups; see *Pedagogy of the Oppressed: 30th Anniversary Edition* (Continuum, 2000).

[12] In thinking this issue through, I drew on an eclectic array of writings that helped me distinguish different forms of power: threat, exchange, and integrative power (Kenneth Boulding, *Three Faces of Power* [Sage, 1990]); actualization and domination power (Riane Eisler, *The Chalice and the Blade: Our History, Our Future* [Harper Collins, 2011]); power as more than a means of coercin or domination (Nancy C. Hartsock, *Money, Sex, and Power* [Northeastern University Press, 1985], chap. 9); sustainable and nonsustainable power (Frances Moore Lappé and Paul

Martin Du Bois, "Power in a Living Democracy," *Creation Spirituality* [September/October, 1992], pp. 23-25, 42); power over, power to, and power with (Starhawk, *Truth or Dare* [Harper Collins, 1989]).

[13] On the importance of equal power, see Peter Bachrach, *The Theory of Democratic Elitism: A Critique* (Little, Brown, and Co., 1967), chaps. 6 and 7. Any provisional inequalities in power that the group creates must be subject to justification. If a group member questions an inequality, the group or the individual with greater power must be able to justify its existence; see Bruce Ackerman, *Social Justice and the Liberal State* (Yale University Press, 1981). On the difficulties surrounding the establishment of fully equal power, see Andrea Baker, "The Problem of Authority in Radical Movement Groups: A Case Study of a Lesbian-Feminist Organization," *Journal of Applied Behavioral Science* 18 (1982), pp. 323-341; Mansbridge, *Beyond Adversary Democracy*, chap. 17.

[14] Dahl, *Democracy and Its Critics*, pp. 126-130. The problem of inclusiveness is faced not only by small groups and communities, but also by nations. For this reason, it becomes necessary to explore models of international democratic decision making; see David Held, "Democracy: From City-states to a Cosmopolitan Order?," *Political Studies* 40 (1992), pp. 10-39. Dennis Thompson also addresses this issue in "Democratic Theory and Global society," *Journal of Political Philosophy, 7* (1999), pp. 111-125.

[15] In *From the Ground Up* (Black Rose Books, 1993), C. George Benello recognizes the necessary interplay between inclusiveness and the distribution of power. All those affected by group decisions "must have a say in the decision-making process.... The trick is to create a system with sufficient delegation of authority and internal differentiation so that not everyone is involved in all decisions all the time" (p. 51).

[16] Michael Walzer, in chapter 7 of *Radical Principles: Reflections of an Unreconstructed Democrat* (Basic Books, 1980), insists that there will always be people falling within the boundaries of inclusiveness who will not attend meetings. In particular, he asks militant activists to respect those who choose to attend fewer (if any) meetings. Their absence does not justify their exclusion; it only complicates the representation of their interests.

[17] John Burnheim, *Is Democracy Possible? The Alternative to Electoral Politics* (University of California Press, 1985), p. 5.

[18] Dahl, *Democracy and Its Critics*, p. 129. When people are deemed incompetent to participate in group deliberation, the group must—to the best of its ability—still take their interests into account. In this vein, some environmental activists have argued that fully democratic groups should take the interests of other species and all forms of life into account. See Van Andruss, Christopher Plant, Judith Plant, and Eleanor Wright (eds.), *Home! A Bioregional Reader* (New Society Publishers, 1990), pp. 70, 95-99. See also John Dryzek, *Deliberative Democracy and Beyond: Liberals, Critics, Contestations* (Oxford University Press, 2000).

[19] Teresa Labov provides an example of a co-op that sacrificed its principle of "openness to the community" (inclusiveness) in order to satisfy its other three principles—cooperativeness, commitment to the group, and harmony. "Ideological Themes in Reports of Interracial Conflict," in Allen D. Grimshaw (ed.), *Conflict Talk* (Cambridge University Press, 1988), pp. 139–159.

[20] Cohen, "Deliberation and Democratic Legitimacy," p. 21. Carol Gould, in *Rethinking Democracy* (Cambridge University Press, 1988), stresses commitment to the democratic process and responsibility for carrying out group decisions. A more extreme statement is provided by Mahatma Gandhi: "A democrat must be utterly selfless. He [sic] must think and dream not in terms of self or party but only of democracy" (*Gandhi: Selected Political Writings* [Hacket, 1995], p. 145, quoted by S. M. Tewari in Krishna Kumar [ed.], *Democracy and Nonviolence* [Gandhi Peace Foundation, 1968], p. 30). By contrast, I argue only that one ought to make a commitment to the democratic process prior to (not to the exclusion of) other commitments to people and principles.

[21] There are at least two different rationales for using formal group bylaws and similar regulations. First, they might be designed to make a subversion of the democratic process too costly. If such rules have force, they would function in the same way that laws against criminal violence restrain malevolent people; see Kenneth Boulding, "Perspectives on Violence," *Zygon* 18 (1983), pp. 425–437. Second, one can view rules as self-restraints that a group of well-meaning but imperfect people voluntarily impose on themselves as protections against making hasty, undemocratic decisions during moments of weakness. In *Democracy and the Ethical Life: A Philosophy of Politics and Community, 2nd Ed.* (Catholic University of America Press, 1990), chap. 10, Claes G. Ryn presents this view with regard to the role of constitutions. Jo Freeman applies this principle to small groups, insisting that groups must formalize their procedures to safeguard democracy; see "The Tyranny of Structurelessness," *Berkeley Journal of Sociology*, 17 (1972–73), 151–165. Critics of bylaws often contend that formal rules are unrealistic. In this view, a group should not try to codify norms that, in reality, must constantly be redeveloped and "owned" by the group members. Ultimately, bylaws can undermine commitment by replacing personal conscience and organic group norms with impersonal, stale doctrine. Thus, a 1656 Quaker document on business meeting policy reads, "These things we do not lay upon you as a rule or form to walk by...for the letter killeth but the Spirit giveth light." Quoted in Francis E. Pollard, Beatrice E. Pollard, and Robert S. W. Pollard, *Democracy and the Quaker Method* (Ballinsdale, 1949), p. 47.

[22] Since no group fully realizes the democratic ideal, an individual is never strictly obligated to follow group decisions. Philosophical anarchists make this argument with regard to governments; however, the potential for small groups to approximate the democratic ideal is much greater than it is for large political systems. If one thinks of obligation in incremental (as opposed to dichotomous) terms, one can recognize that a group's greater embodiment of democratic principles should inspire

a proportionately stronger sense of obligation. For a strong defense of philosophical anarchism, see A. John Simmons, *Moral Principles and Political Obligations* (Princeton University Press, 1981).

[23] James Fishkin, *Democracy and Deliberation* (Yale University Press, 1991), pp. 34–35.

[24] I have sympathy for the view that a commitment to democracy should remain separate from the definition of democracy itself. In this view, commitment can bolster democracy, but one can behave democratically without a commitment to it. Nonetheless, I opt to keep the two intertwined, even after fretting about this problem in the two decades since this book first appeared. The reason is that practicing democratic conventions without a commitment to core principles has an emptiness to it; the democratic rules and procedures are just that—administrative choices without any underlying norms and values. At the level of the small group, that mechanistic conception of democracy seems too subject to willful abuse or careless misappropriation. At some point, the causal relationship between commitment and faithful practice becomes so strong that the former is required to ensure the latter. This has been shown empirically in the context of technology adoption, and it should be even more true in the case of the complex "technology" of small group democracy; see Gerardine DeSanctis and Marshall Scott Poole, "Capturing the Complexity in Advanced Technology Use: Adaptive Structuration Theory," *Organization Science* 5 (1994), pp. 121–147.

[25] As discussed in the preceding footnote, those who wish a simpler definition of democracy might argue that these relational features should be viewed as conducive to (rather than part of) small group democracy. On the contrary, many democratic theorists have stressed the relational component of a fully democratic process; see Benjamin Barber, *Strong Democracy* (University of California Press, 1984) and Carol Gould, *Rethinking Democracy*. In particular, the different forms of relationship presented herein draw heavily on Barber's discussion of "strong democratic talk" in *Strong Democracy* (pp. 173–198). For a clarification with regard to mutuality, see Benjamin Barber, "Reply," *Dissent* 32 (1985), p. 385. For a brief synopsis, see Benjamin Barber, "Political Talk—and 'Strong Democracy,'" *Dissent* 31 (1984), pp. 215–222. John Dewey has gone even farther by arguing that democratic governance is a means towards a democratic form of relationship among people; see David Fott, "John Dewey and the Philosophical Foundations of Democracy," *Social Science Journal* 28 (1991), pp. 29–44; John D. Peters, "Democracy and American Mass Communication Theory: Dewey, Lippman, Lazarsfeld," *Communication* 11 (1989), pp. 199–220. As the literature on deliberative democracy has advanced, Dewey's pragmatic voice on such matters has only grown stronger; see William R. Caspary, "On Dewey, Habermas and Deliberative Democracy," *Journal of Public Deliberation* 4:1 (2008), art. 10.

[26] One of the early and most provocative works on relational communication is Paul Watzlawick, Janet Beavin, and Don Jackson, *Pragmatics of Human Communication:*

A Study of Interactional Patterns, Pathologies, and Paradoxes (Norton, 1967/2011). Therein, the authors coined the now infamous phrase, "One cannot not communicate" (p. 30). The argument was that interaction always has a meaning and an impact on the relationship. Moreover, Samuel Bowles and Herbert Gintis argue that people's actions and interactions constitute them as persons; thus, one's sense of individuality, competence, or group identity can come into existence through proclaiming and interactively affirming its existence. See their book *Democracy and Capitalism: Property, Community, and the Contradictions of Modern Social Thought* (Basic Books, 1986), esp. chaps. 5 and 6. As I briefly discuss in "Undemocratic Discourse: A Review of Theory and Research on Political Discourse" (*Discourse & Society* 4 [1992], p. 473), the relational aspects of democratic discourse resemble existing politeness theories. See Penelope Brown and Stephen Levinson, "Universals in Language Usage: Politeness Phenomena," in Esther N. Goody (ed.), *Questions and Politeness: Strategies in Social Interaction* (Cambridge University Press, 1978), pp. 56–289; Robin T. Lakoff, "The Logic of Politeness; Or Minding Your p's and q's," in C. Colum et al. (eds.), *Papers from the Ninth Regional Meeting of the Chicago Linguistic Society* (Chicago Linguistic Society, 1973), pp. 292–305; Tae-Seop Lim and John W. Bowers, "Facework Solidarity, Approbation, and Tact," *Human Communication Research* 17 (1991), pp. 415–450.

[27] John Dewey, *The Public and Its Problems* (Penn State Press, 2012). See also Peters, "Democracy and American Mass Communication Theory," p. 218. The implicit metaphor in the term "atmosphere" is only a surface feature of the deep literature on the ecology of human interaction. In this view, the maintenance of a hospitable group environment is essential to sustaining certain forms of human interaction—one of which, I argue, is democratic interaction. On the ecology of human communication, see the article by my thesis advisor, C. David Mortensen, "Communication, Conflict, and Culture," *Communication Theory* 1 (1991), pp. 273–293.

[28] Jane J. Mansbridge, *Beyond Adversary Democracy*, pp. 4–5. See also Jane J. Mansbridge, *Beyond Self-Interest* (University of Chicago Press, 1990) and "Feminism and Democracy," *The American Prospect* 1:2 (1990), pp. 126–139. For a more recent case demonstrating this hazard, see Christopher F. Karpowitz and Jane Mansbridge, "Disagreement and Consensus: The Importance of Dynamic Updating in Public Deliberation," in John Gastil and Peter Levine (eds.), *The Deliberative Democracy Handbook* (Jossey-Bass, 2005), pp. 237–253.

[29] Some of the examples of relational talk are excerpts from staff meetings at Mifflin Street Community Co-op, which I discuss in Chapters 4 and 5.

[30] Kenwyn K. Smith and David N. Berg discuss the tensions between the individual and the group in terms of seven paradoxes that small groups face; see "A Paradoxical Conception of Group Dynamics," *Human Relations* 40 (1987), pp. 633–658. Although groups are more commonly associated with the development of a social or group identity, P. G. Friedman suggests that groups can play a vital role in

developing a person's sense of individual identity. "The Limits of Consensus: Group Processes for Individual Development," in Gerald M. Phillips and Julia T. Wood (eds.), *Emergent Issues in Human Decision Making* (Southern Illinois University Press, 1984), pp. 142–160.

[31] Gould, *Rethinking Democracy*, p. 257. On reciprocity and deliberation, see Amy Gutmann and Dennis F. Thompson, *Democracy and Disagreement* (Harvard University Press, 1996). For an application of the reciprocity principle to large-scale democracy and mass communication systems, see Dianne E. Rucinski, "The Centrality of Reciprocity to Communication and Democracy," *Critical Studies in Mass Communication* 8 (1991), pp. 184–194. In the above quote, Gould uses the term "participatory democracy," a term that corresponds to a broad branch of democratic theory that emphasizes the role of public participation in the decision-making process. Prominent writings in this tradition include: Barber, *Strong Democracy*; C. B. Macpherson, *The Life and Times of Liberal Democracy* (Oxford University Press, 1977); Mansbridge, *Beyond Adversary Democracy*; Carole Pateman, *Participation and Democratic Theory* (Cambridge University Press, 1970). Critics have viewed the participatory theory of democracy as dangerous (e.g, Samuel Huntington, "The Democratic Distemper," *Public Interest* 41 [1975], pp. 9–38), unrealistic (e.g., Daniel C. Kramer, *Participatory Democracy: Developing Ideals of the Political Left* [Cambridge, MA: Schenkman Publishing Co., 1972]), and antagonistic to a more deliberative conception of political decision making (Claus Offe and Ulrich K. Preuss, "Democratic Institutions and Moral Resources," in David Held [ed.], *Political Theory Today* [Stanford: Stanford University Press, 1991], pp. 143–171). For a defense of participatory democracy, even with a begrudging acknowledgment of the value of deliberation, see Carole Pateman's presidential address to the American Political Science Association, "Participatory Democracy Revisited," *Perspectives on Politics* 10 (2012), 7–19.

[32] Like the other forms of democratic relationship, the affirmation of competence manifests itself in the form of communication among group members. Thus, the character of a group's talk can indicate the degree to which members' competence is collectively affirmed. This view parallels Ackerman's "neutrality principle," which forbids speakers from asserting that they are morally superior to other members of the collective; see *Social Justice in the Liberal State*, pp. 10–12, 15–17.

[33] Dahl, *Democracy and Its Critics*, p. 98. The assumption of competence relates to the question in Figure 1 about the capability of group members to represent their own interests and participate in democratic deliberation.

[34] Quoted in Robin Morgan, "Chai Ling Talks with Robin Morgan," *Ms.* (September/October, 1990), p. 14. In addition to believing others are competent, one must also presume that oneself is competent at representing one's self-interest and the interests of the group. This belief in oneself is closely related to self-esteem, which plays a vital role in democracy. As Gloria Steinem explains, self-esteem allows a person to trust her own beliefs and conscience. In this way, "...Self-esteem plays as

much a part in the destiny of nations as it does in the lives of individuals...Self-esteem is the basis of any real democracy." *Revolution from Within* (Open Road Media, 1992/2012), pp. 9–10. Even prominent political philosophers have paid a great deal of attention to self-esteem; see John Rawls, *A Theory of Justice* (Harvard University Press, 1971/2009), pp. 440–446; Michael Walzer, *Spheres of Justice* (Basic Books, 1983), pp. 272–280.

[35] Quote from David Spangler, cited in Corinne McLaughlin and Gordon Davidson, *Builders of the Dawn: Community Lifestyles in a Changing World* (Book Publishing Company, 1986/1990), p. 298.

[36] If one is skeptical that things such as word choice can affect a person's group identity, see Samuel L. Gaertner, Jeffrey Mann, Audrey Murrell, and John F. Dovidio, "Reducing Intergroup Bias: The Benefits of Recategorization," *Journal of Personality and Social Psychology* 57 (1989), pp. 239–249. In addition, Ernest Bormann shows how the sharing of group stories can develop mutuality when narratives are jointly developed and understood by group members. "Symbolic Convergence Theory and Communication in Group Decision-Making," in Randy Y. Hirokawa and Marshall Scott Poole (eds.), *Communication and Group Decision-Making* (Sage, 1996), pp. 81–114. In deliberative events, one can track the emergence of collective identity simply by noting the changing incidence of "we" as a self-descriptor; see Roderick Hart and Sharon Jarvis. "We the People: The Contours of Lay Political Discourse," in Maxwell Mccombs and Amy Reynolds (eds.), *The Poll with a Human Face: The National Issues Convention Experiment in Political Communication* (Lawrence Erlbaum, 1999), pp. 59–84.

[37] Gould, *Rethinking Democracy*, p. 106. The tension between individuality and community has received a great deal of attention in recent sociological and philosophical writings, spawning a group of scholars who see themselves as communitarians. See Robert N. Bellah, Richard Madsen, William M. Sullivan, Ann Swidler, and Steven M. Tipton, *Habits of the Heart: Individualism and Commitment in American Life* (University of California Press, 1985/2007); these same authors move from a descriptive tone to a more prescriptive one in *The Good Society* (Random House, 1992). For philosophical essays, see Michael J. Sandel (ed.), *Liberalism and Its Critics* (New York University Press, 1984), part 2. For recent communitarian writings, one can peruse the journal, *The Responsive Community Quarterly*, which ran from 1990–2004.

[38] Mutuality encompasses an identification with others, which some intriguing social scientific experiments suggest constitutes much of the basis of altruistic behavior. See C. Daniel Batson, Judy G. Batson, Cari A. Griffitt, and Sergio Barrientos, "Negative-State Relief and the Empathy-Altruism Hypothesis," *Journal of Personality and Social Psychology* 56 (1989), pp. 922–933; C. Daniel Batson, Janine L. Dyck, J. Randall Brandt, Judy G. Batson, Anne L. Powell, M. Rosalie McMaster, and Cari Griffitt, "Five Studies Testing Two New Egoistic Alternatives to the Empathy-Altruism Hypothesis," *Journal of Personality and Social Psychology* 55 (1988), pp. 52–77. Also

see Michael E. Morrell, *Empathy and Democracy: Feeling, Thinking, and Deliberation* (Pennsylvania State University Press, 2010).

[39] Though Irving Janis has suggested that group cohesion can contribute to the practice of "groupthink" or faulty collective decision making and judgment (*Groupthink: Psychological Studies of Policy Decisions and Fiascos* [Houghton Mifflin, 1982]), comprehensive reviews of the research on groupthink have found no association between group cohesion and the existence of groupthink; see, for example, Won Woo Park, "A Review of Research on Groupthink," *Journal of Behavioral Decision Making* 3 (1990), pp. 229–245. In fact, meta-analyses have found that, on average, social scientific experiments show a positive relationship between cohesiveness and group productivity; see Daniel J. Beal, Robin R. Cohen, Michael J. Burke, and Christy L. McLendon, "Cohesion and Performance in Groups: A Meta-analytic Clarification of Construct Relations," *Journal of Applied Psychology* 88 (2003): 989–1004; Stanley M. Gully, Dennis J. Devine, and David J. Whitney, "A Meta-analysis of Cohesion and Performance Effects of Level of Analysis and Task Interdependence," *Small Group Research* 26 (1995), pp. 497–520; and Charles R. Evans and Kenneth L. Dion, "Group Cohesion and Performance: A Meta-analysis," *Small Group Research* 22 (1991), pp. 175–186.

[40] Just as some have argued that cohesive groups are unproductive groups, some have argued that happy people tend to be lousy decision makers because they fail to reason systematically. Fortunately, this dim view of the human condition has not received strong empirical support. Diane M. Mackie and Leila T. Worth, "Processing Deficits and the Mediation of Positive Affect in Persuasion," *Journal of Personality and Social Psychology* 57 (1989), pp. 27–40.

[41] Mansbridge, *Beyond Adversary Democracy*, p. 9.

[42] Barber, *Strong Democracy*, p. 189; see also Barber, *The Conquest of Politics* (Princeton University Press, 1988), pp. 147–150. See also Rawls' discussion of the "principle of fraternity;" *A Theory of Justice*, p. 105.

[43] Michael Walzer argues that democratic citizens are expected to "be tolerant of one another." This is probably as close as we can come to that 'friendship' which Aristotle thought should characterize relations among members of the same political community;" see *Radical Principles*, p. 62. At the very least, democratic citizens avoid bursts of rudeness toward their fellow citizens. As an example of the rending effects of such incivility, note the insightful comments of a parking lot attendant, lamenting the behavior of some drivers: "The rudeness, especially as it is so often directed at me, rankles. There is...an evolutionary process at work in this distinctly urban rudeness: a perhaps natural shyness or insecurity aggravated by big-city emotional distance; this becomes reserve, becomes suspicion, becomes indifference, becomes finally incivility, and, at its extremes, inhumanity;" Mark Heisenberg, "A View from the Booth," *Utne Reader* (January/February, 1993), p. 134.

[44] This concern for civil behavior has spawned many academic centers, such as the National Institute for Civil Discourse that arose in Arizona after the shooting of

Congresswoman Gabrielle Giffords in 2011. See C. W. von Bergen, Martin S. Bressler, and George Collier, "Creating a Culture and Climate of Civility in a Sea of Intolerance," *Journal of Organizational Culture, Communication & Conflict* 16 (2012), 95–114; "Symposium: Political Discourse, Civility, and Harm," *Arizona Law Review* 54:2 (2012), pp. 345–480. On the importance of subtlety in distinguishing civil from uncivil discourse, partly with reference to the Arizona case, see Thomas W. Benson, "The Rhetoric of Civility: Power, Authenticity, and Democracy," *Journal of Contemporary Rhetoric* 1 (2011), pp. 22–30. For a contemporary overview, see Susan Herbst, *Rude Democracy: Civility and Incivility in American Politics* (Temple University Press, 2010).

[45] This claim is one that lacks direct causal verification, though research on deliberative processes shows the high degree of correlation between analytic rigor and democratic social relations, albeit not with evidence of whether their influence is reciprocal or directional. See Katherine R. Knobloch, John Gastil, Justin Reedy, and Katherine Cramer Walsh, "Did They Deliberate? Applying an Evaluative Model of Democratic Deliberation to the Oregon Citizens' Initiative Review," *Journal of Applied Communication Research* 41 (2013), pp. 105–125; and John Gastil, "What Counts as Deliberation? Comparing Participant and Observer Ratings" in Lyn Carson, John Gastil, Janette Hartz-Karp, and Ron Lubensky (eds.), *The Australian Citizens' Parliament and the Future of Deliberative Democracy* (Pennsylvania State University Press, 2013), pp. 95–107. Also, the view that deliberative analysis and democratic relations are mutually reinforcing fits with evidence of the generally salutary effects of deliberation; see Heather Pincock, "Does Deliberation Make Better Citizens?" in Tina Nabatchi, John Gastil, Michael Weiksner, and Matt Leighninger (eds.), *Democracy in Motion: Evaluating the Practice and Impact of Deliberative Civic Engagement* (Oxford University Press, 2012), pp. 135–162. The claim also connects, albeit loosely, with the association between extraverted/conscientious social behavior and deliberation; see John Gastil, Laura Black, and Kara Moscovitz, "Ideology, Attitude Change, and Deliberation in Small Face-to-face Groups," *Political Communication* 25 (2008), pp. 23–46.

[46] This definition draws on the work of small-group researcher Randy Y. Hirokawa. "Group Communication and Decision-making Performance: A Continued Test of the Functional Perspective," *Human Communication Research* 14 (1988), 487–515. Similar views of deliberation are provided by John Dewey, *How We Think* (Heath & Co., 1910); Charles R. Beitz, *Political Equality: An Essay in Democratic Theory* (Princeton University Press, 1989), p. 114; Charles W. Anderson, *Pragmatic Liberalism* (University of Chicago Press, 1994), esp. pp. 164–165, chap. 10. I have elaborated this conception of deliberation in my own research; see *Political Communication and Deliberation*, and Stephanie Burkhalter, John Gastil, and Todd Kelshaw, "A Conceptual Definition and Theoretical Model of Public Deliberation in Small Face-to-face Groups," *Communication Theory* 12 (2002), 398–422. Not surprisingly, the satisfaction of Gouran and Hirokawa's functions generally correlates

with sound decision making; see Hirokawa, "Group Communication and Decision-Making Performance." More generally, interactive methods of group decision making (as opposed to the non-interactive techniques some theorists and practitioners have employed) tend to result in higher quality group decisions, better average individual decisions, and an "assembly effect" (a group decision better than any one individual's decision or combination thereof). Brant R. Burleson, Barbara J. Levine, and Wendy Samter, "Decision-making Procedure and Decision Quality," *Human Communication Research* 10 (1984), pp. 557–574.

[47] For a concise overview of deliberative theory, see Simone Chambers, "Deliberative Democratic Theory," *Annual Review of Political Science* 6 (2003), 307–326. Jurgen Habermas' work on the public sphere and other subjects provided some of the foundation for deliberative theory; see *The Structural Transformation of the Public Sphere: An Inquiry into a Category of Bourgeois Society*, trans. Thomas Burger with Frederick Lawrence (MIT Press, 1991). For a review of this work, as well as criticisms and extensions, see Craig Calhoun (ed.), *Habermas and the Public Sphere* (MIT Press, 1992).

[48] On the importance of the jury in both philosophical and empirical theories of deliberation, see John Gastil, E. Pierre Deess, Philip J. Weiser, and Cindy Simmons, *The Jury and Democracy: How Jury Deliberation Promotes Civic Engagement and Political Participation* (Oxford University Press, 2010).

[49] Fishkin, *Democracy and Deliberation*, pp. 30–31.

[50] Ibid., pp. 25, 29.

[51] Cohen, "Deliberation and Democratic Legitimacy," pp. 22–23. In an earlier essay, Cohen presents an essentially similar model of deliberative democracy and examines the economic system that would accompany it. "The Economic Basis of Deliberative Democracy," *Social Philosophy & Policy* 6 (1988), pp. 25–50. Chapter 3 will discuss decision rules in more detail.

[52] On equality of participation in deliberative groups, see Joseph Bonito, Renee Meyers, John Gastil, and Jennifer Ervin, "Sit Down and Speak Up: Stability and Change in Group Participation," in Lyn Carson, John Gastil, Janette Hartz-Karp, and Ron Lubensky (eds.), *The Australian Citizens' Parliament and the Future of Deliberative Democracy* (Pennsylvania State University Press, 2013), pp. 120–130.

[53] One reason people value their silence is that it allows contemplation. As Robert Scott writes, "Orwell's 1984 depicts a society in which the freedom of thought is even controlled, because one cannot contemplate, one is constantly inundated with party slogans and Government Newspeak words.... Winston Smith, although he was nearly continually quiet, had no right to silence" ("Rhetoric and Silence," *Western Speech* 36 [1972], p. 154).

On the other hand, "silence is oppressive when it is characteristic of a dominated group [or subgroup], and when the group is not allowed to break its silence by its own choosing;" Adam Jaworski, "How to Silence a Minority: The Case of Women," *International Journal of the Sociology of Language* 94 (1992), p. 27. In Quaker meetings, it is customary to call for a few minutes of silence and reflection both before meetings and in the case of strong controversy. To have the intended effect, such silence "must be willingly agreed, and not felt as a kind of hostile constraint;" Pollard et al., *Democracy and the Quaker Method*, p. 44.

[54] Dahl, *Democracy and Its Critics*, p. 109. Alice Sturgis, in her elaboration of the principles underlying parliamentary procedure, calls this the "right of discussion." She writes, "Each member of the assembly has the right to speak freely without interruption or interference provided the rules are observed. The right of members to 'have their say,' or to 'have their day in court,' is as important as their right to vote;" *Standard Code of Parliamentary Procedure, 4th Ed.* (McGraw-Hill, 2000), p. 9.

[55] Cohen, "Deliberation and Democratic Legitimacy," p. 21.

[56] Some of the best contemporary work on the micro-dynamics of small group democracy comes from experimental work, such as Christopher F. Karpowitz, Tali Mendelberg, and Lee Shaker, "Gender Inequality in Deliberative Participation," *American Political Science Review* 106 (2012), pp. 533–547. That particular study shows that under majority rule, women have equal voice only when they make up a sizeable proportion of the members; under consensus procedure, the equality norm prevails.

[57] This notion of meaningful opportunities is analogous to Rawls' discussion of the worth of liberty, which depends on one's ability to take advantage of one's rights and liberties; see *A Theory of Justice*, pp. 204–205.

[58] This discussion is based, in part, on an extension of Habermas' notion of communicative competence; see Jürgen Habermas, *Legitimation Crisis*, trans. T. A. McCarthy (Beacon Press, 1975), and *Communication and the Evolution of Society* (Polity Press, 1979/1991). For critical discussions, see Anthony Giddens, "Jurgen Habermas," in Quentin Skinner (ed.), *The Return of Grand Theory in the Human Sciences* (Cambridge University Press, 1990), pp. 121–139; T. A. McCarthy, "A Theory of Communicative Competence," *Philosophy of the Social Sciences* 3 (1973), 135–156. Anderson, in *Pragmatic Liberalism* (pp. 199–202), provides a more concrete definition of deliberative competence. For an extension of this idea to media use and large-scale democracy, see Oscar H. Gandy, "The Political Economy of Communication Competence," in Vincent Mosco and Janet Wasko (eds.), *The Political Economy of Information* (University of Wisconsin Press, 1988), pp. 108–124. For social scientific theory and research on interpersonal and small group communicative competence, see James C. McCroskey and Virginia P. Richmond, "Communication Apprehension and Small Group Communication," in Robert S. Cathcart and Larry A. Samovar, *Small Group Communication, 5th Ed.* (William C. Brown, 1988), pp. 405–420; Malcolm R. Parks, "Interpersonal Communication and the Quest for Personal Competence," in Mark L. Knapp and Gerald R. Miller (eds.), *Handbook of Interpersonal Communication* (Sage, 1985), pp. 171–201; Dean E. Hewes, Michael Roloff, Sally Planalp, and David R. Seibold, "Interpersonal Communication Research: What Should We Know?" in Gerald M. Phillips and Julia

T. Wood (eds.), *Speech Communication: Essays to Commemorate the 75th Anniversary of the Speech Communication Association* (Southern Illinois University Press, 1990), pp. 130–180.

[59] Dahl, *Democracy and Its Critics*, p. 109, stresses the combination of equal with adequate opportunities. I will discuss the issue of time constraints in Chapter 6.

[60] These distinctions among the different forms of speech draw heavily on Barber, *Strong Democracy*, pp. 178–197.

[61] Dahl, *Democracy and Its Critics*, p. 113. The large-scale analogy is the relatively amorphous national "agenda." The media plays a crucial role in setting the nation's agenda; for a discussion see David Protess and Maxwell McCombs (eds.), *Agenda Setting: Readings on Media, Public Opinion, and Policymaking* (Lawrence Erlbaum Associates, 1991); Marc Raboy and Peter A. Bruck (eds.), *Communication for and Against Democracy* (Black Rose Books, 1989); Robert Entman, *Democracy Without Citizens* (Oxford University Press, 1989).

[62] I use the term "debate" alongside "discussion" and "deliberation" because each has an important role in small group democracy. Some writers choose to draw a stark contrast between "debate" and other words, such as "dialogue." Shelley Berman does this, painting a rather dim portrait of debate; see "Comparison of Dialogue and Debate," *Focus on Study Circles: The Newsletter of the Study Circles Resource Center* (Winter, 1993), p. 9; for similar contrasts, see Bruno Lasker's *Democracy through Discussion* (H. W. Wilson Co., 1949), pp. 16–18, passim; Pollard et al., *Democracy and the Quaker Method*, pp. 26–27. I recognize that group debates can become disruptive, divisive, or downright dangerous, but they can also be respectful and productive. By using debate as a synonym for deliberation, discussion, and dialogue, I wish to emphasize that fully democratic group meetings might commonly involve the constructive disagreements and arguments that can make debate a worthwhile activity.

[63] The agenda of a demos is never permanently set, as explained by Barber in *Strong Democracy*: "...Strong democratic talk places its agenda at the center rather than at the beginning of its politics. It subjects every pressing issue to continuous examination and possible reformulation. Its agenda is, before anything else, its agenda. It thus scrutinizes what remains unspoken, looking into the crevices of silence for signs of an unarticulated problem, a speechless victim, or a mute protester" (p. 182).

[64] Lappé and DuBois, in their essay "Power in a Living Democracy," use the term "political imagination" in a sense that is similar to reformulation, as I have defined it. It also corresponds to what media scholars call "issue framing." As an example of the importance of issue frames, in "Framing Responsibility for Political Issues: The Case of Poverty," *Political Behavior* 12 (1990), pp. 19–40, Shanto Iyengar studies the effects of different thematic frames on one's view of poverty. Iyengar explains that "how people think about poverty" depends on "how the issue is framed. When news media presentations frame poverty as a general outcome, responsibility for poverty is

assigned to society-at-large; when news presentations frame poverty as a particular instance of a poor person, responsibility is assigned to the individual. Similar framing effects are documented in the 1986 General Social Survey where the amount of public assistance deemed appropriate for a poor family varies with the description of the family" (p. 19).

[65] Barber, *Strong Democracy*, p. 193.

[66] See Jane J. Mansbridge, Janette Hartz-Karp, Matthew Amengual, and John Gastil, "Norms of Deliberation: An Inductive Study," *Journal of Public Deliberation* 2:1 (2006), art. 7.

[67] This parallels the "right of information" that underlies democratic parliamentary procedures: "Every member has the right to know the meaning of the question before the assembly and what its effect will be;" Sturgis, *Standard Code*, p. 9; see also Manin, "On Legitimacy and Political Deliberation," pp. 351–353. A similar principle underlies some laws in large-scale political systems, such as The Freedom of Information Act in the United States. Likewise, there are many efforts to make government information more accessible, transparent, or even interactive; see, for example, Chung-pin Lee, Kaiju Chang, and Frances Stokes Berry, "Testing the Development and Diffusion of E-Government and E-Democracy: A Global Perspective," *Public Administration Review* 71 (2011), 444–454. For an early proposal to "provide equal opportunity for every citizen to gather information" on questions of interest, see Michael Margolis, *Viable Democracy* (New York: MacMillan Press, 1979), pp. 161–169.

[68] The failure to establish and draw on an adequate information base can prove quite costly. Moreover, if a group member possesses faulty information, communicating it to the rest of the group can be counterproductive. See Randy Y. Hirokawa and Dirk R. Scheerhorn, "Communication in Faulty Group Decision-making," in Randy Y. Hirokawa and Marshall Scott Poole (eds.), *Communication and Group Decision Making* (Sage, 1986), pp. 63–80; Dennis S. Gouran and Randy Y. Hirokawa, "Counteractive Functions of Communication in Group Decision-making," in Randy Y. Hirokawa and Marshall Scott Poole (eds.), *Communication and Group Decision Making* (Sage, 1986), pp. 81–90.

[69] Li Lu, Y. Connie Yuan, and Poppy Lauretta McLeod, "Twenty-five Years of Hidden Profiles in Group Decision Making: A Meta-analysis," *Personality and Social Psychology Review* 16, (2012), pp. 54–75.

[70] The responsibility to make important information public is a clearly-recognized principle among advocates of large-scale democratic government. As communication scholar Jay Blumer writes, democratic theory holds that "ordinary citizens should be sufficiently equipped, informationally, to hold decision-makers effectively to account;" "Communication and Democracy: The Crisis Beyond and the Ferment Within," *Journal of Communication* 33 (1983), p. 169. See also Gandy, "The Political Economy of Communication Competence;" Edward Herman and Noam

Chomsky, *Manufacturing Consent* (Random House, 2011); Raboy and Bruck, *Communication for and Against Democracy.*

[71] Here I side with those who favor sharper conceptual distinctions between deliberation and democracy, per se. Though small group democracy requires deliberation, the imperative is the maintenance of democratic norms, with deliberation occurring to the extent possible and necessary, often within time constraints (see Chapter 6).

[72] Even if a speaker adds no new information or argument to the discussion, there is intrinsic value in the simple act of articulating one's own perspective on an issue. This process can connect the individual with both the group and the content of the group discussion; it can help people understand one another, as well as the subject at hand. For this reason, Follett suggested holding public "experience meetings" that would connect detailed policy information with people's daily lives. *Creative Experience*, chap. 12.

[73] Lynn M. Sanders, "Against Deliberation," *Political Theory* 25:3 (1997), pp. 23–24. The meaning of "articulation" used herein parallels Sanders' notion of "testimony," which she views as a corrective for the excessive emphasis on "deliberation." Karen Tracy likewise emphasizes the importance of robust extra-deliberative speech, which she calls "reasonable hostility," in *Challenges of Ordinary Democracy* (Pennsylvania State University Press, 2011).

[74] Mansbridge, "Feminism and Democracy," p. 136. Similarly, Pollard et al. (*Democracy and Quaker Method*, p. 23) insist "the very attempt to state an idea clearly may clarify it in the mind of the person who holds it."

[75] This definition of persuasion comes from Gerald R. Miller, "On Being Persuaded: Some Basic Distinctions," in Michael Roloff and Gerald R. Miller (eds.), *Persuasion* (Sage, 1980), pp. 1–28. For an overview of research on persuasion, see James Price Dillard and Michael Pfau (eds), *The Persuasion Handbook: Developments in Theory and Practice* (Sage, 2002).

[76] Walzer, *Spheres of Justice*, p. 304. See also Ackerman, *Social Justice and the Liberal State*; Manin, "On Legitimacy and Deliberation."

[77] Cohen, "Deliberation and Democratic Legitimacy," p. 22.

[78] See Ackerman, *Social Justice and the Liberal State*, pp. 4, 7, 11.

[79] Dahl has tried to show a connection between the deliberative view and his "criterion of enlightened understanding." This criterion asks that one be able to provide reasons for one's view, but it also requires that to the extent possible, citizens in a demos must undertake (1) systematic research and (2) self-reflection. "My 'reasons'," Dahl writes, "might meet all the public tests of acceptability and yet not be good reasons—not in my interests—because they are based on an impoverished understanding of my own needs and wants;" "A Rejoinder," *Journal of Politics* 53 (1991), p. 230.

[80] See Morrell, *Empathy and Democracy*, and Michael Neblo's unpublished essay, "Impassioned Democracy: The Role of Emotion in Deliberative Theory," which he

presented at the Democracy Collaborative Affiliates Conference in Washington, D.C. Many theorists have characterized emotion as playing a constructive role in deliberation, including John Dewey ("Human Nature and Conduct," in Jo Ann Boydston [ed.], *John Dewey: The Middle Works, 1899–1924, Vol. 14* [Southern Illinois University Press, 1983/2008], pp. 138–139); John Dryzek (*Deliberative Democracy and Beyond: Liberals, Critics, Contestations* [Oxford University Press, 2000], p. 52); Simone Chambers ("Rhetoric and the Public Sphere: Has Deliberative Democracy Abandoned Mass Democracy?" *Political Theory* 37 [2009], p. 339); Iris Marion Young ("Communication and the Other: Beyond Deliberative Democracy," in Seyla Benhabib [ed.], *Democracy and Difference: Contesting the Boundaries of the Political* [Princeton University Press, 1996], pp. 64–65); and Bryan Garsten (*Saving Persuasion: A Defense of Rhetoric and Judgment* [Harvard University Press, 2009], pp. 135–139).

[81] These examples are taken from my essay "Undemocratic Discourse." The emphasis on a rational basis for persuasion parallels a distinction made in the literature on persuasion between systematic, reasoned attitude change and changes due to heuristic or unconscious processing of peripheral cues, such as the features of the speaker. For an inventory of heuristic processes relied on by professional persuaders, see Robert B. Cialdini, "Compliance Principles of Compliance Professionals: Psychologists of Necessity," in Mark P. Zanna, James M. Olson, and C. Peter Herman (eds.), *Social Influence: The Ontario Symposium, Vol. 5* (Psychology Press, 1987/2014), pp. 165–184; on the effects of emotional appeals, see Ira Roseman, Robert P. Abelson, and Michael F. Ewing, "Emotion and Political Cognition: Emotional Appeals in Political Communication," in Richard R. Lau and David O. Sears (eds.), *Political Cognition* (Psychology Press, 1986), pp. 279–294. For some, the potential for manipulation makes democracy altogether undesirable. Thus, Thomas Hobbes described democracy as "no more than an aristocracy of orators, interrupted sometimes with the temporary monarchy of one orator" ("De Corpore Politico, or The Elements of the Law: Moral & Politick," in *Hobbs's Tripos, in Three Discourses, 3rd ed.* [Matt. Gilliflower, Henry Rogers Booksellers, 1684], p. 165). Reflecting on this quote, Walzer agrees that "democratic politics is a monopoly of politicians" (*Spheres of Justice*, p. 304). By contrast, I take the view that appropriate norms and group procedures might preclude the outright dominance of the most verbally gifted members of the demos. At the very least, such dominance is far from inevitable even in less than fully democratic groups. At least with regard to participation rates, the ability of structured deliberation to mitigate inequality can be seen in actual groups and forums; see Joseph A. Bonito, John Gastil, Jennifer N. Ervin, and Renee A. Meyers, "At the Convergence of Input and Process Models of Group Discussion: A Comparison of Participation Rates across Time, Persons, and Groups," *Communication Monographs* 81 (2014), pp. 179–207, and Joseph A. Bonito, Renee Meyers, John Gastil, and Jennifer Ervin, "Sit down and Speak up: Stability and Change in Group Participation," in Lyn Carson, John Gastil, Janette Hartz-Karp, and

Ron Lubensky (eds.), The Australian Citizens' Parliament and the Future of Deliberative Democracy (Pennsylvania State University Press, 2013), pp. 120-130.

[82] Robert A. Kraig, *The Hitler Problem in Rhetorical Theory: A Speculative Inquiry* (Unpublished manuscript, University of Wisconsin-Madison, 1992), pp. 42–43. Kraig argues for striking a balance between ends and means, stressing the long-term effects of one's present means. In this view, "The practical application of rhetorical ethics...can be understood as a perpetually unresolved dialectic. A rhetor would be ethical when he/she struggled to discover good and effective means of persuasion in any given case" (p. 42). For a similar view of ends and means, see Peter Bachrach and Aryeh Botwinick, *Power and Empowerment: A Radical Theory of Participatory Democracy* (Temple University Press, 1992), pp. 118–119.

[83] This conception of voting must be distinguished from definitions that limit it to majority rule. Julia T. Wood, for example, distinguishes between "consensus" and "voting" as methods of making decisions; see "Alternative Methods of Group Decision Making," in Robert S. Cathcart and Larry A. Samovar, *Small Group Communication, 5th Ed.* (William C. Brown, 1988), pp. 185–191.

[84] Dahl, *Democracy and Its Critics*, p. 111.

[85] Barber, *Strong Democracy*, pp. 192, 193. The importance of dissent is shown by the ingenuity and determination of subordinate political discourse. Members of subordinate groups frequently attempt to express their opposition even at the risk of severe punishment by authorities. See James C. Scott, *Domination and the Arts of Resistance: Hidden Transcripts* (Yale University Press, 2008), esp. chap. 6. In cases of inescapable oppression, people have no threat of "exit"—only the power of "voice" (what I call dissent). In democratic groups, the commitment to the democratic process implies a willingness to rely on "voice" rather than "exit" so long as the group remains democratic. See Albert O. Hirschman, *Exit, Voice, and Loyalty* (Harvard University Press, 1970).

[86] As Frances Moore Lappé and Paul Martin DuBois insist in "Power in a Living Democracy" (p. 42), "The first art of democracy is active listening." Other authors have also noted the transformative effects of listening and being heard; see Trena M. Cleland, "Living Democracy," *In Context* No. 33 (1992), pp. 35–36, and Harry C. Boyte, *Commonwealth* (The Free Press, 1989), p. 148. For an extended discussion of different kinds of listening and their role in democracy, see Michael Osborn and Suzanne Osborn, *Alliance for a Better Public Voice* (National Issues Forums Institute, 1991).

[87] Once again, this relates to Dahl's aforementioned criterion of enlightened understanding. *Democracy and Its Critics*, pp. 111–112. On the importance of Dahl's Criterion and the dynamic character of preferences (or interests), see James G. March, "Preferences, Power, and Democracy," in Ian Shapiro and Grant Reeher (eds.), *Power, Inequality, and Democratic Politics* (Boulder, CO: Westview Press, 1988), pp. 50–66.

[88] Braybrooke, "Changes of Rules, Issue-circumspection, and Issue-processing," in David Baybrooke (ed.), *Social Rules: Origin, Character, Logic, Change* (Westview Press, 1998), p. 76.

[89] Pollard et al., *Democracy and the Quaker Method*, p. 45.

[90] See Shane J. Ralston, "Dewey and Goodin on the Value of Monological Deliberation," *Ethics & Politics* 12 (2010), pp. 235–255.

[91] Bellah et al., *The Good Society*, p. 254.

[92] Barber, *Strong Democracy*, p. 175.

[93] See Mansbridge, "Feminism and Democracy." Thus, we can't measure deliberation on this basis; see Laura Black et al., "Methods for Analyzing and Measuring Group Deliberation."

[94] Lappé and DuBois, "Power in a Living Democracy," p. 42. On listening affecting the listener, see also Brenda Ueland, "Tell Me More: On the Fine Art of Listening," *Utne Reader* No. 54 (November/December 1992), pp. 104–109.

[95] Dahl, *Democracy and Its Critics*, p. 131.

Chapter 3

[1] The fact that the "tyranny of the majority" is a perennial problem associated with the democratic process underscores the historical association of democracy with simple majority rule. See, for example, Robert A. Dahl, *Democracy and Its Critics* (Yale University Press, 1989), pp. 171–173. For this reason alone, it is important to stress that small group democracy encompasses different decision rules, including consensus and proportional outcomes. In the original addition, those were the only ones included, but in this second addition, I have added random selection, which has a long tradition in democratic politics; see Lyn Carson and Brian Martin, *Random Selection in Politics* (Greenwood, 1999).

[2] Unspoken disagreement on procedure can be seen in zero-history groups, such as those in Kevin L. Sager and John Gastil, "Reaching Consensus on Consensus: A Study of the Relationships Between Individual Decision-making Styles and Use of the Consensus Decision Rule," *Communication Quarterly* 47:1 (1999), pp. 67–79. More subtle differences in the interpretations of norms and rules can also arise even in the most highly structured parliamentary groups or the most intimate consensus-based groups.

[3] Quote from Michel Avery, Barbara Stribel, Brian Auvine and Lonnie Weiss, *Building United Judgment* (Center for Conflict Resolution, 1981), p. 1. For an academic history of consensus, see W. K. Rawlins, "Consensus in Decision-making Groups: A Conceptual History," in Gerald M. Phillips and Julia T. Wood (eds.), *Emergent Issues in Human Decision Making* (Southern Illinois University Press, 1984), pp. 19–39. For the history of consensus in political theory and a critical evaluation of it, see Douglas W. Rae, "The Limits of Consensual Decision," *American*

Political Science Review 69:4 (1975), pp. 1270–1294. For a more positive view, see Kirkpatrick Sale, *Human Scale* (G. P. Putnam's Sons, 1980), pp. 501–504.

[4] On Quaker decision making, see Michael J. Sheeran, *Beyond Majority Rule* (Philadelphia Yearly Meeting, 1983); Francis E. Pollard, Beatrice E. Pollard, and Robert S. W. Pollard, *Democracy and the Quaker Method* (Ballinsdale, 1949). On the usefulness of the Quaker method for other groups, see Pollard et al., Ibid., chap. 5. On other quasi-democratic decision making procedures with a heavy spiritual influence, numerous examples are provided in Corinne McLaughlin and Gordon Davidson, *Builders of the Dawn: Community Lifestyles in a Changing World* (Sirius Publishing, 1986). Many Quakers don't view their decision-making process as an example of "consensus" or "democracy." For these Friends, the religious element makes the Quaker process distinct; for example, see the letters under "Not Just Consensus" in *Friends Journal* (February, 1993), p. 5. One unique feature of the Quaker method, as opposed to most versions of consensus in use, is the powerful role of the clerk of the Meeting. Sheeran, in *Beyond Majority Rule*, writes at length about the clerk's responsibility for "discerning" the "sense of the meeting"—and the potential for abusing this responsibility. Some Quaker meetings have procedural safeguards against a clerk's ability to distort decisions, such as a one-fifth vote to overrule the clerk's decision; see, for example, Pollard et al., *Democracy and the Quaker Method*, p. 144.

[5] These guidelines, purportedly written by William Bacon Evans, are adapted from the *Powell House Newsletter* 1 (August, 1964). I thank Christopher Densmore for bringing them to my attention.

[6] That gesture was popularized during the Occupy Wall Street movement. Alex Klein, "Jazz Hands and Waggling Fingers: How Occupy Wall Street Makes Decisions," *Daily Intelligencer* (October 12, 2011), accessed June 20, 2014. The "Occupy movement hand signals" Wikipedia page provides even more detail on the meaning of these gestures.

[7] Consensus can be used with a set of highly structured procedures or a more anarchistic approach. For examples of each, see descriptions of Philadelphia's Movement for a New Society and the Auroville Community in South India in McLaughlin and Davidson, *Builders of the Dawn*, pp. 162–168, 173–178. For an at length description of a methodical discussion procedure that draws on consensus principles, see Bruno Lasker, *Democracy Through Discussion* (H. W. Wilson Co., 1949), part III. As a cautionary note, at least one investigation has found that inexperienced consensus groups using unstructured discussion methods have more difficulty integrating the information held by different group members; see Garold Stasser and William Titus, "Pooling of Unshared Information in Group Decision Making: Biased Information Sampling During Discussion," *Journal of Personality and Social Psychology* 48:6 (1985), pp. 1467–1478.

[8] Advocates of consensus sometimes give "compromise" a pejorative meaning, contrasting it with the pursuit of a genuine common ground. It is in this sense that

Pollard et al. insist that Quaker business meetings don't have "any special tendency to result in mere compromise between different points of view"; *Democracy and the Quaker Method*, p. 61.

[9] Sheeran, *Beyond Majority Rule*, pp. 65–71. On blocking consensus and the alternatives to blocking, see Avery, Stribel, Auvine and Weiss, *Building United Judgment*, chap. 5.

[10] Mary Ann Renz, "The Meaning of Consensus and Blocking for Cohousing Groups" *Small Group Research* 37:4 (2006), pp. 351–76.

[11] On full veto power and the U.N. Security Council, see Jane J. Mansbridge, *Beyond Adversary Democracy* (University of Chicago Press, 1983), chap. 18. In Julia T. Wood's terminology, the U.N. format is closer to "negotiation" than consensus, because it involves no attempt to find common ground or create a collective identity; see "Alternative Methods of Group Decision Making," in Robert S. Cathcart and Larry A. Samovar (eds.), *Small Group Communication: a Reader, 5th Ed.* (William C. Brown, 1988), 187–188.

[12] The dearth of research on group-chosen decision rules is remarkable given the importance of this choice for groups, and the absence of primary studies of this sort accounts for the absence of a useful meta-analysis on the subject. Some point out that most of the research on consensus and small groups treats "consensus" as an outcome—a product of group discussion rather than a group process. Thus, the majority of studies on small group consensus are not relevant to the question of how the consensus process affects groups and their members. See RoLayne S. DeStephen and Randy Y. Hirokawa, "Small Group Consensus: Stability of Group Support of the Decision, Task Process, and Group Relationships," *Small Group Behavior* 19:2 (1988), pp. 227–239; also see Sager and Gastil, "Reaching Consensus on Consensus." One variable I don't discuss is the "productivity" of groups using a consensus, majority rule, or proportional outcomes decision rules. "Productivity" is a rather broad variable, and the few studies that have compared majority rule and consensus are far from conclusive on the question. See Randy Y. Hirokawa, "Does Consensus Really Result in Higher Quality Group Decisions?" in Gerald M. Phillips and Julia T. Wood (eds.), *Emergent Issues in Human Decision Making* (Southern Illinois University Press, 1984), pp. 40–49. Consensus may be more advantageous in a group negotiation context, since it tends to result in more mutually beneficial decisions. Two recent studies have produced evidence supporting this view; Leigh L. Thompson, Elizabeth Mannix, and Max H. Bazerman, "Group Negotiation: Effects of Decision Rule, Agenda, and Aspiration," *Journal of Personality and Social Psychology* 54:1 (1988), pp. 86–95; and Elizabeth Mannix, Leigh L. Thompson, and Max H. Bazerman, "Negotiation in Small Groups," *Journal of Applied Psychology* 74:3 (1989), pp. 508–517. Like these two articles, the vast majority of social scientific studies cited herein have been conducted with groups of college students. In the typical design, the group members have little or no experience working with one another. These factors make many studies somewhat artificial, a problem that has plagued research on small

groups for decades, as small group communication scholar Ernest G. Bormann has observed on more than one occasion; "The Paradox and Promise of Small Group Research," *Speech Monographs* 37:3 (1970), pp. 211–216; "The Paradox and Promise of Small Group Communication Revisited," *Central States Speech Journal* 31:3 (1980), pp. 214–220. This conventional methodology also makes it more difficult to generalize the findings to the full variety of group settings—most of which don't consist of three or four unacquainted college students discussing a hypothetical problem for one or more hours. Nonetheless, the careful research designs in many of these studies make their findings suggestive or, at the very least, thought-provoking. I encourage readers to conduct their own inclusive and contextually sensitive research on small group democracy. There is little research on the subject, per se, and careful study of existing groups would greatly improve our understanding of the democratic process in small groups. As for the social scientists in this area, a movement has begun toward doing more ethnographic research on groups; see, for example, Larry R. Frey, *Group Communication in Context: Studies of Bona Fide Groups* (Psychology Press, 2004).

[13] A wealth of evidence supports the notion that, on average, group members are more satisfied with the consensus method than with majority rule. See Charlan Nemeth, "Interactions Between Jurors as a Function of Majority vs. Unanimity Decision Rules," *Journal of Applied Social Psychology* 7:1 (1977), pp. 38–56; Martin F. Kaplan and Charles E. Miller, "Group Decision Making and Normative Versus Informational Influence: Effects of Type of Issue and Assigned Decision Rule," *Journal of Personality and Social Psychology* 53:2 (1987), pp. 306–313. A similar study reports the same findings and also notes that even group members holding the minority viewpoint were more satisfied with the decisions reached in consensus groups than in those using majority rule; Norbert L. Kerr, Robert S. Atkin, Garold Stasser, David Meek, Robert W. Holt, James H. Davis, "Guilt Beyond a Reasonable Doubt: Effects of Concept Definition and Assigned Decision Rule on the Judgments of Mock Jurors," *Journal of Personality and Social Psychology* 34:2 (1976), pp. 282–294.

[14] John Gastil, E. Pierre Deess, Philip J. Weiser, and Cindy Simmons, *The Jury and Democracy: How Jury Deliberation Promotes Civic Engagement and Political Participation* (Oxford University Press, 2010).

[15] See Lynne Kelly and Cynthia F. Begnal, "Group Members' Orientations Toward Decision Processes," in Gerald M. Phillips and Julia T. Wood (eds.), *Emergent Issues in Human Decision Making* (Southern Illinois University Press, 1984), pp. 63–79.

[16] Some of the best contemporary work on the micro-dynamics of small group democracy comes from experimental work, such as Christopher F. Karpowitz, Tali Mendelberg, and Lee Shaker, "Gender Inequality in Deliberative Participation," *American Political Science Review* 106:3 (2012), pp. 533–547. That particular study shows that under majority rule, women have equal voice only when they make up a

sizeable proportion of the members; under consensus procedure, the equality norm prevails regardless.

[17] Critics of consensus maintain that the process suppresses conflict, preventing the airing of minority viewpoints. In this view, majority rule is a better method for ensuring that the minority has its say. For evidence supporting this view, see Gideon Falk, "An Empirical Study Measuring Conflict in Problem-solving Groups Which Are Assigned Different Decision Rules," *Human Relations* 35:12 (1982), pp. 1123–1138. In a similar study, Gideon and Shoshana Falk also argue that majority rule is better than a unanimity rule at minimizing the influence of the most powerful group member; "The Impact of Decision Rules on the Distribution of Power in Problem-solving Teams with Unequal Power," *Group and Organization Studies* 6:2 (1981), pp. 211–223.

[18] Studies finding greater commitment to consensus group decisions include Nemeth, "Interactions Between Jurors," Dean Tjosvold and Richard H. G. Field, "Effects of Social Context on Consensus and Majority Vote Decision Making," *Academy of Management Journal* 26:3 (1983), pp. 500–506.

[19] Warren Watson, Larry K. Michaelsen, and Walt Sharp, "Member Competence, Group Interaction, and Group Decision Making: A Longitudinal Study," *Journal of Applied Psychology* 76:6 (1991), pp. 803–809. Some critics hold that consensus is inherently flawed. For a brief, impassioned argument against consensus, see D. G. Clark, "Consensus or Stalemate?" *National Parliamentarian* 53:1 (1992), p. 7.

[20] Anne Gero identifies the existence of an "antidisagreement norm" in her study of business and social work students, "Conflict Avoidance in Consensual Decision Processes," *Small Group Behavior* 16:4 (1985), pp. 487-499.

[21] Quantitative studies of inexperienced groups support this view. For instance, comparisons of majority rule and consensus mock juries have found that consensus groups take more time to reach decisions; Nemeth, "Interactions Between Jurors;" Kerr et al., "Guilt Beyond a Reasonable Doubt;" Charles E. Miller, "Group Decision Making under Majority and Unanimity Decision Rules," *Social Psychology Quarterly* 48:1 (1985), pp. 51–61. In addition, qualitative studies of experienced consensus groups, such as the Clamshell Alliance, have found that the process tends to take more time; see Gary L. Downey, "Ideology and the Clamshell Identity: Organizational Dilemmas in the Anti-nuclear Power Movement," *Social Problems* 33:5 (1986), pp. 357–373. The simplest theoretical explanation for why consensus takes longer than majority rule is that it is usually easier to get a smaller number of people to agree; thus, in groups of equal size, consensus requires more people to agree (or, at least, accept a decision); see Benjamin Radcliff, "Majority Rule and Impossibility Theorems," *Social Science Quarterly* 73:3 (1992), p. 515.

[22] The argument that time spent on one issue takes it away from deliberation on another comes from Thomas Christiano, "Freedom, Consensus, and Equality in Collective Decision Making," *Ethics* 101:1 (1990), p. 167.

[23] Jane J. Mansbridge, "A Paradox of Size," in C. George Benello, *From the Ground Up* (South End Press, 1992), p. 166. To counterbalance the tendency to favor the status quo, a group can put expiration dates on its decisions. Caroline Estes explains that Alpha Farm makes "temporary decisions on a number of occasions, usually trying the decision for a year and then either making a final decision or dropping it entirely;" "Consensus Ingredients," in Fellowship for Intentional Community and Communities Publications Cooperative (eds.), *Intentional Communities: A Guide to Cooperative Living* (Communities Publications Cooperative, 1990), p. 81. This "favoritism toward the status quo" can also be viewed as caution, which is entirely appropriate in many contexts. For instance, a study using actual jurors found that after watching a videotape of a trial, groups using consensus were more likely than groups using majority rule to reach not guilty or hung verdicts (relatively cautious, compared to guilty verdicts); Robert Buckhout, Steve Weg, and Vincent Reilly, "Jury Verdicts: Comparison of 6- vs. 12-Person Juries and Unanimous vs. Majority Decision Rule in a Murder Trial," *Bulletin of the Psychonomic Society* 10:3 (1977), pp. 175–178.

[24] For this insight I owe thanks to Mary Giovagnoli. The classic on parliamentary procedure is Henry M. Robert, *Robert's Rules of Order Newly Revised, 11th Ed.* (Da Capo Press, 2011). A popular, more streamlined alternative is Alice Sturgis, *Standard Code of Parliamentary Procedure, 4th Ed.* (McGraw-Hill, 2000). For a general critique of the majority rule method of decision making in small groups, see Avery, Stribel, Auvine and Weiss, *Building United Judgment*, pp. 4–7.

[25] This is a longstanding argument against majority rule. If one presumes that, at a given point in time, people have different preferences, majority rule, compared to all other decision rules, is the most responsive to individual preferences (presuming the body has an odd number of members and the choice is among only two alternatives); Philip D. Straffin, Jr., "Majority Rule and General Decision Rules," *Theory and Decision* 8:4 (1977), pp. 351–360. If one ignores the role of deliberation and changing preferences, this can be proven mathematically; see Straffin, "Majority Rule," and Mark Gradstein, "Conditions for the Optimality of Simple Majority Decisions in Pairwise Choice Situations," *Theory and Decision* 21:2 (1986), pp. 181–187. A more readable presentation of this view is provided by Bruce Ackerman, *Social Justice in the Liberal State* (Yale University Press, 1980), chap. 9. Ackerman uses rather humorous dialogues to make the case for using majority rule when "good-faith" disagreements exist.

[26] Once again, it is useful to think of these decision rules as a technology imperfectly adopted by groups, to varying degrees. Though developed in relation to more sophisticated technologies, the structurational approach to technology adoption is apt when thinking about groups failing to use decision rules effectively. See Gerardine Desanctis and Marshall Scott Poole, "Capturing the Complexity in Advanced Technology Use: Adaptive Structuration Theory," *Organization Science* 5:2 (1994), pp. 121–147.

---

[27] On the mutually reinforcing relationship between unstable majorities and pluralist politics, see Nicholas R. Miller, "Pluralism and Social Choice," *American Political Science Review* 77:3 (1983), pp. 734–747. On a large social scale, Northern Ireland provides an example of the fate of a permanent minority; see Anthony Arblaster, *Democracy* (Open University Press, 1987), pp. 70–72. When the composition of the majority does not change over time and the views of the opposition are markedly different from those of the majority, a proportional outcome scheme, discussed below, might be a more democratic method of decision making. In developing this idea, I drew on Arend Lijphart, *Democracies: Patterns of Majoritarian and Consensus Governments in Twenty-One Countries* (Yale University Press, 1984), pp. 21–23. He has updated that with his newer volume, *Patterns of Democracy: Government Forms and Performance in Thirty-Six Countries* (Yale University Press, 2012). A related concept in the group and organizational literature is the idea of a fault line that divides subgroups, often to the detriment of the smaller one; see Dora C. Lau and J. Keith Murnighan, "Interactions Within Groups and Subgroups: The Effects of Demographic Faultlines," *Academy of Management Journal* 48 (2005), pp. 645–659.

[28] See Alfie Kohn, *No Contest* (Houghton Mifflin, 1986).

[29] Robert H. McKenzie, "Learning to Deliberate and Choose," *Public Leadership Education* 4 (1991), p. 11.

[30] In response to a majority court opinion, a dissenting Supreme Court justice expressed this view: "It is said that there is no evidence that majority jurors will refuse to listen to dissenters whose votes are unneeded for conviction. Yet human experience teaches that polite and academic conversation is no substitute for the earnest and robust argument necessary to reach unanimity." Those words are from Justice Douglass, with Justices Marshall and Brennan, in *Johnson v. Louisiana*, 406 U.S. 356, 389 (1972), quoted in Nemeth, "Interactions Between Jurors," p. 40. In a study investigating this issue, Nemeth found some support for Justice Douglass' view; consensus groups engaged in more conflict and participants were more likely to change their minds. Similarly, Kerr et al., in "Guilt Beyond a Reasonable Doubt," found that in half of the mock juries using majority rule, deliberation was ended after the first decisive poll, despite the presence of a vocal minority. More generally, the very nature of majority rule makes it more likely that minority viewpoints will emerge and be dominated by majorities. Thompson et al. ("Group Negotiation") found that majority-rule negotiation groups were more likely to form dominant coalitions and reach decisions that worked against the interests of group minorities.

[31] Leon Mann, Charlotte Tan, Crisetta MacLeod-Morgan, and Anne Dixon, "Developmental Changes in Application of the Majority Rule in Group Decisions," *British Journal of Developmental Psychology* 2:3 (1984), pp. 275–281.

[32] On the application of the proportionality principle, see Arend Lijphart, *Democracy in Plural Societies* (Yale University Press, 1977), pp. 38–41. The proportional outcome approach to decision making has proven effective in the past, even for large-scale social groups, such as Switzerland and The Netherlands, both of which

use "consociational" political systems that incorporate proportional outcomes. See Lijphart, *Democracies* and *Democracy in Plural Societies*; Mansbridge, *Beyond Adversary Democracy*, pp. 265–268.

[33] The proportional outcomes method is probably closer to consensus than majority rule; thus, Lijphart's definition of the "consensus model of democracy," which includes proportional outcomes, is contrasted with majority rule; see *Democracies*, pp. 23–30.

[34] Mannix et al. ("Negotiation in Small Groups") conducted a direct test of the benefits of sequential-agendas versus package agendas (simultaneously reaching decisions on different issues, making them part of a single agenda item). They found that package agendas resulted in more mutually beneficial decisions for the members of small negotiation groups, whether the groups used majority rule or consensus decision rules.

[35] On the disadvantages of proportional outcomes and consociationalism in large-scale systems, see Lijphart, *Democracy in Plural Societies*, pp. 47–52.

[36] This discussion is adapted from my book *The Group in Society* (2010) with the permission of Sage Publications.

[37] On random selection in politics, see Carson and Martin, *Random Selection in Politics*. Perry Deess (personal communication, March 11, 2008) reminded me that the drawing of straws, in particular, often serves to assign an unpleasant task—a kind of election that nobody wants to win.

[38] Sue Major Holmes, "Tied Elections a Game of Chance in New Mexico," *Associated Press* (November 17, 2000).

[39] Acts 1: 20–26 (New International Version). Heather Serrano conducted background research on this topic.

[40] For a discussion on multichoice and two-step voting formats, see Benjamin Barber, *Strong Democracy* (University of California Press, 1984), pp. 286–289. For a more detailed discussion of the multichoice format and its use in Switzerland, see Benjamin Barber, *The Death of Communal Liberty* (Princeton University Press, 1974).

[41] See James Lull and Joseph Cappella, "Slicing the Attitude Pie: A New Approach to Attitude Measurement," *Communication Quarterly* 29:2 (1981), pp. 67–80; Bernard Manin, "On Legitimacy and Political Deliberation," trans. Elly Stein and Jane Mansbridge, *Political Theory* 15:3 (1987), p. 350.

[42] In fact, the existence of multiple alternatives raises a problem for majority rule voting. If head-to-head votes show that majorities favor A over B, favor B over C, and favor C over A, which is the preferred policy? For a clear discussion of this problem, see Dahl, *Democracy and Its Critics*, pp. 144–146. This paradox is irresolvable, but, as Benjamin Radcliff argues in "Majority Rule and Impossibility Theorems," this should be seen as a limitation on democratic bodies using majority rule—not as a reason to abandon such a process.

---

[43] I thank George Gastil for providing detailed information on the "Earlham '85" ballots.

[44] This case will be discussed more in Chapter 8. See Mark Warren and Hilary Pearse (eds.), *Designing Deliberative Democracy: The British Columbia Citizens' Assembly* (Cambridge University Press, 2008).

[45] See James H. Davis, Mark Stasson, Kaoru Ono, and Suzi Zimmerman, "Effects of Straw Polls on Group Decision Making: Sequential Voting Pattern, Timing and Local Majorities," *Journal of Personality and Social Psychology* 55:6 (1988), pp. 918–926; James H. Davis, Tatsuya Kameda, Craig Parks, Mark Stasson, and Suzi Zimmerman, "Some Social Mechanics of Group Decision Making: The Distribution of Opinion, Polling Sequence, and Implications for Consensus," *Journal of Personality and Social Psychology* 57:6 (1989), pp. 1000–1012.

[46] Social choice theorists, rather soberly, refer to deceptive voting behavior as "strategic voting." On its unavoidability, see David Miller, "Deliberative Democracy and Social Choice," *Political Studies* 40:s1 (1992), pp. 58–59.

[47] Some of the details of Martha's Rules of Order have changed over the years. The namesake cooperative, Martha's Co-op, currently uses a different version. I thank Jeff Haines for clarifying the details of Martha's Rules. For brief summaries of Martha's Rules and other alternative procedures, see Avery, Stribel, Auvine and Weiss, *Building United Judgment*, pp. 101–106. Some critics of procedures like Martha's Rules argue that it is an "impure" form of consensus, because it allows a majority to rule. In response, many ardent advocates of consensus emphasize that consensus does not require unanimity. Defining it as such underemphasizes the importance of practices such as "standing aside" from a decision. See Virginia Coover, Ellen Deacon, Charles Esser, and Christopher Moore, *Resource Manual for a Living Revolution* (New Society Publishers, 1978), pp. 52–53; Estes, "Consensus Ingredients," pp. 80–81.

Chapter 4

[1] Quoted in Seymour M. Lipset, Martin Trow, and James Coleman, *Union Democracy* (Anchor, 1956), p. 463.

[2] At the staff's request, I have used pseudonyms for the names of the staff members, but not for the store. I ask readers to respect the anonymity of the staff. To maintain that anonymity, I have refrained from providing richer personal descriptions of individual staff members. These relatively impersonal presentations might leave the reader with the impression that the staff members are, in Ray's words, "worker drones." Rest assured: The staff lead normal lives outside work. For those who for some reason read my Masters thesis, I changed two pseudonyms since I first discussed Mifflin Co-op in "Democratic Deliberation: A Redefinition of the

Democratic Process and a Study of Staff Meetings at a Co-Operative Workplace," *Masters Abstracts* 30-04M (1992), 1114 (University Microfilms No. 1348177). "Laura" was previously "Lulu," and "Norma" was referred to as "Sarah." Lulu was, admittedly, a silly name to use. My bad. I have no recollection of why Sarah was problematic. To any Sarah reading this and taking offense, remember that there's no accounting for taste.

[3] The quote comes from page 3 of Michael Bodden's history of the Co-op, which was originally distributed as a stapled, unpublished booklet with the title, *A Twenty Year History of the Mifflin Street Community Co-op* (1990). The out-of-print history was posted more than a decade later, after perhaps a light edit, as *People's History: A History of the Mifflin Street Community Co-op* (Unpublished, 1992). Bodden's history of the Co-op is an important document, simply because it exists. As Dennis K. Mumby explains, organizational narratives do more than "simply inform organization members about the values, practices, and traditions to which their organization is committed. Rather, they help to constitute the organizational consciousness of social actors by articulating and by embodying a particular reality, and subordinating or devaluing other modes of 'organizational rationality.'" In this sense, Mifflin Co-op's democratic features are partly a result of its historical image as a democratic organization. See "The Political Function of Narrative in Organizations," *Communication Monographs* 54:2 (1987), p. 125.

[4] Mifflin's decision to employ a democratic method of decision making relates to the decision tree in Figure 1. The staff's decisions are of concern to all group members, whose interests are considered equal. Staff are also willing to presume that each member is competent and committed to preserving the democratic process. While the staff is concerned with the store's financial prosperity, it believes that this goal is best served by using a democratic system. In addition, the staff's statement of purpose views fully democratic decision making as an end in itself; the Mifflin staff hopes to serve as an example for other co-ops.

[5] In my thesis ("Democratic Deliberation," pp. 68–72), I discuss in more detail the process I used to select Mifflin Co-op over other groups. For other examples of communities pursuing democratic methods of decision making, see John Case and Rosemary C. R. Taylor (eds.), *Co-ops, Communes, and Collectives: Experiments in Social Change in the 1960s and 1970s* (Pantheon Books, 1979); Corinne McLaughlin and Gordon Davidson, *Builders of the Dawn: Community Lifestyles in a Changing World* (Sirius Publishing, 1986); Elaine Sundancer, *Celery Wine: The Story of a Country Commune* (Community Publications Cooperative, 1973), pp. 91–94; Arthur E. Morgan, *The Small Community: Foundation of Democratic Life* (Transaction Books, 2013); and Richard Fairfield (ed.), *The Modern Utopian: Alternative Communities of the '60s and '70s* (Process, 2010). On Quaker business meetings, see Michael J. Sheeran, *Beyond Majority Rule* (Philadelphia Yearly Meeting, 1983). A wonderful volume on decision-making processes in community/political action is Francesca Polletta, *Freedom Is an Endless Meeting: Democracy in American Social*

Movements (University of Chicago Press, 2002); see also Case and Taylor, *Co-ops, Communes, and Collectives*; Gary L. Downey, "Ideology and the Clamshell Identity: Organizational Dilemmas in the Anti-nuclear Power Movement," *Social Problems* 33:5 (1986), pp. 357–373; Jane J. Mansbridge, *Beyond Adversary Democracy* (University of Chicago Press, 1983); the drafting of the Port Huron Statement in James Miller, *Democracy Is in the Streets: From Port Huron to the Siege of Chicago* (Simon & Schuster, 1987); Sara M. Evans and Harry C. Boyte, *Free Spaces* (Harper & Row, 1992). Among the many existing case studies of democracy in larger workplaces are those on Spain's Mondragon cooperatives; see Roy Morrison, *We Build the Road as We Travel* (New Society Publishers, 1991); William F. Whyte and Kathleen K. Whyte, *Making Mondragon: The Growth and Dynamics of the Worker Cooperative Complex* (ILR Press, 1988); C. George Benello, *From the Ground Up* (South End Press, 1992), chap. 8. See also Len Krimerman and Frank Lindenfeld, *When Workers Decide: Workplace Democracy Takes Root in America* (New Society Publishers, 1991), Lipset et al., *Union Democracy*, and Mansbridge, *Beyond Adversary Democracy*. For case studies from the field of social work with relevance to small group democracy, see Judith A. B. Lee (ed.), *Group Work with the Poor and Oppressed* (Haworth Press, 1989); Erik K. Laursen and Thomas F. Tate, "Democratic Group Work," *Reclaiming Children and Youth* 20:4 (2012), pp. 46–51. Examples of attempts to conduct classrooms and schools democratically can be found in Walter Parker, *Teaching Democracy: Unity and Diversity in Public Life* (Teachers College Press, 2003), and Mary A. Hepburn (ed.), *Democratic Education in Schools and Classrooms* (National Council for the Social Studies, 1983), chaps. 3, 4, and 6.

[6] Helen Schwartzman, *The Meeting: Gatherings in Organizations and Communities* (Plenum, 1989), p. 239.

[7] Whenever a researcher makes observations, it is important to gauge the effect of the observation on the observed. In the case of Mifflin Co-op, the staff and I concluded that the presence of cameras didn't have a large net effect on deliberation during meetings. For further discussion of this issue, see Gastil, "Democratic Deliberation," pp. 123–126. For additional reading on case-study methodology, see Robert K. Yin, *Case Study Research, 5th Ed.* (Sage, 2013), and John Brewer and Albert Hunter, *Multimethod Research: A Synthesis of Styles* (Sage, 1989). Though my methodology involved soliciting staff feedback on several occasions, I take sole responsibility for this portrayal of Mifflin Co-op.

[8] Quotes from a September 21, 2014 interview with Norm Stockwell.

[9] Like any other social entity, the staff was surely influenced by cultural forces, which I discuss in relation to communication styles in Chapter 5 and more broadly in Chapter 6. Staff could have identified additional ways they would have liked to change the store, were it not for the social disapproval (and loss of customers) such changes would create; for a further discussion of external constraints on group democracy, see Chapter 6.

[10] I once observed a community improvement group meeting where the group members arranged themselves in a circle, with the exception of one member, who sat just outside the circle. The room permitted this woman to join the circle, but she chose to sit outside it. During the meeting, group members made little eye contact with her, and the few times she tried speaking, she was usually ignored. The woman sitting outside the circle had the same formal status as the other members, yet during the meeting I observed, she was clearly an outsider, both figuratively and literally. In the decades since, I have witnessed many groups with inner and outer rings, particularly within universities; those in the outer ring, often arranged along the walls of the room, do speak up, but it is a safe bet that those seated "at the table" are more likely to speak and exercise influence in the discussion. The seating arrangement may lack independent causal force; it may simply be another indicator of pre-existing differences in power (or interest) in the group process. That said, the question begs for an experimental test. For tips for using space democratically, see Rick Arnold, Bev Burke, Carl James, D'Arcy Martin, and Barb Thomas, *Educating for a Change* (Doris Marshall Institute for Education and Action, 1991), pp. 118–119. For academic discussions of the significance of seating and other features of the physical group setting, see: Judee K. Burgoon, "Spatial Relationships in Small Groups," in Robert S. Cathcart and Larry A. Samovar (eds.), *Small Group Communication, 5th Ed.* (William C. Brown, 1988), pp. 351–366; and L. L. Cummings, George P. Huber, and Eugene Arendt, "Effects of Size and Spatial Arrangements on Group Decision Making," *Academy of Management Journal* 17:3 (1974), pp. 460–475.

[11] To make this chapter more concise and readable, excerpts from the transcripts have been edited. In many cases, redundancies, filled pauses (e.g., "um," "uh"), and digressions have been removed, and grammatical errors have been corrected. For unedited excerpts, see Gastil, "Democratic Deliberation."

[12] Though tempted to condense them with ellipses, I chose to leave the Co-op dialogues exactly the same in this second edition as in the first. I do so for the sake of continuity.

[13] A verbal commitment to democracy can't be taken for granted. One might presume that most U.S. citizens could identify fundamental democratic principles, but in-depth interviews with citizens have revealed widely varying abilities to articulate the meaning of democracy. See Michael Binford, "The Democratic Political Personality: Functions of Attitudes and Styles of Reasoning," *Political Psychology* 4:4 (1983), pp. 663–684; Robert E. Lane, *Political Ideology* (The Free Press, 1962). Shawn W. Rosenberg, Dana Ward, and Stephen Chilton, *Political Reasoning and Cognition* (Duke University Press, 1988), esp. chap. 4; and Pamela Johnston Conover, Ivor M. Crewe, and Donald D. Searing, "The Nature of Citizenship in the United States and Great Britain: Empirical Comments on Theoretical Themes," *Journal of Politics* 53:3 (1991), pp. 800–832. Some groups will openly express hostility towards democracy, and others will hint at such disdain. I have observed more than one group that was

ostensibly democratic but governed rather autocratically, with the chair acknowledging this as though it were a jest or point of pride.

[14] Mifflin Co-op staff agreed to participate in my Masters thesis research on the condition that I seek publication of its findings. When I started to revise the thesis into a book, they and I both had the same press in mind—New Society Publishers, which was itself co-operative business. New Society published the first edition and marketed it successfully, to the delight of the staff, who have in this book left a legacy that, unfortunately, outlived the Co-op itself.

[15] For a lengthy discussion of the coding methodology I employed, see Gastil, "Democratic Deliberation," pp. 90–110. For suggesting additional ways of observing relational communication and deliberation, I would like to thank the Mifflin staff and some of my former students, including Kevin Fischer, Cathy Pollack, Sarah Mohs, and Brian Costigan.

[16] This brief description of nonverbal behavior at Mifflin Co-op does not do justice to the rich information that is available in a group's nonverbal behavior. See Peter A. Anderson, "Nonverbal Communication in the Small Group," in Robert S. Cathcart and Larry A. Samovar (eds.), *Small Group Communication, 5th Ed.* (William C. Brown, 1988), pp. 333–350. Nonverbal behavior often proves less tractable than one might expect, with ambiguous meanings and effects; see, for example, Judith A. Hall, Erik J. Coats, and Lavonia Smith LeBeau, "Nonverbal Behavior and the Vertical Dimension of Social Relations: A Meta-analysis." *Psychological Bulletin* 131:6 (2005), pp. 898–924. Nonetheless, efforts are afoot to automate the coding of nonverbals, which could produce sufficiently rich datasets to reveal a more powerful role for these variables; see Daniel Gatica-Perez, "Automatic Nonverbal Analysis of Social Interaction in Small Groups: A Review," *Image and Vision Computing* 27:12 (2009), pp. 1775–1787.

[17] In a September 21, 2014 interview, former co-op member Norm Stockwell noted that "the 'turnips' benefits system wound up being the same one adopted by WORT-FM years later." He currently works at that community radio station where they simply call these benefits "longevity bonuses." He explained that "it's a lump-sum bonus based on the number of hours you worked rather than some arbitrary validation of your worth as an employee." The main difference is that the radio station "doesn't have a vegetable name for it."

[18] This was not the only time that Co-op staff made self-conscious references to democracy in the presence of my cameras, but it was the only instance that doing so sounded, to my ears, as a self-serving appropriation of the language of democracy.

[19] The tension between individuality and mutuality is commonplace in many small egalitarian groups. The section on unequal involvement and commitment in Chapter 5 provides further discussion of this problem at Mifflin Co-op. For examples of this tension in other groups, see McLaughlin and Davidson, *Builders of the Dawn*, pp. 62–65. For a theoretical discussion of this tension, see Kenwyn K. Smith and David N.

Berg, "A Paradoxical Conception of Group Dynamics," *Human Relations* 40:10 (1987), pp. 633–658.

[20]Amy, Kate, and others questioned Norma's interpretation of the grandfather clause. I investigated the matter by reading records from past Co-op meetings, but these proved inadequate: Notes from the critical meeting are not sufficiently precise to resolve the issue. That discovery reminded the Co-op staff (and me) of the need for more vigilant note-taking during meetings.

[21] That said, she did leave shortly thereafter, though almost all of the other staff moved on from their Co-op jobs in the course of a decade.

[22] The numbers in Figure 2 are adjusted for imbalances in absences and the performance of facilitation and notetaking duties. See Gastil, "Democratic Deliberation," pp. 108–110.

[23] On the importance of interruptions and their varied forms in group discussions, see Lynn Smith-Lovin and Charles Brody, "Interruptions in Group Discussions: The Effects of Gender and Group Composition," *American Sociological Review* 54:3 (1989), pp. 424–435. On gender effects more generally in group deliberation, see Christopher F. Karpowitz, Tali Mendelberg, and Lee Shaker, "Gender Inequality in Deliberative Participation," *American Political Science Review* 106:3 (2012), pp. 533–547.

[24] Sam and Laura may have spoken less than others, but they were capable of influencing the group. These two were candidates for group clowns, since they had developed a knack for playing with language and drawing laughter. As just one example, Sam and Laura played a role in popularizing the term "turnip," a name that has become the sole label for the Co-op policy I have called "tenure incentives." As Robert D. Rossel argues, "Laughter is an acknowledgment by others that an individual has momentarily gained the upper hand against the conventions of language, and thus of reality by means of linguistic artistry—for the moment persuading the rest that things are not as they seem.... One indicator of the pecking order in a group may be a simple assessment of whose statements are laughed at by whom.... In addition, some individuals are more capable than others of coining words that capture the moment and go on to become widely distributed tokens in the group.... This ability to coin new words and cultivate special meanings that become part of the group vocabulary is often associated with the ability to get people to laugh." Quote from Rossel's article, "Word Play: Metaphor and Humor in the Small Group," *Small Group Behavior* 12 (1981), pp. 130–133. The humor surrounding "turnips" also provided some ambiguity that can be productive for groups working through difficult questions; see Joann Keyton and Stephenson J. Beck, "Examining Laughter Functionality in Jury Deliberations," *Small Group Research* 41 (2010), pp. 386-407.

[25] During the six meetings I observed, staff members never dissented, but since the Co-op made most decisions through consensus, this is not surprising. Nevertheless, dissent does occur on occasion. Under its system of consensus, the Co-op allows a

staff member to accept a decision without endorsing it. This happened in the case of tenure incentives, with Louis accepting but disagreeing with the final decision. After the last meeting I observed, Louis did choose to express his disagreement with the decision after it had been finalized. As a result, the staff reopened the issue for further discussion and revised its policy.

[26] On the use of these and other linguistic devices in political discourse, see John Gastil, "Undemocratic Discourse: A Review of Theory and Research on Political Discourse," *Discourse & Society* 3:4 (1992), pp. 469–500.

[27] Dean E. Hewes, "A Socio-egocentric Model of Group Decision-making," in Randy Y. Hirokawa and Marshall Scott Poole (eds.), *Communication and Group Decision Making* (Sage, 1986), pp. 265–291. Hewes' grim perspective on groups inspired considerable research but has not withstood the data that came subsequently; see, for example, Joseph A. Bonito, and Renee A. Meyers, "Examining Functional Communication as Egocentric or Group-centric: Application of a Latent Group Model," *Communication Monographs* 78:4 (2011), pp. 463–485. More generally, however, Hewes' complaint remains salient because so little small group research looks at dynamic group behavior; see Roy F. Baumeister, Kathleen D. Vohs, and David C. Funder, "Psychology as the Science of Self-reports and Finger Movements: Whatever Happened to Actual Behavior?" *Perspectives on Psychological Science* 2:4 (2007), pp. 396–403.

[28] Despite its success with democratic procedures, I refrain from calling Mifflin Co-op, or any other existing group, a "democratic" group. As defined herein (see Chapters 1–2), the democratic ideal is unattainable; the Co-op can never be fully democratic. Recall that Robert A. Dahl has attempted to resolve this difficulty with regard to large-scale political systems by coining the term "polyarchy." Perhaps a similar term should be developed for small groups, such that some groups could fully qualify for a descriptive term other than "democratic." Herein, I have refrained from referring to any existing group as "fully democratic." On polyarchy, see Dahl, *Democracy and Its Critics* (Yale University Press, 1989).

Chapter 5

[1] On the logic behind the critical case study approach, see Robert K. Yin, *Case Study Research: Design and Methods, 5th Ed.* (Sage, 2013), p. 51. Since the study of Mifflin Co-op, I found additional evidence suggesting that the obstacles to small group democracy identified in this chapter are encountered by a wide variety of groups; see John Gastil, "Identifying Obstacles to Small Group Democracy," *Small Group Research* 24:1 (1993), pp. 5–27; portions of this chapter are adapted from that article.

[2] Oscar Wilde quoted in Michael Walzer, *Radical Principles: Reflections of an Unreconstructed Democrat* (Basic Books, 1980), p. 129. Walzer also provides a humorous sketch of the real activities of Karl Marx's ideal socialist citizen, who is constantly running from one meeting to the next. Walzer's parodies have some basis

in fact. Corinne McLaughlin and Gordon Davidson found that many communities have faced similar problems, which they call "workaholism" or "meeting-itis"; *Builders of the Dawn: Community Lifestyles in a Changing World* (Sirius Publishing, 1986), pp. 76–77. It may not be the amount of time, per se, but the amount of time in excess of expectations. Thus, Jane J. Mansbridge argues that groups that frequent or long meetings are not as much of a problem for groups that "expect to spend a lot of time in decision making, and can value that time as interaction with friends." "Time, Emotion, and Inequality: Three Problems of Participatory Groups," *Journal of Applied Behavioral Science* 9:2-3 (1973), p. 357.

[3] A cynical reader might suspect that long meetings at Mifflin Co-op reflect a desire for longer work hours and, consequently, more take-home pay. This suspicion is unwarranted, since the staff is not paid for attending its mandatory Monday night meetings. As compensation for attendance, the staff receive the ten percent volunteer discount at the store; however, the discount requires only four hours of work, whereas staff spend between eight and twelve hours a month in Monday meetings.

[4] When taken to extremes, exceedingly long (or frequent) meetings can reduce group members' willingness to attend meetings at all, which creates an inclusiveness problem. Some groups, such as university faculty, are jealous guards of their time, and if members perceive that meetings take too long, they will choose to cancel or sporadically attend meetings. See Daniel C. Kramer, *Participatory Democracy: Developing Ideals of the Political Left* (Schenkman Publishing Co., 1972), pp. 122–127; also see Francesca Polletta, *Freedom Is an Endless Meeting: Democracy in American Social Movements* (University of Chicago Press, 2002).

[5] Surprisingly little research has been done on self-facilitation, per se. An exception is the interest in this phenomenon in Group Decision Support Systems, which use software to enhance group decision making. See, for example, Constantin-Bala Zamfirescu, "An Agent-oriented Approach for Supporting Self-facilitation for Group Decisions," *Studies in Informatics and Control* 12:2 (2003), pp. 137–148.

[6] In retrospect, it is remarkable that judges only recently began permitting juries to take notes during trials. Among other things, this frees jurors to pay attention to what is said next, after writing a note on what they just heard. See Michael Dann, Valerie P. Hans, and David H. Kaye, "Can Jury Trial Innovations Improve Juror Understanding of DNA Evidence?," *Judicature* 90:4 (2006), pp. 152–156, and Larry Heuer and Steven Penrod. "Increasing Juror Participation in Trials Through Note Taking and Question Asking." *Judicature* 79:5 (1995), pp. 256–262.

[7] For a classic facilitation guide concerned with democratic process, see Brian Auvine, Betsy Densmore, Mary Extrom, Scott Poole, and Michel Shanklin, *A Manual for Group Facilitators* (Center for Conflict Resolution, 1977). A more modern version is Sam Kaner and Lenny Lind, *Facilitator's Guide to Participatory Decision-making* (Jossey-Bass, 2007). For a guide produced by one of the most successful community-organizing foundations, see Sandy Schuman, *The IAF*

Handbook of Group Facilitation: Best Practices from the Leading Organization in Facilitation (Jossey-Bass, 2005).

[8] On the inevitability of unequal involvement and its effects on democratic decision making, see Walzer, *Radical Principles*, chap. 9; Mansbridge, "Time, Emotion, and Inequality," pp. 361–367; Anne Phillips, *Engendering Democracy* (Pennsylvania State University Press, 1991), and "Must Feminists Give Up on Liberal Democracy?" *Political Studies* 40:s1 (1992), pp. 74–75, 79.

[9] When power differences are slight, there may be a danger in exaggerating those differences and accusing marginally more powerful group members of hoarding power. Kate said she became frustrated when she was criticized for her level of knowledge and authority in the Co-op. She pointed out that she has encouraged others to take on more responsibilities, but she occasionally perceived one or more members resisting the power and influence offered to them.

[10] In a subsequent interview, Norma speculated that her lower level of commitment to the store may have been the result of how she felt treated by the staff in the past. She said that she thought others initially viewed her as less competent and less committed, so as a result, she behaved in these ways. Regardless of the veracity of the claim, it raises the issue of self-fulfilling expectations, particularly with regard to sustaining a member's commitment and competence.

[11] In the view of some staff members, the situation at Mifflin Co-op related to the more general problem of apathy. Political apathy exists in large quantities on social scales both large and small. In small groups, as in large societies, it obstructs fully participatory decision making. See Kramer, *Participatory Democracy*, chap. 6; Walzer, *Radical Principles*, chap. 9; Phillips, *Engendering Democracy*, esp. chap. 5. More recently, see Nina Eliasoph, *Avoiding Politics: How Americans Produce Apathy in Everyday Life* (Cambridge University Press, 1998).

[12] In another group I observed, some members would conduct extended side-conversations during meetings. Known as "caucusing," this practice is doubly disruptive, since it also removes the caucus members from the ongoing meeting discussion. Within larger social units, however, it can become necessary and helpful to permit the formation of enclaves that help sub-groups articulate their particular interests in relation to the general well-being of the organization or society. Christopher F. Karpowitz, Chad Raphael, and Allen S. Hammond IV, "Deliberative Democracy and Inequality: Two Cheers for Enclave Deliberation among the Disempowered," *Politics & Society* 37:4 (2009), pp. 576–615.

[13] Few high schools, and relatively few colleges and universities, require training in public speaking as part of the curriculum. At Penn State, where I now teach, a course in public speaking has been required for every undergraduate student for decades, and though students often dread the course, many seniors who avoided taking it until their last semester have remarked afterward that it was one of the most important experiences of their four years in college.

[14] Research I have conducted with colleagues at the University of Arizona has shown that highly structured deliberative environments can do a great deal to equalize participation, even over the course of just four days. In our study of the Australian Citizens' Parliament, we found that the quieter participants became more vocal, and vice versa. See Joseph A. Bonito, Renee Meyers, John Gastil, and Jennifer Ervin, "Sit down and Speak up: Stability and Change in Group Participation," in Lyn Carson, John Gastil, Janette Hartz-Karp, and Ron Lubensky (eds.), The Australian Citizens' Parliament and the Future of Deliberative Democracy (Pennsylvania State University Press, 2013), pp. 120-130.

[15] None of the Mifflin Co-op staff had a severe speech impediment, so it has not had to deal with this special difficulty. I have observed a small planning board with a member who required a great deal of time and energy to speak clearly. With practice, the other board members learned to understand his utterances, and they showed patience in letting him finish his sentences. Despite this difference in speaking ability, it appeared that the board member was treated as an equal member of the group. The example simply shows that groups are capable of accommodating wide ranges of speaking abilities.

[16] Joseph L. Chesebro argues that people vary considerably in both their appetite and aptitude for conversation in an essay that argues for the advantages of taking a person-centered approach to listening; see "The Relationship Between Listening Styles and Conversational Sensitivity," *Communication Research Reports* 16:3 (1999), pp. 233–238.

[17] The introverted style discussed by Amy and Louis has similarities with shyness or reticence. In an extreme form, this amounts to a fear of speaking in groups. On the varieties and effects of such fear, as well as ways of overcoming it, see James C. McCroskey and Virginia P. Richmond, "Communication Apprehension and Small Group Communication," in Robert S. Cathcart and Larry A. Samovar, *Small Group Communication, 5th Ed.* (William C. Brown, 1988), pp. 405–420. A wave of recent books has made a forceful argument for the bias against introversion in modern society; see, for example, Susan Cain, *Quiet: The Power of Introverts in a World That Can't Stop Talking* (Broadway Paperbacks, 2013).

[18] On the intersection of cultural, moral, and stylistic differences in communication, see W. Barnett Pearce and Stephen W. Littlejohn. *Moral Conflict: When Social Worlds Collide* (Sage, 1997).

[19] Other writers have lamented the variety of personal conflicts that plague small groups and communities. See Mansbridge, "Time, Emotion, and Inequality," pp. 358–361; McLaughlin and Davidson, *Builders of the Dawn*, chap. 3.

[20] Since the first edition of *Democracy in Small Groups*, a vast literature has grown on the regulation of emotion using various physiological measures. At least one meta-analytic summary of these studies suggests that suppressing one's experience of emotion (or thoughts about the emotional event) can prove counterproductive, whereas suppressing the expression of an emotion can be functional. See Thomas L.

Webb, Eleanor Miles, and Paschal Sheeran, "Dealing with Feeling: A Meta-analysis of the Effectiveness of Strategies Derived from the Process Model of Emotion Regulation," *Psychological Bulletin* 138:4 (2012), pp. 775–808. On the positive and negative roles of emotion in deliberation, see Simon Thompson and Paul Hoggett, "The Emotional Dynamics of Deliberative Democracy," *Policy & Politics* 29:3 (2000), pp. 351–364.

[21] Meta-analytic results show a variety of modest differences consistent with Kate's assessment of the male members of the Co-op. See Nicole M. Else-Quest, Janet Shibley Hyde, H. Hill Goldsmith, and Carol A. Van Hulle, "Gender Differences in Temperament: A Meta-analysis," *Psychological Bulletin* 132:1 (2006), pp. 33–72. The relationship of gender to motional self-disclosure data is discussed in Leslie R. Brody and Judith A. Hall, "Gender, Emotion, and Expression," in Michael Lewis and Jeannette M. Haviland-Jones (eds.), *Handbook of Emotions 2nd Ed.* (Guilford Press, 2000), pp. 338–349.

[22] For another take on the appropriate expression of hostility in public deliberation, see Karen Tracy, *Challenges of Ordinary Democracy* (Pennsylvania State University Press, 2011).

[23] For a typology of methods for resolving conflicts, see Richard W. Fogg, "Dealing with Conflict: A Repertoire of Creative, Peaceful Approaches," *Journal of Conflict Resolution* 29:2 (1985), pp. 330–358. There now exist dozens of handbooks and guides for managing conflict, particularly in couples, groups, and organizations. See, for example, Gary T. Furlong, *The Conflict Resolution Toolbox: Models & Maps for Analyzing, Diagnosing, and Resolving Conflict* (Wiley, 2005). On the intersection of conflict resolution and deliberative democracy, see Hiro N. Aragaki, "Deliberative Democracy as Dispute Resolution? Conflict, Interests, and Reasons," *Ohio State Journal on Dispute Resolution* 24:3 (2009): 407–480.

[24] Additional suggestions for dealing with problems like those in Table 2 are provided in Avery, Stribel, Auvine and Weiss, *Building United Judgment* (Center for Conflict Resolution, 1981), chap. 13.

[25] The distinction between staff and shift workers remains an uncomfortable one for some staff. For instance, one provision of the Co-op insurance policy reads, "Shift workers at the Co-op, *though dearly appreciated*, are exempt from this policy..." (italics added).

[26] In seeing the connection between architecture and democracy, Mifflin Co-op joins the likes of Frank Lloyd Wright and many others, including my cousin Raymond W. Gastil, who co-edited with Zoë Ryan *Open: New Designs for Public Space* (Princeton Architectural Press, 2004). See also Allan Greenberg, *The Architecture of Democracy: American Architecture and the Legacy of the Revolution* (Rizzoli, 2006) and Bruce Brooks Pfeiffer, *Frank Lloyd Wright: Building for Democracy* (Taschen, 2004).

[27] The staff's desire to sit in a circle makes sense, since people communicate more often with people facing them than with those adjacent to them. A rectangular or irregular seating arrangement reduces the number of people one can face without

shifting or craning one's neck. See L. L. Cummings, George P. Huber, and Eugene Arendt, "Effects of Size and Spatial Arrangements on Group Decision Making," *Academy of Management Journal* 17:3 (1974), pp. 460–475.

[28] The wording of the final clause of the dismissal policy also suggests the Co-op's continuing commitment to democratic deliberation: "If for some reason, the Board rejects the staff's recommendation, it must ask the Collective to reconsider the firing and *give reasons why* to the Collective. Likewise, when the Collective recommends dismissing an employee, it must explain to the Board its reasons for recommending the dismissal" (italics added). The stress placed on reasons parallels the emphasis placed on reasoned argument in Chapter 2 of this book and the emphasis on reason-giving in deliberative democratic theory generally; see Amy Gutmann and Dennis Thompson, *Why Deliberative Democracy?* (Princeton University Press, 2004). For more academic accounts of how to locate reason-giving in deliberative democratic theory, see James Bohman and Henry S. Richardson, "Liberalism, Deliberative Democracy, and 'Reasons That All Can Accept,'" *Journal of Political Philosophy* 17:3 (2009), pp. 253–274, and Luigi Pellizzoni, "The Myth of the Best Argument: Power, Deliberation, and Reason," *British Journal of Sociology* 52:1 (2001), pp. 59–86.

[29] In the recent past, there had been another staff member besides Norma who had switched shifts and taken vacations in a similar manner, so some staff viewed this as a recurring problem.

[30] The new staff clearly understood meeting procedures. This came partly from experience and partly from the information provided by other staff members. To aid the learning process, Sam and Kate wrote a three page description of staff meeting procedures to complement the materials in the Co-op's training manual.

[31] Many authors have stressed the productive role that conflict can play in groups. Frances Moore Lappé and Paul Martin DuBois believe that "creative controversy" is critical for a democracy. "It brings to light the interest and values that must be incorporated if proposed solutions are to work;" "Power in a Living Democracy," *Creation Spirituality* (September/October, 1992), p. 42. For a more general treatment of the social purposes of conflict, see Lewis Coser, *The Functions of Social Conflict* (Free Press, 1956). On conflict and cohesion in groups generally, see John Gastil, *Group in Society* (Sage, 2010), pp. 171–179. Contemporary research on groups often shows evidence of productive conflict profiles, as in Karen A. Jehn and Elizabeth A. Mannix, "The Dynamic Nature of Conflict: A Longitudinal Study of Intragroup Conflict and Group Performance," *Academy of Management Journal* 44:2 (2001), pp. 238–251. A meta-analysis, however, suggests a wide range of negative associations between various dimensions of conflict and performance; see Carsten K. W. De Dreu and Laurie R. Weingart, "Task versus Relationship Conflict, Team Performance, and Team Member Satisfaction: A Meta-analysis," *Journal of Applied Psychology* 88:4 (2003), pp. 741–749.

Chapter 6

[1] Though there does not exist, nor can there exist, a generic optimal group size, researchers have given the question considerable thought. One of the most pertinent recent studies suggests that smaller is better, at least in terms of productivity and group development, even when making fine comparisons between, say, six- versus ten-person groups; Susan A. Wheelan, "Group Size, Group Development, and Group Productivity," *Small Group Research* 40:2 (2009), pp. 247–262. For research on a wider array of groups small and large, even across species, see Jens Krause and Graeme D. Ruxton, *Living in Groups* (Oxford University Press, 2002), and H. Ronald Pulliam and Thomas Caraco, "Living in Groups: Is There an Optimal Group Size?" in J. R. Krebs and N. B. Davies (eds.), *Behavioural Ecology: An Evolutionary Approach 2nd Ed* (Wiley-Blackwell, 1984), 122–147.

[2] This idea often appears in academic literature as "the iron law of oligarchy," a concept that Pamela S. Tolbert revisited in an entry by the same title in the *Encyclopedia of Social & Political Movements* (Wiley Blackwell, 2013). [3] Those who deviate from the group risk becoming labeled as deviants from the "in group" norms, which groups use to contrast themselves against outsiders. See Dominic Abrams, Michael A. Hogg, Steve Hinkle, and Sabine Otten, "The Social Identity Perspective on Small Groups," in Marshall Scott Poole and Andrea B. Hollingshead (eds.), *Theories of Small Groups: Interdisciplinary Perspectives* (Sage, 2005), pp. 99–138.

[4] See Robert A. Dahl and Edward R. Tufte, *Size and Democracy* (Stanford University Press, 1973).

[5] A sense of political self-confidence is vital to active engagement in public life; see Sidney Verba, Kay Lehman Schlozman, and Henry E. Brady, *Voice and Equality: Civic Voluntarism in American Politics* (Harvard University Press, 1995). To some extent, the deliberative democratic project aims to address this alienation problem in mass society; see Katherine R. Knobloch, "Public Sphere Alienation: A Model for Analysis and Critique," *Javnost—The Public* 18:4 (2011), pp. 21–37.

[6] On interpersonal trust and group size, see Shane Soboroff's University of Iowa doctoral dissertation, *Group Size and the Trust, Cohesion, and Commitment of Group Members* (Iowa Research Online, 2012).

[7] For an example of the negative association between group size and cooperativeness, see Anthony J. Stahelski and Ruth Ann Tsukuda, "Predictors of Cooperation in Health Care Teams," *Small Group Research* 21:2 (1990): 220–233.

[8] An example of such size effects in work teams comes from Caroline Aubé, Vincent Rousseau, and Sébastien Tremblay, "Team Size and Quality of Group Experience:

The More the Merrier?" *Group Dynamics: Theory, Research, and Practice* 15:4 (2011): 357–375.

[9] Heterogeneity can actually enhance group productivity, but as group size increases, that benefit diminishes. See Jonathon N. Cummings, Sara Kiesler, Reza Bosagh Zadeh, and Aruna D. Balakrishnan. Group Heterogeneity Increases the Risks of Large Group Size A Longitudinal Study of Productivity in Research Groups"Group Heterogeneity Increases the Risks of Large Group Size A Longitudinal Study of Productivity in Research Groups." *Psychological Science* 24 (2013): 880–890. More generally, see Scott Page, *The Difference: How the Power of Diversity Creates Better Groups, Firms, Schools, and Societies* (Princeton University Press, 2008).

[10] In a classic set of experiments, Solomon Asch graphically showed the power of conformity pressures in larger groups. He had undergraduate students say which of three lines on a card was longest; the student had to answer the question after all other members in the group—in collaboration with the experimenter—had given an incorrect answer. The participants in the study were more likely to give the wrong answer if there were more confederates answering before them. "Opinions and Social Pressure," in Elliot Aronson (ed.), *Readings about the Social Animal* (W. A. Freeman, 1962), pp. 3-12. The conformity effect owing to group size is more acute in face-to-face groups in which members can see each other's votes; see Rod Bond, "Group Size and Conformity," *Group Processes & Intergroup Relations* 8:4 (2005), 331–354.

[11] It is true enough that courtesy norms do not ensure civility in parliamentary bodies, but the idea remains a good one, even though they are too often abused or ignored; see Chapter 5 in my book, *Political Communication and Deliberation* (Sage, 2008).

[12] As groups grow even larger, it becomes necessary to make explicit appeals to "superordinate" identities, such as all being members of the same nation. This worked effectively at the Australian Citizens' Parliament, and it has likely served the same purpose at other deliberative events. See Andrea Felicetti, John Gastil, Janette Hartz-Karp, and Lyn Carson, "Collective Identity and Voice at the Australian Citizens' Parliament," *Journal of Public Deliberation* 8:1 (2012), art. 5; and Janette Hartz-Karp, Patrick Anderson, John Gastil, and Andrea Felicetti, "The Australian Citizens' Parliament: Forging Shared Identity through Public Deliberation," *Journal of Public Affairs* 10:4 (2010), 353–371. On superordinate identity and culture generally, see Samuel L. Gaertner, John F. Dovidio, Jason A. Nier, Christine M. Ward, and Brenda S. Banker, "Across Cultural Divides: The Value of a Superordinate Identity," in Deborah A. Prentice and Dale T. Miller (eds.), *Cultural Divides: Understanding and Overcoming Group Conflict* (Russell Sage Foundation, 1999), pp. 173–212.

[13] This process has been used in numerous deliberative groups, small and large. For examples of public meetings conducted in this way, see Katherine R. Knobloch, John Gastil, Justin Reedy, and Katherine Cramer Walsh, "Did They Deliberate? Applying an Evaluative Model of Democratic Deliberation to the Oregon Citizens' Initiative

Review," *Journal of Applied Communication Research* 41:2 (2013), pp. 105–125; Carolyn J. Lukensmeyer, Joe Goldman, and Steven Brigham, "A Town Meeting for the Twenty-first Century," in John Gastil and Peter Levine (eds.), *The Deliberative Democracy Handbook* (Wiley, 2005), pp. 154–163; and Lyn Carson, John Gastil, Janette Hartz-Karp, and Ron Lubensky (eds.), *The Australian Citizens' Parliament and the Future of Deliberative Democracy* (Pennsylvania State University Press, 2013).

[14] Even small groups, however, commonly exist as embedded entities within larger networks, organizations, and (always) societies, as I argue throughout *The Group in Society* (Sage, 2010), esp. chap. 2. See also Gary Alan Fine, *Tiny Publics: A Theory of Group Action and Culture* (Russell Sage Foundation, 2012).

[15] I thank Paul Klinkman for providing information on the Clamshell Alliance. On the successes and failures of the Alliance and its Congress, see Gary L. Downey, "Ideology and the Clamshell Identity: Organizational Dilemmas in the Anti-nuclear Power Movement," *Social Problems* 33:5 (1986), pp. 357–373. Notice that despite its size, the Alliance used consensus effectively. I personally witnessed an effective, large consensus group, when I helped facilitate a gathering of Madison residents who had come together to protest the Gulf War. The large group (approximately one hundred people) came up with a wide variety of ideas for action, and small subgroups discussed each proposal. When the large group reconvened, the two most popular proposals were debated. Within a half hour, consensus was reached on a plan that effectively incorporated the two points of view. That evening, the demonstration went according to plan, and the participants (most of whom had not attended the meeting) appeared satisfied with the way it was conducted.

[16] See Lukensmeyer et al., "A Town Meeting for the Twenty-first Century." For more on such technology, including Group Decision Support Systems, see the following section in this chapter on "Geographically Dispersed Groups."

[17] Age, ethnicity, income, and education may influence panelists' ability to adapt to a more digital format, with those with less access to digital technology and less technological skill more likely to face difficulty; see M. Kay Cresci, Hossein N. Yarandi, and Roger W. Morrell, "The Digital Divide and Urban Older Adults," *Computers Informatics Nursing* 28:2 (2010), pp. 88–94, and Ellinor Larsson, Maria Larsson-Lund, and Ingeborg Nilsson, "Internet Based Activities (IBAs): Seniors' Experiences of the Conditions Required for the Performance of and the Influence of These Conditions on Their Own Participation in Society," *Educational Gerontology* 39:3 (2013), pp. 155–167.

[18] On the variety of choices made when designing online deliberation, see Todd Davies and Reid Chandler, "Online Deliberation Design: Choices, Criteria, and Evidence," in Tina Nabatchi, Michael Weiksner, John Gastil, and Matt Leighninger (eds.), *Democracy in Motion: Evaluating the Practice and Impact of Deliberative Civic Engagement* (Oxford University Press, 2012), pp. 103–131. Also see Scott Wright and

John Street, "Democracy, Deliberation and Design: The Case of Online Discussion Forums," *New Media & Society* 9:5 (2007), pp. 849–869.

[19] On the primacy (and complexity) of face-to-face interaction, see Jonathan H. Turner, *Face to Face: Toward a Sociological Theory of Interpersonal Behavior* (Stanford University Press, 2002). The topic of electronic meetings is not as new as some might imagine. For an early review of research on this issue, see Robert Johansen, Jacques Vallee, and Kathleen Spangler, "Teleconferencing: Electronic Group Meetings," in Robert S. Cathcart and Larry A. Samovar (eds.), *Small Group Communication, 5th Ed.* (William C. Brown, 1988), pp. 140–154.

[20] On the potential advantages of online deliberation, see the review and original evidence presented by Vincent Price, "Citizens Deliberating Online: Theory and Some Evidence" in Todd Davies and Seeta Pena Gangadharan (eds.), *Online Deliberation: Design, Research, and Practice* (University of Chicago Press, 2009), pp. 37–58. For an early and optimistic view of online discussion's potential to mitigate differences in status and expertise, see Vitaly J. Dubrovsky, Sara Kiesler, and Beheruz N. Sethna, "The Equalization Phenomenon: Status Effects in Computer-mediated and Face-to-face Decision-making Groups," *Human-Computer Interaction* 6:2 (1991), pp. 119–146. For more disappointing results in recent research reports, see Jason A. Delborne, Ashley A. Anderson, Daniel Lee Kleinman, Mathilde Colin, and Maria Powell, "Virtual Deliberation? Prospects and Challenges for Integrating the Internet in Consensus Conferences," *Public Understanding of Science* 20:3 (2011), pp. 367–384, and Kim Strandberg and Kimmo Grönlund, "Online Deliberation and Its Outcome—Evidence from the Virtual Polity Experiment," *Journal of Information Technology & Politics* 9:2 (2012), pp. 167–184.

[21] Most of the research on "deliberation online" looks at loosely-coupled networks and ephemeral discussions, rather than the internal dynamics of ongoing groups. For a critical overview of this work, see Stephen Coleman and Giles Moss, "Under Construction: The Field of Online Deliberation Research," *Journal of Information Technology & Politics* 9:1 (2012), pp. 1–15.

[22] See Laura W. Black, Howard T. Welser, Dan Cosley, and Jocelyn M. DeGroot, "Self-governance through Group Discussion in Wikipedia: Measuring Deliberation in Online Groups," *Small Group Research* 42:5 (2011), pp. 595–634.

[23] Most of the research on this phenomenon compares what aren't necessarily groups, per se, but loosely-coupled networks. See, for example, Daniel Halpern and Jennifer Gibbs, "Social Media as a Catalyst for Online Deliberation? Exploring the Affordances of Facebook and YouTube for Political Expression," *Computers in Human Behavior* 29:3 (2013), pp. 1159–1168.

[24] For a view that recasts some "flaming" as provocative civil discourse, see Zizi Papacharissi, "Democracy Online: Civility, Politeness, and the Democratic Potential of Online Political Discussion Groups." *New Media & Society* 6:2 (2004), pp. 259–283. On the frequency of negativity in online political discussion, see Young Min Baek, Magdalena Wojcieszak, and Michael X. Delli Carpini, "Online versus Face-to-

face Deliberation: Who? Why? What? With What Effects?" *New Media & Society* 14:3 (2012), pp. 363–383.

[25] For ideas on how to distribute responsibility in online groups, see Brian Butler, Lee Sproull, Sara Kiesler, and Robert Kraut, "Community Effort in Online Groups: Who Does the Work and Why?" in Suzanne Weisband (ed.), *Leadership at a Distance: Research in Technologically-supported Work* (Psychology Press, 2008), pp. 171–193.

[26] Helen Schwartzman, *The Meeting: Gatherings in Organizations and Communities* (Plenum, 1989).

[27] Saniye Tugba Bulu, "Place Presence, Social Presence, Co-presence, and Satisfaction in Virtual Worlds," *Computers & Education* 58:1 (2012), pp. 154–161.

[28] Quote from Michael Schudson, "The Limits of Teledemocracy," *The American Prospect* 11 (1992), p. 44.

[29] Minsun Shim, Joseph N. Cappella, and Jeong Yeob Han, "How Does Insightful and Emotional Disclosure Bring Potential Health Benefits? Study Based on Online Support Groups for Women With Breast Cancer," *Journal of Communication* 61:3 (2011), pp. 432–454.

[30] Emma A. Jane, "'Your a Ugly, Whorish, Slut,'" *Feminist Media Studies* 14:4 (2014), pp. 531–546. Also see Amy Binns, "Don't Feed the Trolls!" *Journalism Practice* 6:4 (2012), pp. 547–562.

[31] On the importance of being face-to-face during meetings, see Mansbridge, *Beyond Adversary Democracy* (University of Chicago Press, 1983), chap. 19. On the limits of noninteractive techniques, see Brant R. Burleson, Barbara J. Levine, and Wendy Samter, "Decision-making Procedure and Decision Quality," *Human Communication Research* 10:4 (1984), pp. 557–574.

[32] This was part of the story from the online groups that preceded the face-to-face meetings of the Australian Citizens' Parliament; see Brian Sullivan and Janette Hartz-Karp, "Grafting an Online Parliament onto a Face-to-face Process," in Lyn Carson, John Gastil, Janette Hartz-Karp, and Ron Lubensky (eds.), *The Australian Citizens' Parliament and the Future of Deliberative Democracy* (Pennsylvania State University Press, 2013), pp. 49–62.

[33] See Black et al., "Self-governance through Group Discussion in Wikipedia."

[34] Craig R. Scott, "Communication Technology and Group Communication," in Lawrence R. Frey (ed.), *The Handbook of Group Communication Theory and Research* (Sage, 1999), pp. 432–472.

[35] Already, online groups can be seen generating some of the civic benefits associated with face-to-face meetings; see Seong-Jae Min, "Online vs. Face-to-face Deliberation: Effects on Civic Engagement," *Journal of Computer-Mediated Communication* 12:4 (2007), pp. 1369–1387.

[36] Unstable membership, in a nutshell, makes it more difficult for groups to work effectively. One factor in this is "social integration," whereby different group members become an integrated group or team. See Gerben S. van der Vegt, Stuart Bunderson, and Ben Kuipers, "Why Turnover Matters in Self-managing Work

Teams: Learning, Social Integration, and Task Flexibility," *Journal of Management* 36:5 (2010), pp. 1168–1191. The social integration of new members becomes a critical task for any group that wishes to sustain itself over time; see Eleanor F. Counselman, "Leadership in a Long-term Leaderless Women's Group," *Small Group Research* 22:2 (1991), pp. 240–257. For a more prosaic discussion of the importance of integrating new members, see Starhawk, *Truth or Dare: Encounters with Power, Authority, and Mystery* (Harper & Row, 1986).

[37] For the larger variety of small groups that exist online, there may be an exception to this rule. So long as an online group's stable core membership shares a strong democratic commitment, online groups may also benefit from steady member turnover, with those uncommitted to the work of democracy departing effortlessly, to be replaced by newcomers who might share the group's interest in democratic process. See Laura Dabbish, Rosta Farzan, Robert Kraut, and Tom Postmes, "Fresh Faces in the Crowd: Turnover, Identity, and Commitment in Online Groups," in *Proceedings of the ACM 2012 Conference on Computer Supported Cooperative Work* (ACM, 2012), pp. 245–248.

[38] See Abrams et al., "The Social Identity Perspective on Small Groups."

[39] The Madison Community Co-op Board had a sizable member turnover every semester. To maintain bonds among members, "light and lively" activities were planned for the intermissions during board meeting. Activities included making up a story together, forming a human pretzel, and comparing hobbies and backgrounds. For books on group games, see Wayne Rice and Mike Yaconelli, *Play It!* (Zondervan Publishing House, 1986), and Andrew Fluegelman (ed.), *The New Games Book* (Headlands Press, 1976).

[40] As one example, see Michael Huspek and Kathleen E. Kendall, "On Withholding Political Voice: An Analysis of the Political Vocabulary of a 'Non-political' Speech Community," *Quarterly Journal of Speech* 77:1 (1991), pp. 1–19. For a review including this and other studies relevant to the issue of discourse, see John Gastil, "Undemocratic Discourse: A Review of Theory and Research on Political Discourse," *Discourse & Society* 3:4 (1992), pp. 469–500.

[41] A study by Arie W. Kruglanski and Donna M. Webster suggests the validity of these concerns. Groups under greater time pressure appear more likely to reject deviation and reward conformity. This problem may be exacerbated in very noisy group environments. "Group Members' Reactions to Opinion Deviates and Conformists at Varying Degrees of Proximity to Decision Deadline and of Environmental Noise," *Journal of Personality and Social Psychology* 61:2 (1991), pp. 212–225.

[42] Hermann Hesse, *Siddhartha* (New Directions, 1951), p. 46.

[43] For further discussion of these issues, see Joyce Rothschild-Whitt, "Conditions for Democracy: Making Participatory Organizations Work," in John Case and Rosemary C. R. Taylor (eds.), *Co-ops, Communes, and Collectives: Experiments in Social Change in the 1960s and 1970s* (Pantheon Books, 1979), pp. 215–244.

44 Structuration theory provides a rich conceptual framework for understanding power relationships. On the pervasiveness and character of power structures, see Anthony Giddens, *Central Problems in Social Theory* (University of California Press, 1979), and *The Constitution of Society* (University of California Press, 1984). For an application of Giddens' terminology to small groups, see Marshall Scott Poole, Robert D. McPhee, and David R. Siebold, "Group Decision-Making as a Structurational Process," *Quarterly Journal of Speech* 71:1 (1985), pp. 74–102.

45 A wonderful new book summarizes years of research on "implicit social cognition"—the unconscious ways we make inferences about people in our social world; see Mahzarin R. Banaji and Anthony G. Greenwald, *Blind Spot: Hidden Biases of Good People* (Delacorte Press, 2013). For an overview of this subject more generally, see John F. Dovidio, Miles Hewstone, Peter Glick, and Victoria M. Esses, *The SAGE Handbook of Prejudice, Stereotyping and Discrimination* (SAGE, 2010). On the history of theory and research on stereotyping, see Arthur G. Miller, "Historical and Contemporary Perspectives on Stereotyping," in Arthur G. Miller (ed.), *In the Eye of the Beholder: Contemporary Issues in Stereotyping* (Praeger, 1982), pp. 1–40. Cognitive psychology has created new conceptions of stereotyping and the potential for reversing stereotypical thinking patterns. See Patricia Devine, "Automatic and Controlled Processes in Prejudice: The Role of Stereotypes and Personal Beliefs," in A. R. Pratkanis, S. J. Breckler, and A. G. Greenwald (eds.), *Attitude Structure and Function* (Erlbaum, 1989), pp. 181–212; David J. Schneider, "Social Cognition," *Annual Review of Psychology* 42 (1991), pp. 527–561.

46 These dynamics can shape the community and organizational context of the group, which has indirect but powerful effects on the group's prospects for democratic deliberation; see, for example, Robert Chaskin, Amy Khare, and Mark Joseph, "Participation, Deliberation, and Decision Making: The Dynamics of Inclusion and Exclusion in Mixed-income Developments," *Urban Affairs Review* 48:6 (2012), pp. 863–906. On the influence of socioeconomic class on group deliberation, see Mansbridge, *Beyond Adversary Democracy*, esp. pp. 107–114, 199–208. On race, see William Labov, "The Logic of Nonstandard English," in Frederick Williams (ed.), *Language and Poverty: Perspectives on a Theme* (Markham Publishing, 1970). For an overview of earlier literature on these subjects, see Howard Giles and John M. Wiemann, "Language, Social Comparison, and Power," in Charles R. Berger and Steven H. Chaffee (eds.), *Handbook of Communication Science* (Sage, 1987), pp. 350–384.

47 Christopher F. Karpowitz, Tali Mendelberg, and Lee Shaker, "Gender Inequality in Deliberative Participation," *American Political Science Review* 106:3 (2012), pp. 533–547. On gender and democracy, see Jane J. Mansbridge, "Feminism and Democracy," *The American Prospect* 2 (1990), pp. 126-139; Carole Pateman, "Feminism and Democracy," in Graeme Campbell Duncan (ed.), *Democratic Theory and Practice* (Cambridge University Press, 1983), pp. 204-217; Anne Phillips, *Engendering*

Democracy (Pennsylvania State University, 1991); Sanders, Lynn M. "Against Deliberation." *Political Theory* 25:3 (1997), pp. 347–376.

[48] On the existence of gender differences in confidence at persuasive ability, see Patricia H. Andrews, "Gender Differences in Persuasive Communication and Attributions of Success and Failure," *Human Communication Research* 13:3 (1987), pp. 372-385. On controlling behavior, see Judi B. Miller, "Patterns of Control in Same-sex Conversations: Differences between Women and Men," *Women's Studies in Communication* 8 (1985), pp. 62-69. On males' more domineering use of interruptions in group discussion, see Lynn Smith-Lovin and Charles Brody, "Interruptions in Group Discussions: The Effects of Gender and Group Composition," *American Sociological Review* 54:3 (1989), pp. 424-435. On men's greater likelihood to use autocratic leadership styles, see Alice H. Eagley and Blair T. Johnson, "Gender and Leadership Style: A Meta-analysis," *Psychological Bulletin* 108:2 (1990), pp. 233-256. For a textbook overview of gender and communication, see Julia T. Wood, *Gendered Lives, 10th Ed.* (Cengage Learning, 2011). For a very general and accessible treatment of the wide range of gender differences in conversational style, see Deborah Tannen, *You Just Don't Understand* (Ballantine, 1990). It should be noted that many studies have not found communication differences based on differences in biological sex. For example, see Cynthia S. Burgraf and Alan L. Sillars, "A Critical Examination of Sex Differences in Marital Communication," *Communication Monographs* 54:3 (1987), pp. 276-294; Kathryn Dindia, "The Effects of Sex of Subject and Sex of Partner on Interruptions," *Human Communication Research* 13:3 (1987), pp. 345-371. Thus, it is important to move beyond the simple sex-difference approach to this subject. One must consider the complex relationship between sex, socialization into gender roles, and adult differences in communication behavior. See Howard Giles and Richard L. Street, "Communicator Characteristics and Behavior," in Mark L. Knapp and Gerald R. Miller (eds.), *Handbook of Interpersonal Communication* (Beverly Hills, CA: Sage, 1985), pp. 212-216. Evidence suggests the importance of the mediating influence of socialization into gender roles with regard to group communication, as noted by Scott Seibert and Leopold Gruenfeld, "Masculinity, Femininity, and Behavior in Groups," *Small Group Research* 23:1 (1992), pp. 95-112.

[49] Anthony Mulac, L. B. Studley, John M. Wiemann, and James J. Bradac, "Male/Female Gaze in Same-sex and Mixed-sex Dyads: Gender-Linked Differences in Mutual Influence," *Human Communication Research* 13:3 (1987), pp. 323-343; Anthony Mulac, John M. Weimann, Sally J. Widenmann, and Toni W. Gibson, "Male/Female Language Differences and Effects in Same-Sex and Mixed-Sex Dyads: The Gender-Linked Language Effect," *Communication Monographs* 55:4 (1988), pp. 315-335. See also James J. Bradac, M. O'Donnel, and Charles H. Tardy, "Another Stab at a Touchy Subject: Affective Meaning of Touch," *Women's Studies in Communication* 7 (1984), 38-50.

---

[50] Shirley Ardener, "Introduction: The Nature of Women in Society" in Shirley Ardener (ed.), *Defining Females* (Croom Helm, 1978), p. 21. See also Adam Jaworski, "How to Silence a Minority: The Case of Women," *International Journal of the Sociology of Language* 94:1 (1992), pp. 27-41.

[51] Studies finding biases toward males include Dore Butler and Florence Geis, "Nonverbal Affect Responses to Male and Female Leaders: Implications for Leadership Evaluations," *Journal of Personality and Social Psychology* 58:1 (1990), pp. 48-59, and Robert L. Duran and Rodney A. Carveth, "The Effects of Gender-Role Expectations Upon Perceptions of Communicative Competence," *Communication Research Reports* 7:1 (1990), pp. 25-33. More encouraging findings are reported by Craig Johnson and Larry Vinson, "'Damned if you Do, Damned if you Don't?': Status, Powerful Speech, and Evaluations of Female Witnesses," *Women's Studies in Communication* 10:1 (1987), pp. 37-44. The latter study set up a mock budget-allocation process, and undergraduates gave female witnesses higher credibility ratings and financial awards when they "spoke in a forceful manner" (pp. 41-42).

[52] Charles Derber, *The Pursuit of Attention: Power and Ego in Everyday Life* (Oxford University Press, 2000). Giles and Street ("Communicator Characteristics and Behavior," pp. 214-215) argue that communication differences between the genders tend to reflect women's lower social status or their different communication networks. See also Kalbfleisch, Pamela J., and Michael J. Cody, eds. *Gender, Power, and Communication in Human Relationships* (Psychology Press, 1995).

[53] This is tantamount to the task of consciousness raising groups; see Catharine A. MacKinnon, *Toward a Feminist Theory of the State* (Harvard University Press, 1989), chap. 5.

[54] Many authors have stressed the importance of dialogue even in deliberative groups: see Barge, J. K., "Enlarging the meaning of group deliberation: From discussion to dialogue" in L.Frey (ed.), *New directions in group communication* (Sage, 2002), pp. 159–178. See W. Barnett Pearce and Stephen W. Littlejohn. *Moral Conflict: When Social Worlds Collide* (Sage, 1997); Laura W. Black "Deliberation, Storytelling, and Dialogic Moments," *Communication Theory* 18:1 (2008): 93–116; and Stephanie Burkhalter, John Gastil, and Todd Kelshaw, "A Conceptual Definition and Theoretical Model of Public Deliberation in Small Face-to-face Groups," *Communication Theory* 12:4 (2002), 398-422.

Chapter 7

[1] Bruno Lasker, *Democracy through Discussion* (H. W. Wilson Co., 1949), p. 3.
[2] In this second edition, I expand on the discussion of each of these aspects of democratic society because the literature on each has expanded substantially in the past twenty years. None of these topics has received sustained attention in democratic theory, but they have caught the attention of many scholars and

democratic reformers. Substantially more work in the theory and practice of democracy has aimed to make public meetings more deliberative, as discussed in Chapter 8.

[3] Hopefully, it doesn't lead to murder, as Hitchcock would have us imagine. I think instead of memorable exchanges I've had with strangers on trains, planes, and even in a shared rental car (after a cancelled flight). We don't always seize such opportunities, but the Internet has made such encounters more palatable even to those who need more personal space when traveling.

[4] In other cases, there may be a need for more secluded conversation, as when members of oppressed social groups desire to speak only with people in the same situation to better understand their situation and imagine remedies. Christopher F. Karpowitz, Chad Raphael, and Allen S. Hammond IV, "Deliberative Democracy and Inequality: Two Cheers for Enclave Deliberation among the Disempowered," *Politics & Society* 37:4 (2009), pp. 576–615.

[5] That free flowing element is one that facilitators associate with deliberation generally; see Jane J. Mansbridge, Janette Hartz-Karp, Matthew Amengual, and John Gastil, "Norms of Deliberation: An Inductive Study," *Journal of Public Deliberation* 2:1 (2006) art. 7.

[6] See Anthony Giddens, "Jürgen Habermas," in Quentin Skinner (ed.), *The Return of Grand Theory in the Human Sciences* (Cambridge University Press, 1985), pp. 121-139; Jürgen Habermas, *Communication and the Evolution of Society* (Beacon Press, 1979). John Wilson goes a step farther by defining conversation as the condition of participants having equal speaking opportunities. Communication that violates this rule is not, by his definition, conversation. See *On the Boundaries of Conversation* (Permagon Press, 1989).

[7] H. Paul Grice, "Logic and Conversation," in P. Cole and J. L. Morgan (eds.), *Syntax and Semantics 3: Speech Acts* (Academic Press, 1975), pp. 113-128. For a more detailed analysis of democratic conversation, see my book *Political Communication and Deliberation* (Sage, 2008), pp. 19-29, brief portions of which are adapted for this section.

[8] Comedians make good use of norm violations to shock listeners, as in the joke once related to me by a New Mexico politician. A lobbyist grabs a senator by the arm and begins to argue forcefully for a new piece of legislation. The senator becomes suspicious and says, "Hey, hold on. I think you're lying to me." "Sure, sure," the lobbyist says with a nod, "but hear me out."

[9] Charles Derber, *The Pursuit of Attention: Power and Individualism in Everyday Life* (Oxford University Press, 1979), pp. 16-17. Derber's portrait of conversations bears considerable resemblance to Hewes' model of group discussion, except where Derber sees a narcissist, Hewes imagines more mundane indifference toward the social environment; Dean E. Hewes, "A Socio-Egocentric Model of Group Decision Making," in Randy Y. Hirokawa and Marshall Scott Poole (eds.), *Communication and Group Decision Making* (Sage, 1986), pp. 265-291. Research building on the

work of Derber and others has continued to explore "conversational discrimination" and "participation shifts," as in Gibson, David R. "Participation shifts: Order and differentiation in group conversation," *Social forces* 81:4 (2003): 1335-1380. Though Derber focuses on conversants seeking attention, much more is at stake in conversation, such as social influence and relationships maintenance; see Guerin, Bernard. "Language Use as Social Strategy: A Review and an Analytic Framework for the Social Sciences," *Review of General Psychology* 7:3 (2003): 251–298.

[10] Derber, *The Pursuit of Attention*, pp. 17-19.

[11] Derber, *The Pursuit of Attention*, p. 35. See also Anita L. Vangelisti, Mark L. Knapp, and John A. Daly, "Conversational Narcissism," *Communication Monographs* 57:4 (1990), pp. 251-274.

[12] Robinson, Dawn T., and Lynn Smith-Lovin. "Getting A Laugh: Gender, Status, and Humor in Task Discussions," *Social Forces* 80:1 (2001), pp. 123–158.

[13] Robert D. Putnam, *Bowling Alone* (Simon and Schuster, 2001).

[14] Katherine Cramer Walsh, *Talking About Politics: Informal Groups and Social Identity in American Life* (University of Chicago Press, 2004), p. 233. Also see Michael Schudson, "Why Conversation Is Not the Soul of Democracy," *Critical Studies in Mass Communication* 14:4 (1997), pp. 1–13.

[15] Diana C. Mutz and Paul S. Martin, "Facilitating Communication Across Lines of Political Difference: The Role of Mass Media," *American Political Science Review* 95:1 (2001), pp. 97–114.

[16] Holbert, Lance R., William L. Benoit, Glenn J. Hansen, and Wei-Chun Wen. "The Role of Communication in the Formation of an Issue-based Citizenry," *Communication Monographs* 69:4 (2002), pp. 296–310. See also, Pattie, Charles, and Ron Johnston. "Talk as a Political Context: Conversation and Electoral Change in British Elections, 1992-1997," *Electoral Studies* 20:1 (2001), pp. 17–40.

[17] Huckfeldt, Robert and John Sprague, *Citizens, Politics, and Social Communication: Information and Influence in an Election Campaign* (Cambridge University Press, 1995).

[18] Papacharissi, Zizi. "Democracy Online: Civility, Politeness, and the Democratic Potential of Online Political Discussion Groups," *New Media & Society* 6:2 (2004), 259–283.

[19] Stromer-Galley, Jennifer. "New Voices in the Public Sphere: A Comparative Analysis of Interpersonal and Online Political Talk," *Javnost The Public* 9:2 (2002), pp. 23–42.

[20] Nina Eliasoph goes so far as to argue that the more public an exchange, the less public spirited we might expect it to be; see "Making a fragile public: A talk-centered study of citizenship and power," *Sociological Theory*, 14:3 (1996), pp. 262–289.

[21] Jack M. McLeod, Dietram A. Scheufele, and Patricia Moy, "Community, Communication, and Participation: The Role of Mass Media and Interpersonal Discussion in Local Political Participation," *Political Communication* 16:3 (1999), pp. 315–336. and Robert O. Wyatt, Elihu Katz, and Joohan Kim, "Bridging the Spheres:

Political and Personal Conversation in Public and Private Spaces," *Journal of Communication* 50:1 (2000), pp. 71–92.

[22] Patricia Moy and John Gastil, "Predicting Deliberative Conversation: The Impact Of Discussion Networks, Media Use, and Political Cognitions," *Political Communication* 23:4 (2006), pp. 443–360.

[23] William A. Gamson, *Talking Politics* (Cambridge University Press, 1992) p. 175.

[24] For a cautionary argument against being too didactic about proper online discourse, see Stephen Coleman and Giles Moss, "Under Construction: The Field of Online Deliberation Research," *Journal of Information Technology & Politics* 9:1 (2012), pp. 1–15. A similar caution augurs against limiting our study of political conversation to its deliberative (or non-deliberative) features; see William P. Eveland, Alyssa C. Morey, and Myiah J. Hutchens, "Beyond Deliberation: New Directions for the Study of Informal Political Conversation from a Communication Perspective," *Journal of Communication* 61:6 (2011) pp. 1082–1103.

[25] Diana C. Mutz, *Hearing the Other Side: Deliberative versus Participatory Democracy* (Cambridge University Press, 2006).

[26] Quotes are from pp. 133 and 139 from Kerry Burch, "Eros as the Educational Principle of Democracy," *Studies in Philosophy and Education* 18:3 (1999), pp. 123–142.

[27] See Jane Mansbridge, *Beyond Adversary Democracy* (University of Chicago Press, 1983) and Benjamin Barber, *Strong Democracy* (University of California Press, 1984). The concept of love has deep roots in other modern democratic theories, such as those of Arendt; see, for example, Chiba, Shin. "Hannah Arendt on Love and the Political: Love, Friendship, and Citizenship," *The Review of Politics* 57:3 (1995), pp. 505–535.

[28] Gary Alan Fine, *Tiny Publics: A Theory of Group Action and Culture* (Russell Sage Foundation, 2012).

[29] Carole Pateman, "Feminism and Democracy," in Graeme Duncan (ed.), *Democratic Theory and Practice* (Cambridge University Press, 1983), p 216.

[30] Erich Fromm, *The Art of Loving* (Harper & Row, 1956), pp. 46, 55.

[31] Fromm, *The Art of Loving*, pp. 20, 21. So long as one relational partner views the other as something other than a competent and independent individual, the relationship will also lack truly mutualistic bonds. Mitchell Aboulafia makes this argument by applying the Hegelian master-slave dialectic to male-female relationships. True acknowledgement of one's independent existence can only come from another independent being; thus, the master and the slave can't receive recognition from one another until they reject their master-slave relation and become equals. Similarly, male-female relationships are incomplete until prevailing patterns of male-domination are rejected. "From Domination to Recognition," in Carol Gould (ed.), *Beyond Domination* (Rowman & Allanheld, 1984), pp. 175-185.

[32] Quoted in Susan Moller Okin, *Justice, Gender, and the Family* (Basic Books, 2008), p. 42. On unequal power in marriage, see Carol Gould, "Private Rights and Public

Virtues: Women, the Family, and Democracy," in Carol Gould (ed.), *Beyond Domination* (Rowman & Allanheld, 1984), pp. 3-18; Catharine A. MacKinnon, *Toward a Feminist Theory of the State* (Harvard University Press, 1989).

[33] M. P. Johnson and R. M. Milardo, "Network Interference in Pair Relationships: A Social Psychological Recasting of Slater's Theory of Social Regression," *Journal of Marriage and the Family* 46:4 (1984), pp. 893-899.

[34] Bettina Brickell, Robert Huckfeldt, and John Sprague, *Gender Effects on Political Discussion: The Political Networks of Men and Women*, paper presented at the Annual Meeting of the Midwest Political Science Association, Chicago, IL, April, 1988.

[35] Pateman, "Feminism and Democracy," p. 213.

[36] Fromm, *The Art of Loving*, p. 132.

[37] Richard Flacks, *Making History: The American Left and the American Mind* (Columbia University Press, 1988), p. 240.

[38] Nancy Burns and Kay Lehman Schlozman, *The Private Roots of Public Action: Gender, Equality, and Political Participation* (Harvard University Press, 2001).

[39] Ronald Inglehart and Pippa Norris. *Rising Tide: Gender Equality and Cultural Change around the World* (Cambridge University Press, 2003).

[40] Ellen Lamont, "Negotiating Courtship Reconciling Egalitarian Ideals with Traditional Gender Norms," *Gender & Society* (published online before print, September 23, 2013).

[41] One organization tracking changes in the law is Freedom to Marry. The most relevant Wikipedia page also has regular updates.

[42] Daniel C. Lewis, "Direct Democracy and Minority Rights: Same-Sex Marriage Bans in the US States," *Social Science Quarterly* 92:2 (2011), pp. 364–383.

[43] Claire Snyder provides a sustained argument for marriage equality in *Gay Marriage and Democracy: Equality for All* (Rowman & Littlefield, 2006).

[44] Gregory M. Herek, "Anti-Equality Marriage Amendments and Sexual Stigma," *Journal of Social Issues* 67:2 (2011), pp. 413–426.

[45] Robert A. Dahl addresses this issue in *Democracy and Its Critics* (Yale University Press, 1989). Some have advocated lowering the voting age to sixteen, but the maturity argument recommends against doing so, as argued by Tak Wing Chan and Matthew Clayton, "Should the Voting Age Be Lowered to Sixteen? Normative and Empirical Considerations," *Political Studies* 54:3 (2006), pp. 533–558.

[46] Modern theories of political socialization, however, assume that civic education flows both from parent to child and vice versa; see Michael McDevitt and Steven Chaffee, "From Top-down to Trickle-up Influence: Revisiting Assumptions about the Family in Political Socialization," *Political Communication* 19:3 (2002), pp. 281–301.

[47] Classic writings by John Dewey on the subject include *Democracy and Education: An Introduction to the Philosophy of Education* (MacMillan, 1916) and *Education Today* (G. P. Putnam's & Sons, 1940), esp. chap. 5. See also Amy Gutman's

Democratic Education (Princeton University Press, 1987). On democracy and elementary school education, see Jarrod S. Hanson and Ken Howe, "The potential for deliberative democratic civic education," *Democracy and Education* 19:2 (2011), Polly Greenberg, "Why Not Academic Preschool (Part 2): Autocracy or Democracy in the Classroom?" *Young Children* 47:3 (1992), pp. 54-64, and "Parents as Partners in Young Children's Development and Education: A New American Fad? Why Does It Matter?" *Young Children* 44:4 (1992), pp. 61-75; Emma E. Holmes, "Democracy in Elementary School Classes," *Social Education* 55:3 (1991), pp. 176-178; Shirley A. Kessler, "Alternative Perspectives on Early Childhood Education," *Early Childhood Research Quarterly* 6:2 (1991), pp. 193-196.

[48] On the importance of political knowledge, see Michael X. Delli Carpini and Scott Keeter *What Americans Know about Politics and Why It Matters* (Yale University Press, 1996).

[49] Walter C. Parker, *Teaching Democracy: Unity and Diversity in Public Life* (Teachers College Press, 2003).

[50] Walter Parker, "Feel Free to Change Your Mind. A Response to "The Potential for Deliberative Democratic Civic Education," *Democracy and Education*, 19:2 (2011) Art. 9 p. 2.

[51] Rahima C. Wade, "Voice and Choice in a University Seminar: The Struggle to Teach Democratically," *Theory & Research in Social Education* 27:1 (1999), p. 90.

[52] Erik K. Laursen and Thomas F. Tate, "Democratic Group Work," *Reclaiming Children and Youth* 20:4 (2012), pp. 46–51.

[53] This example was provided to me by one of the teachers at the Meeting School, my brother George Gastil.

[54] Dana Mitra, Stephanie Serriere and Donnan Stoicovy, "The Role of Leaders in Enabling Student Voice," *Management in Education* 26:3 (2012), pp. 104–112.

[55] John Stuart Mill quoted in Pateman, "Feminism and Democracy," p. 211. On the treatment of the family in modern moral and political philosophy, see Okin, *Justice*, esp. pp. 8-10.

[56] For theorizing on democratic parenting, see Smiljka Tomanović, "Negotiating Children's Participation and Autonomy within Families," *The International Journal of Children's Rights* 11:1 (2003), pp. 51–71. Constance Flanagan, "Developmental Roots of Political Engagement," *PS: Political Science and Politics* 36:2 (2003), pp. 257-262.

[57] The size of the effect, however, was small relative to the impact of parents' authoritarianism and other characteristics. Marta Miklikowska and Helena Hurme, "Democracy begins at home: Democratic parenting and adolescents' support for democratic values," *European Journal of Developmental Psychology* 8:5 (2011), pp. 541-557.

[58] These findings come from William S. Aquilino and Andrew J. Supple, "Long-term effects of parenting practices during adolescence on well-being outcomes in young adulthood," *Journal of Family Issues* 22:3 (2001), pp. 289-308, and Ciara Smalls,

"African American adolescent engagement in the classroom and beyond: The roles of mother's racial socialization and democratic-involved parenting," *Journal of youth and adolescence* 38:2 (2009), pp. 204-213.

[59] The idea that democratic "motherhood" (or parenting generally) is a citizen responsibility comparable to other forms of public service comes from Carole Pateman, "Political Obligation, Freedom and Feminism," *American Political Science Review* 86:1 (1992), pp. 181-182; Anne Phillips, "Must Feminists Give Up on Liberal Democracy?" *Political Studies* 40:suppl (1992), p. 71.

[60] George Lakoff makes this argument in *Moral Politics: How Liberals and Conservatives Think* (University of Chicago Press, 2002), when he contrasts the conservative metaphor of the ideal society having "strict fathers" versus the liberals' image of a society populated by "nurturing parents." The idea is that both ideologies take those approaches not only in families but also in government and other social institutions.

[61] One early attempt to develop a definition of democratic families is Mary Stewart Lyle's *Adult Education for Democracy in Family Life* (Iowa State College Press, 1944). On the benefits of raising children democratically, see Robert N. Bellah, Richard Madsen, William M. Sullivan, Ann Swidler, Steven M. Tipton, *The Good Society* (Alfred A. Knopf, 1991), pp. 256-261; Martin Gold and Denise S. Yanof, "Mothers, Daughters, and Girlfriends," *Journal of Personality and Social Psychology* 49:3 (1985), pp. 654-659.

[62] Cameron W. Meredith, "Democracy in the Family," *Individual Psychology: Journal of Adlerian Theory, Research and Practice* 42:4 (1986), p. 609. In the first edition, I had also noted Adlerian therapists' interest in the notion of the "democratic family," which was loosely defined in works such as James W. Croake, "An Adlerian View of Life Style," *Journal of Clinical Psychology* 31:3 (1975), pp. 513-518. On the problematic nature of the Adlerian view, see the discussion of work by Shlomit Oryan later in this chapter.

[63] During World War II, Lyle (*Adult Education for Democracy in Family Life*, p. 10) offered a similar understanding of the democratic family. In her study, she defined democracy as "a quality of human relationships characterized by respect for individuality, by sharing in policy-making as well as in efforts to achieve the goals jointly determined, and by confidence in intelligence as the means of resolving conflicts and meeting situations successfully."
More recently, Richard M. Merelman argued that the real basis of sophisticated political thought is moral and cognitive development during childhood. The key factors necessary for the development of ideology are (a) maintaining a parental consensus on basic values within the family and the child identifying her/himself with this consensus and (b) giving the child responsibility, psychological discipline, and warmth, coupled with low frustration and anxiety. According to Merelman, these high standards are rarely met in our childhood, and that is why few citizens in the United States have sophisticated political ideologies; see "The Development of

Political Ideology: A Framework for the Analysis of Political Socialization," *American Political Science Review* 63:3 (1971), pp. 1033-1047.

[64] Nancy J. Chodorow, *The Reproduction of Mothering: Psychoanalysis and the Sociology of Gender* (University of California Press, 1978), p. 7. On negative effects of the maternal stereotype on women, see the chapter on "The Fantasy of the Perfect Mother" (co-authored with Susan Contratto) in Nancy J. Chodorow's *Feminism and Psychoanalytic Theory* (Yale University Press, 1989).

[65] Chodorow, *The Reproduction of Mothering*, p. 218.

[66] Steven H. Chaffee, Jack McCleud, and Daniel B. Wackman, "Family Communication Patterns and Adolescent Political Participation," in Jack Dennis (ed.), *Socialization to Politics: A Reader* (John Wiley & Sons, 1973), pp. 349-364. These distinctions parallel the distinction between attitudes serving social-adjustive functions and those serving a value-expressive function. If parents influence which attitudinal functions undergird a child's adherence to democratic values, concept-oriented communication may aid the development of the more enduring and powerful commitment that comes with value-expressive attitude. See John Gastil, "Why We Believe in Democracy: Testing Theories of Attitude Functions and Democracy," *Journal of Applied Social Psychology* 22:6 (1992), pp. 423-450.

[67] Shlomit Oryan and John Gastil, "Democratic parenting: paradoxical messages in democratic parent education theories," 59:1 *International Review of Education* (2013), pp. 1-17. Also see Shlomit Oryan, "The Family Council: Different Styles of Family Deliberation in Two Cultures," *The Journal of Individual Psychology* 70:2 (2014), pp. 128–47. He complete argument comes in Shlomit Oryan's doctoral dissertation, *Democratic Parenting - Education for Parenting in Israel and the U.S.A in the Late Modern Era* (Hebrew University, 2005).

[68] Richard Flacks, *Making History*, p. 3.

[69] Michael MacKuen and Courtney Brown, "Political Context and Attitude Change," *American Political Science Review* 81 (1987), pp. 471-490. For a compilation of years of research on political conversation that shows the power of political disagreement in our social networks, see Robert Huckfeldt, Paul E. Johnson, and John Sprague, *Political Disagreement: The Survival of Diverse Opinions within Communication Networks* (Cambridge University Press, 2004).

[70] Through social media, the speed of these influence cascades may be even greater, even if the intensity of individual interactions might be somewhat diminished.

[71] Vaclev Havel, "Politics and the World Itself," *Kettering Review* (Summer 1992), p. 13. The technical name for the Butterfly Effect is "sensitive dependence on initial conditions," and it appears to be a pervasive phenomenon in the physical world. See James Gleick, *Chaos: Making a New Science* (Viking, 1987), pp. 20-23. For its application to politics, see Shaul R. Shenhay, "Political Narratives and Political Reality," *International Political Science Review* 27:3 (2006), pp. 245–262.

Chapter 8

[1] James Fishkin, *Democracy and Deliberation* (Yale U. Press, 1991), p. 25.

[2] This opening section is adapted from *The Group in Society*, pp. 246-252.

[3] Robert Wuthnow, *Sharing the Journey: Support Groups and America's New Quest for Community* (Simon and Schuster, 1994), p. 4. For research on the civic impact of such groups, see Melissa Katherine Marcello and Robert Perrucci, "Civic Engagement Among Small-Group Participants: Creating Community or Self-Absorption?" *Sociological Spectrum* 29:6 (2009), pp. 677–699.

[4] Wuthnow, *Sharing the Journey*, p. 5.

[5] Wuthnow, *Sharing the Journey*, p. 7.

[6] Kevin D. Dougherty and Andrew L. Whitehead, "A Place to Belong: Small Group Involvement in Religious Congregations." *Sociology of Religion* 72:1 (March 20, 2011), pp. 91–111.

[7] Jürgen Habermas, *An Awareness of What Is Missing: Faith and Reason in a Post-Secular Age* (Polity, 2010).

[8] For an overview, see Andrew Edgar, *The Philosophy of Habermas* (McGill-Queen's Press, 2005).

[9] See Edgar, *The Philosophy of Habermas*, pp. 168–69. The principal texts by Jürgen Habermas on this subject include *Legitimation Crisis* (Beacon Press, 1975), *Communication and the Evolution of Society* (Beacon Press, 1979), and *The Structural Transformation of the Public Sphere* (MIT Press, 1991). For a discussion of (and response to) some of the most trenchant criticism of Habermas, see Lincoln Dahlberg, "The Habermasian Public Sphere: Taking Difference Seriously," *Theory and Society* 34:2 (2005), pp. 111–136.

[10] Robert A. Dahl aptly called this "polyarchy" (rule of the many), a term he contrasts with democracy in *Democracy and its critics* (Yale University Press, 1989).

[11] A very accessible account of this approach is provided in Amy Gutmann and Dennis Thompson, *Why Deliberative Democracy?* (Princeton University Press, 2009), as well as in Matt Leighninger's long-titled *The Next Form of Democracy: How Expert Rule Is Giving Way to Shared Governance-- and Why Politics Will Never Be the Same* (Vanderbilt University Press, 2006).

[12] The figure shows the number of articles found in Academic Search Complete using the search term "Deliberation or Deliberative" AND "Civic OR Citizen OR Political OR Public OR Democracy OR Democratic" in either the title or abstract, limited to peer-reviewed academic journals. Search conducted November 16, 2013. A similar 11/16/13. Communication scholar Damien Pfister pointed out to me that a very similar curve occurs when searching Google Books for titles on "deliberative democracy" over the same time period.

[13] Tina Nabatchi, "An Introduction to Deliberative Civic Engagement," in Tina Nabatchi, John Gastil, Michael Weiksner, and Matt Leighninger (eds.), *Democracy in Motion: Evaluating the Practice and Impact of Deliberative Civic Engagement* (Oxford University Press, 2012), pp. 3–17. Also see John Gastil and Peter Levine (eds.), *The Deliberative Democracy Handbook: Strategies for Effective Civic Engagement in the Twenty-First Century* (Jossey-Bass, 2005).

[14] Thomas Ferraro and Richard Cowan, "Deliberative Senate Gripped by Paralysis," *Reuters* (March 8, 2012).

[15] John Gastil, *Political Communication and Deliberation* (Sage, 2008), p. 133.

[16] When I taught a doctoral seminar at Wayne State University in the summer of 2012, I asked the students to design original deliberative innovations. Robert Richards and I edited the peer-reviewed essays that resulted from that seminar, and these now appear in the *Journal of Public Deliberation*,9:2 (2013).

[17] On the Japanese quasi-jury system, see Hiroshi Fukurai, "Japan's Quasi-Jury and Grand Jury Systems as Deliberative Agents of Social Change: De-Colonial Strategies and Deliberative Participatory Democracy," *Chicago-Kent Law Review* 86 (2011), pp. 789-829. On the American jury system generally, see Neil Vidmar and Valerie P. Hans, *American Juries: The Verdict* (Prometheus Books, 2007). A remarkably broad review of jury research appears in Dennis J. Devine, Laura D. Clayton, Benjamin B. Dunford, Rasmy Seying, and Jennifer Pryce, "Jury Decision Making: 45 Years of Empirical Research on Deliberating Groups," *Psychology, Public Policy and Law* 7:3 (2001) pp. 622–727. For an overview of the jury's relationship to deliberative democracy, see John Gastil, E. Pierre Deess, Philip J. Weiser, and Cindy Simmons, *The Jury and Democracy: How Jury Deliberation Promotes Civic Engagement and Political Participation* (Oxford University Press, 2010).

[18] John Gastil and Robert Richards, "Making Direct Democracy Deliberative through Random Assemblies," *Politics & Society* 41:2 (2013) pp. 253–281.

[19] See Ned Crosby and Doug Nethercutt, "Citizens Juries: Creating a Trustworthy Voice of the People," in John Gastil and Peter Levine (eds.), *The Deliberative Democracy Handbook* (Jossey-Bass, 2005), pp. 111-119, and Ned Crosby and John C. Hottinger, "The Citizens' Jury Process," in *The Book of the States* (2011), pp. 321-325. For a full-length account of the ideas leading to the Oregon CIR, see Ned Crosby, *Healthy Democracy: Bringing Trustworthy Information to the Voters Of America* (Beaver's Pond Press, 2003). I was in conversations with Crosby years earlier and articulated a similar proposal in John Gastil, *By Popular Demand: Revitalizing Representative Democracy through Deliberative Elections* (University of California Press, 2000).

[20] James Fishkin, *When the People Speak: Deliberative Democracy and Public Consultation* (Oxford University Press, 2009).

[21] Thomas E. Cronin, in *Direct Democracy: The Politics of Initiative, Referendum, and Recall* (Havard University Press, 1989) provides a history of the initiative process. A skeptical account appears in David S. Broder, *Democracy Derailed: Initiative*

Campaigns and the Power of Money (Harcourt, 2000), and a more sympathetic view appears in John Matsusaka, *For the Many or the Few: The Initiative, Public Policy, and American Democracy* (University of Chicago Press, 2008) and Shaun Bowler and Todd Donovan, *Demanding Choices: Opinion, Voting, and Direct Democracy* (University of Michigan Press, 1998).

[22] Elizabeth R. Gerber, *The Populist Paradox: Interest Group Influence and the Promise of Direct Legislation,* (Princeton University Press, 1999). Elisabeth R. Gerber and A. Lupia, "Voter competence in direct legislation elections," in S. L. Elkin and K. E. Sotan (eds.), *Citizen competence and democratic institutions* (The Pennsylvania State University Press, 2010), pp. 147-160.

[23] For a review of the 2010 CIR, see Katherine R. Knobloch, John Gastil, Justin Reedy, and Katherine Cramer Walsh, "Did They Deliberate? Applying an Evaluative Model of Democratic Deliberation to the Oregon Citizens' Initiative Review," *Journal of Applied Communication Research* 41(2) (2013), pp. 105–125. A more detailed version appears in John Gastil and Katherine R. Knobloch, *Evaluation Report to the Oregon State Legislature on the 2010 Oregon Citizens' Initiative Review* (University of Washington, 2010). For a review of the 2012 CIR, see Katherine R. Knobloch, John Gastil, Robert Richards, and Traci Feller, *Evaluation Report on the 2012 Citizens' Initiative Reviews for the Oregon CIR Commission* (The Pennsylvania State University, 2012).

[24] Justin Levitt, "Weighing the Potential of Citizen Redistricting," *Loyola of Los Angeles Law Review* 44 (2011), pp. 534–37.

[25] See Richard Gonzales, "Political Battles Still Dog Redistricting In California," *NPR.org* (May 29, 2013), and Eric McGhee and Daniel Krimm, *Test-driving California's Election Reforms* (Public Policy Institute of California, September, 2012).

[26] Noelle McAfee, Robert McKenzie, and David Mathews, *Hard Choices* (Kettering Foundation, 1991), pp. 10-15. The lead author of that booklet has continued to study citizenship and deliberation, influenced by the experience of working closely with the National Issues Forums; see, for example, Noelle McAfee, "Three Models of Democratic Deliberation," *The Journal of Speculative Philosophy* 18 (2004), pp. 44–59.

[27] That study yielded three articles focused on the NIF: John Gastil, "Adult Civic Education through the National Issues Forums: Developing Democratic Habits and Dispositions through Public Deliberation," *Adult Education Quarterly* 54:4 (2004) pp. 308–328. John Gastil and James Price Dillard, "The Aims, Methods, and Effects of Deliberative Civic Education through the National Issues Forums," *Communication Education* 48(3) (1999), pp. 1–14. John Gastil and James Price Dillard, "Increasing Political Sophistication through Public Deliberation," *Political Communication* 16:1 (1999), pp. 3–23. See also, Keith Melville, Taylor L. Willingham and John R. Dedrick, 2005. "National Issues Forums: A Network of Communities," in John Gastil and Peter Levine, (eds.) *The Deliberative Democracy Handbook* (Jossey-Bass, 2005).

[28] To see current projects conducted by these organizations, and to peruse their archives, visit AmericaSpeaks and Everyday Democracy (formerly the Study Circles Resource Center).

[29] For links to many of these, visit the Co-Intelligence Institute or the Resource Center at the National Coalition for Dialogue and Deliberation.

[30] Bruce A. Ackerman and James S. Fishkin, *Deliberation Day* (Yale University Press, 2004).

[31] Too little research has looked at the intricacies of the caucus process. For a favorable overview of their role in the Presidential election, see David P. Redlawsk, Caroline J. Tolbert, and Todd Donovan, *Why Iowa? How Caucuses and Sequential Elections Improve the Presidential Nominating Process* (University of Chicago Press, 2011).

[32] Brian Wampler, *Participatory Budgeting in Brazil: Contestation, Cooperation, and Accountability* (University Park: Pennsylvania State University Press, 2007). See also Boaventura de Sousa Santos, "Participatory Budgeting in Porto Alegre: Toward a Redistributive Democracy," *Politics & Society* 26:4 (1998): 461–510. My colleagues and I were so impressed with the efforts of Josh Lerner and the Participatory Budgeting Project to bring that process to the United States that we awarded them the inaugural Brown Democracy Medal, given by the Pennsylvania State University's McCourtney Institute for Democracy in 2014. That medal will be given each year for innovations in democratic theory and practice.

[33] The details of this proposal appear on pp. 156-160 of the first edition of *Democracy in Small Groups*. The delegates would move up from local to national forums via a tiered structure proposed by Mary Parker Follett, *Creative Experience* (Longmans, Green, & Co., 1924). The representatives who go from one tier to the next would practice what Norberto Bobbio calls "representation by mandate"—the "half-way house between representative and direct democracy;" *The Future of Democracy: A Defence of the Rules of the Game* (Polity Press, 1987), p. 52. The idea for a Delegate House comes from Dahl's call for a "minipopulus" in *Democracy and Its Critics*, p. 340.

[34] This process also made it possible for those members of Congress with districts harmed by the closures to take the floor and protest, ineffectually, the commission's decisions. That opportunity for dissent was a means of giving those representatives political cover without derailing the necessary cuts. See Jerry Brito, "Running for Cover: The BRAC Commission as a Model for Federal Spending Reform," *Georgetown Journal of Law & Public Policy* 9 (2011), pp. 131–141.

[35] Ethan J. Leib, *Deliberative Democracy in America: A Proposal for a Popular Branch of Government* (Pennsylvania State University Press, 2004), 12. For a similar but less detailed proposal, see Simon Threlkeld, "A Blueprint for Democratic Law-making: Give Citizen Juries the Final Say," *Social Policy* 28:4 (1998), pp. 5–9.

[36] Kevin O'Leary, *Saving Democracy: A Plan for Real Representation in America* (Stanford University Press, 2006).

---

[37] Harry Brighouse and Erik Olin Wright, A Proposal to Transform the House of Lords into a Citizens Assembly (Unpublished manuscript, University of Wisconsin-Madison, March, 2006).

[38] The first sustained argument for this idea that I have read comes from Ernest Callenbach and Michael Phillips, *A Citizen Legislature* (Banyan Tree Books, 1985).

[39] For a detailed discussion of these issues, see my earlier book, *By Popular Demand*, esp. chapters 1-3.

[40] See Joseph M. Bessette, *The Mild Voice of Reason: Deliberative Democracy and American National Government* (University of Chicago Press, 1997), and Stephanie Burkhalter's doctoral dissertation, *Talking Points: Message Strategies and Deliberation in the US Congress* (University of Washington, 2007).

[41] Joshua Cohen and Joel Rogers, *On Democracy* (Penguin Books, 1983), pp. 157-158.

[42] That said, Norman H. Nie, in *Education and Democratic Citizenship in America* (University of Chicago Press, 1996), makes the case that much of education's positive impact on civic engagement comes from its sorting effect (i.e., advanced degrees advance the civic standing of those who earn them, versus those who do not); this is less a civic impact than a differentiator. On the precursors of political engagement generally, see Sidney Verba, Kay Lehman Schlozman, and Henry E. Brady, *Voice and Equality: Civic Voluntarism in American Politics* (Harvard University Press, 1995).

[43] The changing legal landscape in the United States makes some previously popular proposals moot, barring constitutional amendment or new Supreme Court rulings. A useful resource for those interested in campaign reform in the United States is the Campaign Finance Reform section of the website for Demos, a non-governmental organization committed to securing equal voice for all citizens in the United States.

[44] C. George Benello, *From the Ground Up* (South End Press, 1992), p. 51. In *Human Scale* (G. P. Putnam's Sons, 1980), Kirkpatrick Sale maintains that "the only true democracy...is direct democracy" (p. 493). In *Democracy Is You: A Guide to Citizen Action* (Harper & Bros., 1953), Richard W. Poston defines democracy as "a process by which free people in a free society are in communication with one another and together mold and control their own destiny at the neighborhood or community level" (p. 8, emphasis added).

[45] Decentralists can learn from successes and failures of direct democracy in existing political systems. On referenda, initiatives, and recall elections, see Thomas E. Cronin, *Direct Democracy* (Harvard U. Press, 1989).

[46] Early visions of this world appeared in Alvin Toffler, *The Third Wave* (Pan MacMillan, 1980), chap. 28. Regardless of any socioeconomic and technological changes in the coming century, it is difficult to see how global government can ensure equal participation and high-quality deliberation. In its defense, such a system addresses the need for international governance. Federal and decentralized systems must address the need for an overarching legal document or governing body that prevents tyranny and human rights violations within smaller nations or regions. For an overview of transnational, global, or "cosmopolitan" democracy, see David Held,

Cosmopolitanism: Ideals and Realities (Polity, 2010). For studies that consider global systems from the standpoint of deliberative democracy, see Randall Germain, "Financial Governance and Transnational Deliberative Democracy," *Review of International Studies* 36:2 (2010) pp. 493–509, and Patrizia Nanz and Jens Steffek, "Assessing the Democratic Quality of Deliberation in International Governance: Criteria and Research Strategies," *Acta Politica* 40:3 (2005) pp. 368–383, and Archon Fung, "Deliberative Democracy and International Labor Standards," *Governance: An International Journal of Policy, Administration, and Institutions* 16:1 (2003) pp. 51–71.

[47] Benello, *From the Ground Up*, p. 51; see also, Jane J. Mansbridge, "A Paradox of Size," in C. George Benello (ed.), *From the Ground Up* (South End Press, 1992), pp. 161, 173, note 3. It is important to accurately portray the "empowerment" that takes place under decentralization. Although an individual can have relatively more influence in a local decision, these decisions are less powerful; the power of a bill prohibiting censorship decreases the smaller the scope of an assembly's jurisdiction. See Robert A. Dahl and Edward R. Tufte, *Size and Democracy* (Stanford University Press, 1973). In reply, the decentralist can argue that citizens are far more interested in setting censorship policy in their own communities; they are willing to relinquish their influence over other communities. When one's civil rights fall owing to the majesty of local law, however, one might pine for a more centralized constitutional authority that protects minority rights from local abrogation.

[48] Susan Clark and Woden Teachout, *Slow Democracy: Rediscovering Community, Bringing Decision Making Back Home* (Chelsea Green, 2012).

[49] See Robert L. Thayer, *LifePlace: Bioregional Thought and Practice* (University of California Press, 2003), Van Andruss, Christopher Plant, Judith Plant, and Eleanor Wright (eds.), *Home! A Bioregional Reader* (New Society Publishers, 1990), and Kirkpatrick Sale, *Dwellers in the Land: The Bioregional Vision* (Sierra Club Books, 1985), esp. chap. 7. I thank Christopher Plant for discussing bioregional visions of political decision making with me. Bioregionalists have focused more on the delineation of political boundaries than the decision-making processes within these. In fact, Sale's version of bioregionalism suggests that democratic principles might even be subordinate to bioregional ideals: "Different cultures could be expected to have quite different views about what political forms could best accomplish their political goals...It is quite possible that an extraordinary variety of political systems would evolve within bioregional constraints, and there is no reason to think that they would necessarily be compatible—or even, from someone else's point of view, good." It is unclear what this passage means, but it shows the need for an explicit discussion of the relationship between bioregionalism and democracy. Finally, note that some recent discussions of bioregionalism have linked it to religious practice; see Ched Myers, *Who Will Roll Away the Stone? Discipleship Queries for First World Christians* (Orbis Books, 1994).

---

[50] The numbers I use are from Edward Goldsmith, "Decentralization," in Andrew Dobson (ed.), *The Green Reader: Essays toward a Sustainable Society* (Mercury House, 1991), p. 76. Also see Sale, *Human Scale*, chap. 7.

[51] On confederalism in general, see Benjamin R. Barber, *Jihad vs. McWorld* (Ballantine Books, 1996); Murray Bookchin, "The Meaning of Confederalism," in Judith Plant and Christopher Plant (eds.), *Putting Power in Its Place* (New Society Publishers, 1992); Frank Bryan and John McClaughry, *The Vermont Papers: Recreating Democracy on a Human Scale* (Chelsea, VT: Chelsea Green, 1989); Kirkpatrick Sale, *Human Scale*; Toffler, *The Third Wave*, chap. 28. These authors dispel the myth that all decentralists advocate pure autarky; instead, they call for semi-autonomous regions that cooperate in joint political and economic activities. Some go even further to argue that it is both impractical and immoral to seek the creation of "pocket utopias." A prosperous community has an ethical obligation to maintain connections with other, less successful communities.

[52] This depiction of the council system is based on C. B. Macpherson, *The Life and Times of Liberal Democracy* (Oxford University Press, 1977), pp. 108-112, and Benello, *From the Ground Up*, pp. 50-53; see also, George Lakey, *Strategy for a Living Revolution* (Grossman, 1973), pp. 162-163. For a tiered system designed to organize the economy through on worker and consumer councils, see Michael Albert and Robin Hahnel, *Socialism Today and Tomorrow* (South End Press, 1981). In "A Paradox of Size," Mansbridge cautions that these systems can create too much psychological distance between citizens and higher councils. Also, higher councils would be unable to operate effectively by mandate; representatives would need considerable leeway to compromise and change their minds during council deliberation.

[53] Burnheim, *Is Democracy Possible?*, esp. pp. 106-124.

[54] T. M. Thomas Isaac and Richard W. Franke, *Local Democracy and Development: The Kerala People's Campaign for Decentralized Planning* (Lanham, MD: Rowman & Littlefield, 2002).

[55] Raymond Fishman and Roberta Gatti, "Decentralization and Corruption: Evidence across Countries," *Journal of Public Economics* 83:3 (2002), pp. 325–345.

[56] Patrick Heller, "Moving the State: The Politics of Democratic Decentralization in Kerala, South Africa, and Porto Alegre," *Politics and Society* 29:1 (2001), pp. 131–163.

[57] For a range of cases, including some driven by elites, see Philip Oxhorn, Joseph S. Tulchin and Andrew Selee, *Decentralization, Democratic Governance, and Civil Society in Comparative Perspective: Africa, Asia, and Latin America*, (Woodrow Wilson Center Press, 2004).

[58] On the idea that articulating an alternative vision can increase the probability of its realization, see Pierre Bourdieu's discussion of "heretical discourse" in *Language and Symbolic Power* (Harvard University Press, 1991), chap. 5.

[59] Sara M. Evans and Harry C. Boyte, *Free Spaces* (Harper & Row, 1992). For similar perspectives on the role of group activity on large-scale social change, see Virginia

Sapiro, "The Women's Movement and the Creation of Gender Consciousness: Social Movements as Socialization Agents," in Orit Ichilov (ed.), *Political Socialization, Citizenship Education, and Democracy* (Teachers College, 1990), pp. 266-280; Lawrence Goodwyn, "Organizing Democracy: The Limits of Theory and Practice," *democracy* 1 (1981), pp. 25-40. On the impact of deliberation generally, see Heather Pincock, "Does deliberation make better citizens?" in Tina Nabatchi, John Gastil, Michael Weiksner, and Matt Leighninger (eds.), *Democracy in Motion: Evaluating the Practice and Impact of Deliberative Civic Engagement* (Oxford University Press, 2012), pp. 135-162.

[60] Harry Boyte, *Commonwealth* (The Free Press, 1989), p. 32.

[61] For more abstract formulations of this concept, see Gary Alan Fine, *Tiny Publics: A Theory of Group Action and Culture* (Russell Sage Foundation, 2012), and Anthony Giddens, *The Constitution of Society* (University of California Press, 1984).

Small Group Exercises

[1] The utility of these exercises likely hinges on one's cultural frame of reference. After I wrote the first edition of this book, officials from the United Nations' Food and Agriculture Organization's People's Participation Programme (PPP) contracted with me to write a manual on group process for the small groups they organized in countries principally in South Asia, Africa, and Latin America. I adapted the text and these exercises for their purposes, and they sent me a small check. I didn't hear from them again for many years. Once the Internet made such things possible, I proto-Googled one of these employers, who had left the now-defunct PPP, and asked whether the exercises had proven useful. The gist of his reply was that the concepts and activities simply failed to translate to rural communities in the southern hemisphere. Duly noted.

[2] This is inspired by Jane Mansbridge's "power circle exercise" in *Beyond Adversary Democracy* (University of Chicago Press, 1983), pp. 183-184.

[3] Clearly, this is a hat-intensive activity, which could serve as a corrective against the fact, noted famously by Monty Python, that people are not wearing enough hats. This deficit may explain some of the appeal of the otherwise unattractive sorting hat in Harry Potter.

[4] Charles Douglas Lummis, "The Radicalism of Democracy," *democracy* 2 (1992), p. 9.

Printed in the USA
CPSIA information can be obtained
at www.ICGtesting.com
LVHW020315110923
757792LV00003B/344